NEIGHBOURS ACROSS THE PACIFIC

NEIGHBOURS ACROSS THE ◻● PACIFIC 🍁

CANADIAN-JAPANESE RELATIONS 1870-1982

KLAUS H. PRINGSHEIM

◢ MOSAIC PRESS

CANADIAN CATALOGUING IN PUBLICATION DATA

Pringsheim, Klaus H., 1923-
  Neighbours across the Pacific : Canadian-Japanese
relations, 1870-1982

Bibliography: p.
Includes index.
ISBN 0-88962-216-7

1. Canada — Relations — Japan — History — 20th century.
2. Japan — Relations — Canada — History — 20th century.

FC251.J3P74 1983   327.71052   C83-098975-7
F1029.J3P74 1983

Published by Mosaic Press, P.O. Box 1032, Oakville, Ontario, L6J 5E9, Canada.

NEIGHBOURS ACROSS THE PACIFIC originally published by Greenwood Press, Westport, CT., USA, 1983

Published with the assistance of the Canada Council and the Ontario Arts Council.

Cover design by Doug Frank.
Printed and bound in Canada

ISBN 0 88962-216-7 paper

Distributed in the United States by Flatiron Books, 175 Fifth Avenue, Suite 814, New York, N.Y. 10010, U.S.A.

Distributed in the U.K. by John Calder (Publishers) Ltd., 18 Brewer Street, London, W1R 4AS, England.

Distributed in New Zealand and Australia by Pilgrims South Press, P.O. Box 5101, Dunedin, New Zealand.

To my wife Hsiuping and my
family, who have been so
patient while I struggled
to finish the book

and

To Raymond Moriyama, who admonished
me not to do a whitewash on the
war years.

Authors must articulate the guilty conscience of their country, because politicians have such clear consciences.

—Rolf Hochhuth, 1965

Contents

Tables

Acknowledgments

The basic research for this history of Canada-Japan relations was carried out between 1977 and 1979 to document the first fifty years of official diplomatic ties (1929–1979) between Ottawa and Tokyo. I am indebted to Donald Page, deputy director of the Historical Division of the Department of External Affairs in Ottawa, for suggesting that I undertake the study and for arranging access to the files and records of the Department of External Affairs, which also provided funding to enable me to travel to Japan and several North American cities to meet with Canadian and Japanese diplomats and officials. F. A. Hart, director of the Historical Division, and Canada's ambassador to Japan, Bruce I. Rankin, were kind enough to provide letters of introduction to Canadian and Japanese diplomats and officials, thus giving me access to many people directly involved in the Canada-Japan relationship. My greatest debt, however, is to these diplomats and officials in both countries who spoke so openly of their experiences and gave so generously of their time and whose insights taught me so much about the subject. Special thanks is owed to Dr. Hugh L. Keenleyside, who read the manuscript chapter by chapter and supplied many suggestions and corrections. Professor Keith A. J. Hay, Col. Robert L. Houston, and N. Gregor Guthrie, my friends at the Canada-Japan Trade Council, have been most supportive in answering questions and providing criticisms. Professor Frank Langdon of the University of British Columbia has also been most helpful. My colleagues in the Department of Political Science at McMaster University, Adam Bromke, Howard Aster, Marshall Goldstein, Roman March, Derry Novak, Peter Potichnyj, and Kim Nossal, all read parts of the manuscript and helped me in editing it for publication. Retired Canadian diplomat Charles J. Woodsworth provided me with a preparatory guide to the Japan files of the Department of External Affairs when the project was first initiated. To all these individuals and many more cited in footnotes, I am most grateful. I would also like to thank Katsura Shindoh, who worked as my research assistant in Tokyo from 1977 to 1979 and transcribed a number of the Japanese-language tapes.

While I am thus indebted to a great many people both in Canada and Japan, I alone must assume responsibility for the material assembled and the conclusions reached. May I finally express my thanks to Dr. George Schwab of the City University of New York for thinking enough of this manuscript to include it in the series under his editorship.

Abbreviations

ACJ	Allied Council for Japan
ANZUS	Australia-New Zealand-U.S. Treaty
BCSC	British Columbia Security Commission
CANDU	Canadian Deuterium Uranium Nuclear Plant
CAPF	Canadian Army Pacific Force
CBAJ	Canadian Businessmen's Association in Japan
CCF	Cooperative Commonwealth Federation
CCJC	Cooperative Committee on Japanese Canadians
CIDA	Canadian International Development Agency
CPR	Canadian Pacific Railroad
DCER	*Documents on Canadian External Relations*
DEA	Department of External Affairs
DEAF	Department of External Affairs files
DEAR	*Department of External Affairs Records*
DISC	Domestic International Sales Corporation
FEAC	Far Eastern Advisory Commission

FEC	Far Eastern Commission
FIRA	Foreign Investment Review Act
GATT	General Agreement on Tariffs and Trade
IATA	International Air Transport Association
IMTFE	International Military Tribunal, Far East
JCCC	Japanese Canadian Citizens Council
JCCD	Japanese Canadian Committee for Democracy
LDP	Liberal Democratic Party (Japan)
MITI	Ministry of International Trade and Industry (Japan)
NJCCA	National Japanese-Canadian Citizens Association
NMEG	Nisei Mass Evacuation Group
NORAD	North American Aerospace Defense Agreement (*previously* North American Air Defense Command Agreement)
OECD	Organization for Economic Cooperation and Development
PJBD	Permanent Joint Board of Defense (Canada-U.S.)
RCMP	Royal Canadian Mounted Police
ROK	Republic of Korea (South Korea)
SCAP	Supreme Commander for the Allied Powers (General MacArthur)
SMEP	Subcommittee on Mineral and Energy Powers (of the Canada-Japan Ministerial Committee)
SSEA	Secretary of State for External Affairs (Canada's Foreign Minister)
USSEA	Under Secretary of State for External Affairs
VCC	Vancouver Consultative Council
VERs	Voluntary Export Restraints
WLMK	William Lyon MacKenzie King

NEIGHBOURS ACROSS THE PACIFIC

1

The Early Years, 1877–1929

The Japanese lived in Japan as an integrated, well-defined nation long before the modern Canadian state came into existence. They had spent more than a thousand years becoming a nation, carrying on a series of internal conflicts that left them little time or energy to develop technology or to extend themselves abroad beyond Korea and some of the islands surrounding the Japanese archipelago. But by the beginning of the seventeenth century, the great Shogun Tokugawa Iyeyasu had made himself and his heirs the masters of all Japan, achieving internal unification and pacification and thus preparing Japan to be a significant member of the growing international community of states that made their mark in more than one hemisphere.[1]

It was in the first decade of the seventeenth century that we hear of Japanese embassies arriving in Acapulco, Mexico, and returning to Japan with glowing reports of the wonders of America. The first Japanese to reach Europe appear to have been four young samurai from Kyushu who visited Rome in 1588, their trip being arranged by Catholic missionaries in Japan. But nothing came of this first expedition to Europe. The first Europeans to set foot in Japan were three Portuguese who landed on Tanegashima off the coast of Kyushu in 1542 and gave the Japanese their first look at what Europeans looked like as well as at Western firearms. Yet, by 1639 the Tokugawa Shogunate proclaimed a policy of seclusion for Japan, forbidding all foreigners entry into Japan and simultaneously forbidding any Japanese to leave the country. Those disregarding this law, be they Japanese adventurers going abroad or foreign sailors shipwrecked on Japan's shores, were to be executed on the spot. The reason for this policy of total isolation was the Tokugawa regime's fear of foreign imperialism, colonialism, or any kind of foreign interference in the internal affairs of the Tokugawa police state. Only a small number of specially licensed Dutch and Chinese ships were permitted each year to land in a designated port (Nagasaki) to carry on a strictly supervised trade in goods and information, which enabled the Tokugawa rulers to keep in touch with events and developments in the outside world. The seclusion of Japan thus initiated was to last for more than two centuries.

Meanwhile, during the eighteenth century an intermittent trade in ginseng, fur, and sealskins provided the occasion for the first tenuous contacts between Western Canada and the Orient. The relative isolation of China, first breached by the Portuguese at the beginning of the sixteenth century (Macao), began to crumble in the last years of the eighteenth century as New England clipper ships joined the Portuguese, Dutch, Spaniards, and British in the lively trade with Canton, Singapore, Manila, Batavia, and Formosa. With China's defeat in the Opium War of 1839–42, China could no longer resist the persistent assaults of foreign traders, missionaries, and soldiers and, in the hundred years that followed, just barely escaped the fate of being reduced to colonial status.

The Japanese, who had preserved their isolation into the 1850s, finally were compelled to yield to the American demands for trade negotiations when Commodore Matthew Perry of the U.S. Navy sailed his flotilla of "black ships" into Tokyo Bay in 1853 and 1854, bringing Japan's seclusion to an end. Great Britain, Russia, France, and other countries soon followed the American example, and the Tokugawa government, having signed the first U.S.-Japan commercial treaty in 1858, was replaced by a rising group of administrators and bureaucrats, mostly from western Japan, who initiated the Meiji restoration in 1868. The restoration marks the founding of the prewar Japanese state, which established a constitutional monarchy with a somewhat flawed parliamentary system and an increasingly Westernized industrial technology.

On July 1, 1867, during the year before the Meiji restoration, Upper and Lower Canada, Nova Scotia, and New Brunswick, all colonies of British North America, had joined together in confederation under the British North America Act. The Canadian federation and Meiji Japan thus came into existence within a few months of one another. By 1871 the province of British Columbia had joined the confederation, and Canada thus became a member of the community of nations bordering on the Pacific Ocean.

As of 1866 Japan granted permission to merchants and students to travel abroad, and some 1,100 passports were issued to Japanese citizens between 1868 and 1875 so that they might go abroad to study in the United States, Britain, France, or Germany. British Columbia had seen an influx of Chinese as early as 1858, when there were gold strikes on the Fraser River. By 1863 some 2,500 Chinese were engaged in mining on Vancouver Island and Victoria seemed destined to become the Canton of the Pacific Northwest.

British interest in opening up the trade routes between the North American continent and the Orient led to renewed attempts between the 1840s and 1870s to find the Northwest Passage. When it became clear that the sea route was not commercially viable, a transcontinental railroad was seen as offering the best hope for commercial advantage, in that it would enable its operator to dominate Britain's trade with China and Japan. The aim was to carry goods in either direction between England and China in a mere thirty-six days. The United States was the first to complete a line, from the East Coast to San Francisco, doing so in 1869, one year after the Meiji restoration and two years after Canadian confederation. On the American lines it was necessary to change trains and companies in Chicago. The Canadian Pacific Railroad (CPR) was thus the first line under single management to be constructed from the East to the West Coast.

It is not precisely known when the first Japanese may have set foot on Canadian territory, but a shipwrecked sailor or fisherman is likely to have been swept away from Japan on the Japan current, subsequently drifting southwards along the North American Pacific Coast. There are reports of several Japanese survivors of these inadvertent trans-Pacific odysseys, dating back as far as 1807, and a number of Japanese landed in what is now British Columbia long before the lifting of the Tokugawa seclusion edict. The first Japanese reputed to have visited North America was one Manjiro

Nakahama, who was picked up by a New England whaler in 1841.[2] He returned to Japan, where he was imprisoned for more than two years, but he eventually turned up as an interpreter between Commodore Perry and the Japanese in 1854.

The first Japanese to settle in Canada, however, appears to have been a stowaway, Manzo "Jack" Nagano, a young sailor from Nagasaki who stepped ashore in New Westminister, B.C., in May 1877 and spent most of the next forty-six years in Canada before returning to Nagasaki in 1923, where he died in May 1924. He raised a family in Canada, and some of his descendants still survive there. His son George Nagano, born in 1891, moved to California around 1915 and was still living there in 1977, when at age eighty he visited Toronto to participate in the celebration of the Japanese-Canadian Centennial, together with his own son Paul Nagano, a Baptist minister in Seattle. The Japanese-Canadian community in Canada proclaimed the year 1977 as the year of the Japanese-Canadian Centennial, in honor of the landing of Manzo Nagano a century earlier. Nagano appears to have been an adventurous, multi-talented person with strong entrepreneurial leanings, trying his luck as a fisherman, longshoreman, and businessman. In 1892 he opened a store in Victoria selling Japanese novelties and goods; later he added a second store and a rooming house, and his businesses appear to have prospered. The erstwhile stowaway later left Victoria and became one of Vancouver's most prominent Japanese Canadians.

Social and economic conditions in early Meiji Japan (the 1870s and thereafter) were such as to make members of the peasantry receptive to the idea of going abroad to make their fortunes. The stories of the wealth to be found in North America that spread all over the world in those days reached Japan as well. It is not surprising then, that on the heels of Manzo Nagano there followed an increasing stream of immigrants, mostly from the more heavily populated prefectures of Western and Southwestern Japan. The sudden rise of unemployment in Japan in the wake of the Sino-Japanese and Russo-Japanese wars provided workers for the surge of industrial development in North America in the aftermath of the U.S. Civil War, as the great transcontinental railroads were completed and both California and British Columbia reached the economic take-off stage. British Columbia needed laborers as urgently as the Japanese emigrants and transient fortune seekers wanted the jobs.

Between 1869 and 1884 most Japanese "emigrants" (105,000) went to Japan's northernmost island of Hokkaido, with some going to the Chinese mainland, although economic conditions there were not notably better than in Japan. A group of 153 Japanese laborers had been illegally transported to Hawaii in 1868 to work in the sugar plantations but encountered working conditions so close to slavery that the Japanese government refused permission for Japanese emigration to Hawaii for the next seventeen years. In 1884, however, permission was granted for emigration to Hawaii by laborers under contract, and soon after that, general emigration of laborers became legal. Close to 180,000 Japanese were to enter Hawaii in the twenty-three years that followed. Others went to the United States, Canada, South America, and Australia—close to another 92,000 for the same period.

It is thus in 1885 that Japanese immigration to Canada really began. Only a handful of Japanese were in British Columbia at that time, most of them having reached Canada's shore by accident, adventure, or adversity. The initial numbers of immigrants were small, and no precise records were kept until the twentieth century. One of the earliest Japanese books on Canada is a kind of guidebook for prospective immigrants, published in Tokyo by Maruzen Shosha Shoten in May 1893. The following fragments provide some insight into the position of Japanese immigrants in Canada at the time.

There are now no less than three or four thousand Japanese living in North America. . . . Only a few of them are merchants . . . with a definite objective. . . . Most are people out to make money by working. . . . Only a few are skilled or experienced. Most of them take work as helpers, dishwashers, servants, cooks, agricultural workers, fishermen, coal miners, or window wipers. . . . There is no one with capital, land, or permanent prospects. . . . If you save your money, and do some work suitable for a Japanese, you can succeed. . . . Many Japanese have been here for several years, and still are barely able to support themselves. . . . As yet there is no association of Japanese in Canada. There are a great many Japanese in Canada who live from hand to mouth and save no money, spending what they make on wine and women. . . .

The behaviour of these Japanese creates the impression that the Japanese are uncultured, interested only in gambling, drinking and wenching. . . . These people are often brought before the courts. . . . When they get sick they have no money to pay for their medicine. . . . These people cannot be called civilized; . . . that is why they are increasingly discriminated against and have even earned the hate of the Americans. Nevertheless, there are some people who like the Japanese, because they have worked with them.[3]

Japanese Consul General Fukashi Sugimura, in a chapter entitled "Some Views for People About to Emigrate to Western Canada,"[4] made some of the following points: He called the climate in British Columbia agreeable to Japanese, pointing out that there were more than ten Japanese settled near the Alaskan border. However, in the cold areas of Canada there were no Japanese; he estimated the population of British Columbia at 150,000 and that of the Northwest Territories at 30,000 and called these areas underpopulated. They were in need of immigrants but wanted whites (Europeans) rather than Orientals. He reported between 3,000 and 5,000 Chinese in British Columbia, with very few in the Northwest Territories. Unlike the Chinese, under the law the Japanese were equal to whites. He estimated that there were some 200 Japanese in British Columbia at that time. Sugimura went on to say that there were two difficulties in organizing the emigration of Japanese into Canada, establishment of legal immigration procedures and improvement of the quality and behavior of the immigrants. Japanese immigrants who came to Canada without knowledge of the customs and language of British Columbia ran into trouble and sometimes did not find work. Sugimura suggested that two steps be taken to alleviate this situation.

1. Establishment of immigration brokerage firms. The brokers would survey conditions in British Columbia and find employment for the immigrants. The immigrants would pay the immigration brokers for their services.

2. Establishment of agricultural companies, which would buy land, develop it, and arrange for people to come and work it.

Sugimura saw these measures as the answer to the troubles of the Japanese immigrants. He further added a series of six propositions as guidelines for future immigration.

1. Immigrants should decide to come as permanent residents.

2. The immigrants should adopt the customs and habits of the people in British Columbia.

3. The immigrants should become Christians; they should go to church, observe the sabbath (Sunday), and conform to Christian customs.

4. The immigrants should raise their standard of living so that they would not be looked down upon by the Occidentals.

5. The immigrants should cultivate a style of living that, unlike that of the Chinese, would not be excessively frugal, so that they would not be despised by other people.

6. The immigrants should bring along Japanese Christian missionaries, to advance the Christian religion within their group and to forbid the immigration of those whose purposes were immoral.

It is easy to imagine that the Sugimura plan might be interpreted by some Occidentals as a Japanese conspiracy to take over British Columbia and as such would be grist for the mills of the exclusionists in the province. There were a thousand or fewer Japanese in Canada as of 1896, and some two thousand by 1897. The lucrative immigration business came to be run by private companies, which obtained contracts for laborers and sent them off to Canada in ever-larger groups. By 1901 some 4,738 Japanese had come as immigrants to Canada, and of these, some 97 percent settled in British Columbia. The first Japanese consulate general in Canada was established in Vancouver in 1889 to look after the affairs of the growing population of Japanese nationals. As the number of Japanese in British Columbia increased in the last decade of the nineteenth century, objections began to be raised to what was perceived by some as an excessive influx of Orientals. In 1885 the dominion government passed legislation levying a head tax of $50 on every Chinese immigrant and limiting the number of Chinese immigrants who might be landed by any one ship to one for every fifty tons of the vessel carrying them. When it was attempted to increase the head tax on the Chinese to $200 in 1891, an amendment was proposed to include Japanese immigrants in this legislation. The motion failed, but it was clear that there were those in British Columbia who strongly objected to the further immigration of Orientals and that the exclusion of Orientals, including the Japanese, from immigration was the eventual aim of these forces.

In this connection it is pertinent to examine some of the reasons why anti-Oriental, or specifically anti-Japanese, feelings would arise among the non-Oriental population in British Columbia. The basic discrimination, which all human beings living in communities practice against those whom they consider to be "outsiders" or newcomers, was reinforced by the fact that Orientals can be physically distinguished from Occidentals by their ethnically stereotypical appearance. Also, the Orientals in British Columbia had been brought in as cheap labor during a time of relatively full employment. As economic activity went into recession, they came to be perceived as unwelcome competition for scarce jobs, pulling down the living standards of those with whom they competed. Employers who profited from exploitation of Oriental labor had no reason to be dissatisfied or resentful, but workers whose jobs or wages were affected by competition from Oriental laborers could quickly blame their misfortunes on the "hordes of Orientals" flooding the British Columbia labor market. It is fairly clear from the tone of a variety of comments on the "Oriental problem" that there was a strong element of racial bigotry contributing to the political agitation against the Orientals.

In 1895 the province of British Columbia excluded the Japanese from the franchise, as it had earlier excluded the Chinese. However, in 1894 Great Britain had signed a treaty of commerce and navigation with Japan. One of the provisions of this treaty specified that subjects of either power were to be granted "full liberty to enter, travel, or reside in any part of the Dominions and possessions of the other contracting party." Since Canada was obliged to conform to imperial policy, it could not pass legislation or enactments that would deny the Japanese the right to enter, live or work in British Columbia. The privy council of the dominion government therefore disallowed those acts of the British Columbia legislature, which were clear violations of the treaty. The Conservative government of Sir MacKenzie Bowell in 1895 expressed Canada's readiness to adhere to the treaty, on condition that the dominion would have control over immigration. When Sir Wilfrid Laurier's government took over in July 1896, it refused to adhere to the treaty because of its misgivings in regard to other aspects of the treaty.

The Japanese government became aware of the emerging confrontation and was prepared to accept Canadian restrictions on immigration. Unemployment among Japanese in British Columbia had meanwhile made immigration to Canada a much less attractive proposition. The Japanese government therefore voluntarily restricted the number of passports to Japanese for Canada in the years from 1901 to 1904 to 447. In Canada, meanwhile, a royal commission had been established to investigate Chinese and Japanese immigration, which brought in its report in 1902.[5]

The report lauded Japan's voluntary restrictions on emigration, voicing the hope that Japan would not revoke that policy. Should Japan do so, the commission recommended the passing of a Natal act.[6] Meanwhile, the press in eastern Canada was critical of British Columbia's anti-Oriental measures. It was also in 1903 that a Japanese consulate general was first established in Ottawa. The virtual halt of Japanese immigration to Canada from 1901 to 1904 did not bring about an alleviation of the confrontation between the anti-Japanese elements and the Japanese in British Columbia, and unsuccessful attempts to legislate Japanese exclusion from certain types of work and a prohibition of further Japanese immigration continued.

The immigrants themselves did not have an easy or particularly pleasant life. They came mostly from farming or fishing backgrounds in Japan and had left their native shores hoping to make money they could send back to Japan or to save to build better lives for themselves in Canada. Many had been recruited by the immigration companies, which made a profit on every immigrant they could deliver, and many had to borrow their passage or sell their possessions in Japan to pay the $50.00 required. Before 1907, almost all the immigrants were male, and their average daily wage was $1.00, most of which they tried to save. The average age of the arriving immigrants was 22.8 years, and many were between the ages of 15 and 19. Upon arrival in Canada they would register with the Japanese consulate, their passports issued by the Japanese government being valid for three years, the general assumption being that they would return to Japan when their passports expired—an assumption that proved to be erroneous in most cases. They worked as fishermen, as coal miners, in the lumber industry, and for the railroads, often underbidding Chinese laborers to get their jobs or shifting from job to job as the opportunities came. They also went into service industries as cooks, servants, hotel boys, and the like. As time went on, however, they spread out into ever-wider fields, including farming, merchandising, and other commercial ventures. The life of Manzo Nagano thus represents a prototype of the Japanese immigrant experience. Some 98 percent of the Japanese immigrants appear to have been literate in Japanese, albeit at a modest level, but the vast majority of them did not speak, read, write, or understand English, which their humble backgrounds in Japan had provided no opportunity to learn, and once in Canada they were too busy working to spend time learning English. Since most of them had no original intention of settling in Canada, their purpose being to earn money and return to Japan, they may also have felt that it would be a waste of time to go beyond the rudiments in English. Associating mostly with their fellow immigrants, they had no social contact with the white community and actually had little need to speak English. Negotiations with employers were carried on by "bosses," who would contract for groups of Japanese laborers for a fee or commission. The inability of the Japanese immigrants to integrate into Canadian society thus had its linguistic, economic, social, and cultural causes and goes some distance to explain the hostility toward them felt by some of the whites. Given the bleakness and uncertainty of the lives they led, the exploitation to which they were subjected by their white employers and their fellow immigrant bosses, and the social and educational handicaps they faced, it is indeed amazing that so many of them stayed and prospered in Canada.

As early as July 27, 1897, when there were only a few hundred Japanese in Canada as yet, an association of Japanese was formed in Vancouver for the protection of the interests of Japanese residents. The original name of the association was Dai Nippon Jin Kai, later (1901) changed to Kanada Nippon Jin Kai (Canadian Association of Japanese) and was officially recognized under that title. The organization opened a number of branches in British Columbia, as well as one in Calgary, Alberta. The total membership reported in 1915 (all branches) was 1,074, rising to 2,821 in 1916 and 3,045 in 1917.[7]

A number of Japanese immigrants were employed in the railroad construction business while the CPR transcontinental line was built. In time they replaced many white and Chinese workers. At one point the president of the CPR resisted a threat by white workers to strike unless the company stopped relying so much on the Japanese. The Japanese railroad employees, meanwhile, soon learned the technical and engineering skills in the railroad business and were employed in these areas as well. Here again they acquired a good reputation for loyal work and diligence, and many of them gained important positions.[8]

It appears that some of the immigrant youngsters, finding themselves with time on their hands in the urban ghettos between jobs, started to gamble, drink, or purchase the favors of prostitutes, thus frittering away their meager earnings and postponing perhaps forever their dreams of returning to Japan.[9] Yet, generally speaking, Japanese immigrants were regarded as cleaner and more law abiding than other Oriental immigrants.

When the Japan Exhibition was opened in Osaka in 1903, there was a display of Canadian goods for possible marketing in Japan. Sidney Fisher, who was minister of agriculture in the Laurier government (1896–1911), attended the exhibition and was later received by the emperor and Japanese government officials. On his return to Canada he gave an enthusiastic report of the commercial prospects but also warned that the matter of Japanese immigration would have to be handled with caution, since the proud and sensitive Japanese would be sure to resent any legislation specifically directed against them. He felt that extensive immigration need not be feared and reported that he had been assured that the restrictions enacted by the Japanese government would be continued. The need for such emigration also receded in Japan as that nation began to prepare for her impending war with Imperial Russia.

The Russo-Japanese War broke out in February 1904 and lasted for seventeen months, during which the Japanese army, at a very high cost in casualties, drove the Russian forces northward into Manchuria and in a spectacular naval battle in the Sea of Japan,

Adm. Heihachiro Togo annihilated Russia's Baltic fleet. At the request of Japan, President Theodore Roosevelt mediated the Treaty of Portsmouth,[10] by which Russia ceded the southern half of the Island of Sakhalin to Japan, acknowledged Japan's "paramountcy" in Korea, and turned over to Japan the Liaotung Leased Territory, the southern half of the Chinese Changchun Railroad, and some coal mines formerly controlled by the Russians, thus giving Japan effective control over southern Manchuria.

Reaction in Canada to Japan's great victory was initially positive, in that "gallant little Japan" had defeated Britain's archenemy, the Russian bear. In British Columbia, however, there were those who viewed the rise of Japan as an increasingly influential Pacific power with some alarm. Japan's imperialistic tendencies, first noted in the Sino-Japanese War of 1894–95, were seen as eventually extending to other areas, such as British Columbia, which had already been "invaded" by so many Japanese immigrants. Meanwhile, in 1906 Laurier's government finally adhered to the Anglo-Japanese treaty of commerce and navigation, thereby bestowing full rights and privileges to Japanese citizens in Canada and once again alarming those who feared excessive Japanese immigration.

These fears were soon to be confirmed, for in the period between the peace of Portsmouth and June 30, 1906, nearly 2,000 Japanese entered Canada, and by March 1907, 2,042 more, thereby almost doubling the number of Japanese in Canada in a mere eighteen months. During the first ten months of 1907 the figure climbed to 8,125 new immigrants for that period alone. Many, if not most, of these new immigrants did not come directly from Japan but from Hawaii, where they had gone in hopes of immigrating to the United States. Unable to go directly, many decided to go by way of Canada, in the hope of easier entry to the United States over the Canadian border or alternatively of remaining in Canada for the time being. The new immigration scare was thus added to the already existing tensions and antagonisms, which had been generated by labor organizing troubles and by disputes between the cannery owners and the fishermen over the price to be paid for fish. More often than not, strikes and price disputes or unemployment troubles would find white laborers squaring off against Orientals, whose greater economic insecurity made them more prone to yield to the demands of the employers. Thus there was a series of touchy situations, with white fishermen in confrontation with Japanese fishermen or white workers pressuring Japanese workers to withdraw from certain kinds of work. Police intervention frequently became necessary to prevent race riots, and the number of ugly incidents mounted.

In spite of these tensions in British Columbia, there appeared to have been good feelings toward Japan in much of the rest of the country. Thus when Prince Sadanaru Fushimi, a cousin of the emperor, made an official visit, landing in Quebec in June 1907 and staying for a month to visit all the major centers in Canada, he was received with popular enthusiasm everywhere. On leaving Canada Prince Fushimi sent a message to the prime minister, thanking him for his warm reception and for the evidence of good will toward Japan.

By August 1907, however, the Asiatic Exclusion League was formed in Vancouver, following similar developments in California, Washington, and Oregon. At a meeting of the league, attended by politicians as well as citizens and workers, a resolution was passed calling the Japanese aggressive and warning that if they were not checked they might eventually control British Columbia. Were they not lowering wage standards in the province, and would they not eventually control its major industries? Once the Japanese became the manufacturing and merchant class, would anything short of war be able to stop the continued stream of Japanese immigrants? Since unemployment was rife at the time, these arguments were most persuasive to labor in British Columbia. Meanwhile, the House of Commons member for Vancouver, R. G. Macpherson, alleged that the Japanese government was responsible for the new waves of immigrants and was sending groups of picked men to take over the country.

The matter went beyond rational discussion, and a kind of hysteria ensued. "Keep Canada Canadian," "British Columbia for the British," and "Keep Out Indigestible Immigrants" were some of the slogans heard. Moreover, the matter had become a highly potent political issue in the February 1907 provincial elections. One newspaper headlined the rumor that fifty thousand Japanese were about to be imported to work on the Grand Trunk Pacific Railroad. The story was a lie, but that did not seem to matter. Macpherson wrote to Prime Minister Sir Wilfrid Laurier on August 20, 1907, to convey the feelings of the exclusionists, who feared that British Columbia was being flooded by masses of Japanese immigrants, who would soon make the province Asiatic.

Sir Wilfrid replied on August 27, 1907.

My Dear Macpherson,

I have your favour of the 20th instant to which I hasten to reply. I am very glad indeed to have this frank expression of your views and I will be equally candid in my answer. My first words to you must be to ask you and our friends to realize that the conditions with regard to the Asiatic question, are not exactly the same as they were twenty years or even ten years ago. Up to that time, the Asiatic when he came to white countries, could be treated with contempt and kicked. This continues to be true yet for all classes of the yellow race, with the exception of the Japanese. The Japanese has adopted European civilization, has shown that he can whip European soldiers, has a navy equal man for man to the best afloat, and will not submit to be kicked and treated with contempt, as his brother from China still meekly submits to.

You say in your letter that there can be no Imperial interests, to outweigh our own in this matter. I submit that it is not only Imperial interests, but Canadian interests and above all British Columbia interests. The Japanese fleet is nearer to the coast of British Columbia than the shores of Great Britain. I also would call your attention to the exaggeration of your statement that in a very short time British Columbia will be Asiatic. If the Japanese were coming here with their women and with a view to permanent settlement, such language could be accepted without exception being taken to it, but as the Jap, like the Chinaman, comes with no women and with the fixed intention of going back to his native country, the spectacle of an Asiatic British Columbia is rather too long drawn. Having said that much, let me now add that I am in communication with the Japanese authorities and I have not given up hope to settle the matter amicably in the sense which you desire. . . . There is an easy way of preventing this Japanese immigration: it is to close the line of steamers now plying between Vancouver and Japan. But if this line is to be maintained, and I do not think the British Columbia people want to have it closed. They still want to sell Canadian goods to the Japs and to have Vancouver continue as it is at present, the point of shipping, and if this is to be maintained there are unavoidably some disadvantages to be expected, along with the profits.

> Believe me as ever,
> my dear Macpherson etc.
> *Laurier*[11]

It appears that Sir Wilfrid's reply, which devastatingly put down Macpherson's attitude, correctly reflected the views both of the Canadian government and of the majority of Canadians outside British Columbia at that time.

Then on September 7, 1907, it was reported that a ship carrying several hundred Japanese was about to arrive in Vancouver the next day. This caused the Asiatic Exclusion League to organize a parade to City Hall, which was near Chinatown. Maj. E. Browne commanded the parading group, which swelled from two thousand to eight thousand by the time it reached City Hall with its banners of "Stand up for a White Canada" and burned an effigy of Lieutenant Governor James Dunsmuir, who was suspected of favoring Oriental immigration to supply laborers for his collieries. An American exclusionist agitator from Seattle gave a particularly inflammatory speech to help matters along. Finally a stone was tossed through the window of a Chinese store, and a hail of missiles of every kind soon followed. Considerable destruction now ensued as the mob moved through Chinatown, but the Chinese residents barricaded their establishments and kept out of sight. The police had been called but were powerless to act.

When the mob reached Little Tokyo and began to smash windows there, they finally met resistance. The Japanese showered them with rocks from rooftops at first, but eventually stood and fought. They had armed themselves with sticks, clubs, knives, and bottles, anything that was handy, and they subjected the attackers to a beating. The attackers then retreated and dispersed. There were some arrests and several people were hurt, but fortunately no one was killed.

The Japanese immediately set up their own patrols and organized for their own defense in case of a recurrence. Another mob gathered the next day, but police were in place and prevented a repetition of the incident. The reaction across Canada was to condemn the rioters and to point out that Orientals, too, were entitled to the equal protection of the laws. It was also feared that there might be adverse effects upon Anglo-Japanese relations. In Vancouver itself a number of Japanese and Chinese went on strike to protest the occurrence, forcing a number of mills and other business establishments to close down temporarily. The atmosphere remained tense for a few days, but no further major trouble resulted. The mutual suspicion and resentment, however, were not relieved, since the factors leading to the riot in the first place continued to exist. Demands for a complete cessation of Oriental immigration therefore continued to be heard.

The Canadian federal government moved quickly, at this point, to minimize the international effects of the Vancouver riots. Laurier wired the mayor of Vancouver as follows:

> His Excellency the Governor General has learned with deepest regret of the indignities and cruelties of which certain subjects of the Emperor of Japan, a friend and ally of His Majesty the King, have been the victims and he hopes that peace will promptly be restored and all the offenders punished.[12]

The government also established a royal commission, headed by William Lyon Mackenzie King, then deputy minister of labor, to look into the losses suffered by the Japanese in Vancouver and eventually a second commission, also headed by King, to look at the methods by which Oriental laborers had been induced to come to Canada. The prime minister personally conferred with Kikujiro Ishii, of the Japanese Foreign Office, and the Japanese Consul General, Tatsugoro Nosse. W. D. Scott, the superintendent of immigration, was subsequently sent to Vancouver, and instructions were given that Japanese landing in Vancouver from Hawaii were not to be excluded, since this would constitute a violation of the Anglo-Japanese Treaty. Finally, the government announced that

Rodolphe Lemieux, then postmaster general and minister of labor, would be sent to Japan to confer with the British ambassador in Tokyo and with members of the Japanese government.

Japanese press reaction to the Vancouver riots had been moderate, and the prompt actions of the Canadian government appeared to satisfy the Japanese. The Japanese consul general had presented an official protest note with a claim for $13,000 to Ottawa; upon investigation the King commission awarded $9,999 to the claimants. On the matter of immigration, the commission determined that 3,619 of the 8,215 Japanese who had landed in British Columbia between January and October 1907 had been admitted to the United States. Of those remaining in Canada, 3,000 had come from Hawaii and 1,641 directly from Japan. The majority of those coming from Japan had been contracted for by Canadian businesses, such as the Canadian Pacific Railway and the Wellington Colliery Company, dealing with emigration companies in Japan. There had thus not in fact been a change in Japanese government policy on emigration, and no Japanese had entered Canada unless some Canadian company asked for them. King further pointed out that the Japanese government could not be held responsible for the influx from Hawaii, since Japan had no control over Japanese citizens beyond its jurisdiction. It is thus clear from the royal commission report that the widely held view that the Japanese government had acted contrary to its previously given assurances on the restriction of immigration to Canada did not hold true.

The mission of Lemieux to Tokyo lasted for over a month, and he succeeded in negotiating with Count Tadasu Hayashi, the Japanese foreign minister, what came to be known as the Gentlemen's Agreement of 1908. The essence of this agreement is contained in a letter from Count Hayashi affirming that while the existing treaty between Japan and Canada absolutely guarantees to Japanese subjects full liberty to enter, travel, and reside in any part of the dominion of Canada, yet it was not the intention of the imperial government to insist upon the complete enjoyment of the rights and privileges guaranteed by those stipulations when that would involve disregard of special conditions that might prevail in Canada from time to time. Japan therefore specifically volunteered to restrict emigration by two sets of regulations. The first of these limited emigrants to the following categories:

1. prior residents in Canada and their wives and children;

2. those engaged by Japanese residents for bona fide personal and domestic service;

3. contract emigrants whose names and the standing of their employers were satisfactorily specified; and

4. agricultural laborers brought in by Japanese landholders in Canada.

All these had to have certificates issued by Japanese consuls in Canada.

The second set specified that Japanese consuls in Canada were not to issue certificates for contract laborers unless these contracts were approved by the Canadian government. Agricultural laborers were limited to ten for each one hundred acres of land owned by the Japanese in Canada. As to domestics and agricultural laborers under these regulations, the Japanese government did not expect that under existing circumstances these two classes would exceed four hundred annually.

It was further understood that there would be direct access to Canada only, no detours by way of Hawaii. The Gentlemen's Agreement did not completely succeed because its provisions were never explained to the public, which mistakenly believed that only four hundred per year were to be admitted in *all* categories. When it became known that more than four hundred had in fact come in, Japan was accused of bad faith. Though this was explained by the dominion officials, public mistrust of Japan persisted. According to the Japanese interpretation of the Gentlemen's Agreement, the limitation of four hundred applied only to domestic servants and agricultural laborers, and not to the wives and children of those already in Canada or of those emigrating. According to this interpretation of the Gentlemen's Agreement, the number of servants and laborers entering Canada from Japan never exceeded 253 in any one year between 1909 and 1921. While the Gentlemen's Agreement of 1908 kept Japanese immigration below 500 per year for 11 of the next 21 years, and below 1,000 for all but one of the remaining ten years (see Table 1), the number of incoming immigrants never ceased to be an issue between the British Columbia provincial government and the dominion government in Ottawa and con-

Table 1
Japanese Immigrants to Canada, 1907–1929

Year	Number	Year	Number	Year	Number
1907	2,042	1915	592	1923	369
1908	7,601	1916	401	1924	448
1909	495	1917	648	1925	501
1910	271	1918	883	1926	421
1911	437	1919	1,178	1927	475
1912	765	1920	711	1928	478
1913	724	1921	532	1929	445
1914	856	1922	471		

Source: Charles J. Woodsworth, *Canada and the Orient*, Appendix B, p. 289.

sequently remained a point of contention between Canada and Japan as well.

In 1909 less than 500 Japanese immigrants entered. The Japanese were beginning to dominate certain industries, however, and exclusionist agitators were quick to publicize any such trends they might detect. Thus by 1911 half the men in gill netting were Japanese. Only those naturalized could get fishing licenses, but many of the Japanese fishermen had dual citizenship, though they were popularly regarded as aliens. By 1912 there were increasing restrictions on licenses designed to keep out the Japanese, new fishing licenses being restricted to whites and Indians.

A new treaty of commerce and navigation was negotiated between Great Britain and Japan on April 3, 1911, and it contained the clause permitting entry, travel, and residence to citizens of both countries in one another's territory, including the stipulation that the treaty would not be applicable to the British dominions unless notice of adherence was given within two years. The Laurier government chose not to accept the new treaty but agreed to continue under the former treaty for another two years, which proved acceptable to Japan. The Laurier government further took the position that the regulation of immigration under the Gentlemen's Agreement was entirely satisfactory to Canada. King, who since 1908 had been sitting in the House as the Laurier government's minister of labor, defended the government's position on the immigration question against attacks that called for a more restrictive approach.

In the general election of 1911, Sir Robert Borden and the Conservatives came to power in Ottawa. Though Borden had often attacked the Liberals on the matter of the Gentlemen's Agreement, he subsequently (in 1913) declared his readiness to adhere to the Anglo-Japanese treaty of 1911, provided that it would not repeal or affect the provisions of the Immigration Act of 1910, which gave Canada the power to bar immigration under certain conditions. The Japanese chose to regard this act as nondiscriminatory, since it applied to all aliens entering Canada, and consequently accepted the proviso. Borden now became a warm defender of the Gentlemen's Agreement, stating that Japan had been observing it "very loyally," and thus the treaty was accepted by Canada as of April 1913, with the Japanese consul general, Takashi Nakamura, giving assurance in writing that Japan fully intended to maintain the controls and limitations she had enforced since 1908. Meanwhile, in July 1911, the Anglo-Japanese Alliance had been renewed, and this was a continuing inducement for the maintenance of cordial relations between Canada and Japan.

When World War I broke out in August of 1914, Japan and Canada were thus linked by the Anglo-Japanese Alliance, the Trade Treaty of 1911 and the Gentlemen's Agreement of 1908, and for once the "immigration blues" receded into the background. The increased demand for workers in British Columbia was also helpful.

As it happened, in July 1914 there was a German naval squadron cruising about in the Pacific, commanded by Adm. Graf von Spee, that had left Kiaochow in China prior to the outbreak of the war. It included the light cruisers *Leipzig, Dresden,* and *Nürnberg*, which were faster and which collectively outgunned Canada's solitary fighting ship in the Pacific, the light cruiser H.M.C.S. *Rainbow*, which was based at Esquimalt, B.C. The *Rainbow* was 300 feet long, displaced 3,600 tons, had a top speed of 20 knots; it carried two six-inch guns, four twelve pounders, two fourteen-inch torpedo tubes, and a complement of 300 men. It had been built in England in 1891 and sold to the Royal Canadian Navy in 1910 for £50,000.00. Hugh L. Keenleyside commented that he thought the *Rainbow* could barely get up enough steam to get out of the harbor.[13]

British Columbia premier Sir Richard McBride apparently felt that, in view of the possibility that the German squadron might bombard Vancouver, *Rainbow* was insufficient protection. He therefore went to Seattle just prior to the outbreak of the war and purchased two small submarines (subsequently named CC1 and CC2), which had been built for the Chilean navy but were not completely paid for. McBride purchased the two submarines for $575,000 each on behalf of the province of British Columbia, thereby adding eight eighteen-inch torpedo tubes to the defense of the British Columbia coast, though it is likely that Spee's squadron would have overpowered even these augmented forces, had he come anywhere near the Canadian coast. Only one of the German ships, the *Leipzig*, intruded into the cool waters of the Northern Pacific, long enough to make a quick coaling call in neutral San Francisco. *Rainbow* was ordered out to challenge the German squadron and, as luck would have it, was unable to find *Leipzig*. The Royal Canadian Navy eventually took over the submarines from the province of British Columbia, thus ending the short history of the British Columbia navy.

Japan, in observance of the Anglo-Japanese Alliance, immediately sent the battleship *Izumo* and the cruiser *Asama* to protect the British Columbia Coast, and England sent the light cruiser *Newcastle*, much to the relief of the population of Vancouver and other communities on the Canadian West Coast. The German squadron had meanwhile moved south to Mexico and Chile and was later sunk by British warships near the Falkland Islands.[14]

Young, Reid, and Carrothers have noted that "a feeling almost approximating goodwill was generated towards the Japanese immigrants in British Columbia" at this time.[15] However, the exclusionists and alarmists in the province were not dead, and when Japan pressed her twenty-one demands upon China in 1915, it was duly noted by those who had always seen Japan as aggressively imperialist and expansionist in the Pacific area. Japan's subsequent actions in occupying parts of Shantung province, which they had seized from the Germans, in seeking to maintain military forces in Siberia after the collapse of Kolchak, and in continuing her drive to dominate Manchuria, seemed to confirm the warnings of those who regarded Japan as a menace that might eventually threaten Canada. During the war, however, these antagonisms were at relatively low ebb, as were those generated by unemployment or wage disputes.

Although not exactly welcomed with open arms, some two hundred Japanese-Canadians volunteered for service with the Canadian armed forces during the war. A total of 197 of them served in the war, and 54 were killed in action. They served with the 209th, the 175th, 191st, and 192nd Battalions and with the 13th Cavalry; all but 10 of the survivors were wounded, and 13 of them received the Military Medal for Bravery.

The reluctance of the British Columbia government to accept military service from the Japanese-Canadian volunteers may in part have been based on the fear that it might lead to a demand for the franchise for the Japanese. Thus the Japanese volunteers were accepted for service in the province of Alberta rather than in their home province of British Columbia. They were in fact permitted to vote in the federal elections while serving in France, but when the returned veterans petitioned for the vote in British Columbia after the war, they were turned down in April 1920, for at the beginning of the twenties the tide of anti-Japanese exclusionist sentiment was on the rise once again in British Columbia.

The Anglo-Japanese Alliance was up for renewal at this time, with Prime Minister Arthur Meighen going to London for the Imperial Conference of 1921, which was to discuss this issue. The exclusionists wanted the treaty terminated so that Canada would gain the right to exclude Japanese immigrants once and for all; a Chinese exclusion act was in fact passed two years later, in 1923.

Canadian opposition to a renewal of the Anglo-Japanese treaty went far beyond the concerns of a few agitators in British Columbia, however. At the level of international politics, Britain was concerned with the maintenance of her power in the Pacific in the face of the increasing power of both Japan and the United States. If the motivation for the alliance of 1902 had been to stop Imperial Russia from dominating the Far East, the motivation for extending the treaty in 1921 might be to stop the United States from becoming the dominant power. War between the United States and Great Britain was not totally unthinkable at that time.

Canada for its part feared that an extension of the alliance might indeed lead to a confrontation between Britain and the United States, and since Canada was most anxious to preserve the U.S. connection, Meighen had to oppose an extension of the alliance. The increasingly negative perception of Japan resulting from the annexation of Korea, the twenty-one demands against China, and

the persistent encroachments of the Japanese imperialist jugger-
naut upon China seemed to validate the claims of the exclusionists
in British Columbia that Japan might eventually encroach upon the
North American continent and that her immigrants were spies and
her fishermen Imperial Navy officers in disguise, dispatched to
chart the British Columbia Coast in preparation for a Japanese invasion. A majority of the press and of members of Parliament were
in fact against the treaty. Thus when Meighen arrived in London in
the summer of 1921 he spoke strongly and persuasively against the
renewal of the alliance. He proposed instead that a conference of
the major powers in the Pacific (Great Britain, the United States,
Japan, and France) be convened.

The British government accepted this suggestion, and the Washington Conference was convened in November of 1921. The resulting
Four Power Treaty was signed on December 13, 1921, with Borden
signing for Canada as a member of the British Empire delegation.
Article 4 of this treaty specified that upon ratification it would
terminate the Anglo-Japanese Alliance.[16] Prime Minister Meighen
could take credit for having set these events in motion.

Thus in the immediate postwar years the confrontation between
the Japanese and the whites in British Columbia was soon reestablished. As soldiers returned and jobs became scarce, Orientals
were once again scrutinized. The increasing birth rate among
Orientals, stimulated by the influx of picture brides from Japan
made possible by the Gentlemen's Agreement, was now seen as the
new menace. The increasing economic success of the Japanese in
the province was also the target of growing jealousy. Returning soldiers described British Columbia as "overrun" by Oriental immigrants. This led eventually to the modification of the Gentlemen's
Agreement in 1924, when the quota of 400 was reduced to 150. A
further modification of the agreement came in 1928, when the
wives and children of Japanese residents were included in the
quota, thus further limiting the number of Japanese immigrants.
Between March 1922 and March 1928 the annual average of Japanese immigrants was 449, of which two-thirds were females. But
some whites in British Columbia were still not satisfied, and so
Prime Minister King obtained further modification of the Gentlemen's Agreement, giving technical control of the movement of Japanese immigrants into the hands of the Canadian representative in

Tokyo. Further immigration of Chinese into British Columbia or the rest of Canada had meanwhile been brought to a halt by the Chinese Exclusion Act of 1923.

A less controversial area of Canada-Japan interaction was trade, which had originally been the incentive for the building of the transcontinental railroads, in the expectation that vast markets for Canada's products would be developed in Japan, China, and other countries of the Far East. There has indeed been a steadily growing volume of large resource exports to Asia from the British Columbia coast, though the dreams of "vast" markets have not really been fulfilled.

As for the trade with Japan in particular, it began quite modestly in the 1870s, increasing every year until 1920, when Canada imported almost $14 million worth of goods while exporting just under $8 million worth to Japan. During this first half-century of trade, Japan consistently sold more goods to Canada than it bought. (See Table 2.) Tea was the principal item shipped from Japan to Canada and accounted for the Japanese trade surplus; silk, pottery, toys, oranges, and other incidentals made up the balance. The Canadian import surplus situation (unfavorable balance of trade) was dramatically turned around by 1925, when Canada enjoyed a three-to-one surplus of exports to Japan. In 1929, when diplomatic relations were finally established, Canada exported $42

Table 2
Canada's Trade with Japan, Selected Years, 1870–1929 (in dollars)

Exports to Japan (5 year average)		Imports from Japan (5 year average)	
1870s	1,000	1870s	311,000
1880	26,891	1880	542,972
1890	26,825	1890	1,258,763
1900	110,735	1900	1,751,415
1910	659,118	1910	1,673,542
1920	7,732,514	1920	13,637,287
1929	42,100,000	1929	12,921,000

Sources: Based on A.R.M. Lower, *Canada and the Far East—1940*, p. 51; the figures from the 1870s and 1929 are from C. J. Woodsworth, *Canada and the Orient*, p. 307.

Note: Dollar values throughout this book are in Canadian dollars.

million worth of goods to Japan while importing only $13 million. This pattern of Canadian export surpluses has never been reversed since 1920.[17]

The reason for the Canadian surpluses lies in Japan's needs and the nature of the complementarity between the two economies. Canada, with its huge territory and abundant natural resources, none of which are sufficiently available in Japan, is a natural supplier to Japan of such resource materials as lumber, forest products, pulp, newsprint, coal, wheat, potash, iron ore, copper, nickel, other nonferrous metals, and a number of agricultural products, such as rapeseed, soybeans, pork, and beef. Japan, with its ever-growing manufacturing industry, serving a population several times that of Canada, needs these resource materials in very great quantities, and so long as Canada can deliver, is most eager to buy. Canada, on the other hand, with its much smaller population, needs only a relatively modest amount of the manufactured goods Japan produces. The permanent deficit Japan has experienced in its trade with Canada is counterbalanced by its excess of exports to other areas, such as the United States.

Canada's first commercial agent in Japan was appointed in 1897. Canada's participation in the exhibition at Osaka in 1903, when Fisher visited Japan, acquainted the Japanese public with a wide range of Canadian goods available for export. As the Japanese began to eat more bread and meat, Canada stood ready as the logical supplier. Meanwhile, the Anglo-Japanese trade treaties to which Canada had adhered made for favorable conditions of trade, including reciprocal most-favored-nation treatment. A trade commissioner was appointed to Yokohama in 1904. In 1923, after the great earthquake in Japan, the Yokohama office was transferred to Kobe. Finally, in 1929, when the Canadian legation in Tokyo was opened, a commercial secretary was appointed to the legation and the future outlook for the development of Japanese-Canadian trade seemed favorable indeed.

Yet another aspect of the Canadian-Japanese relationship has been the work of Canadian missionaries in Japan. Christianity had been prohibited during the Tokugawa feudal period, and the ban on the practice of foreign religions was not officially removed until 1873. It is in this very year that the first two Canadian missionaries arrived in Japan, both Methodists, the Reverend Davidson Macdonald and the Reverend George Cochrane. Church of England missionaries, Presbyterians, and Roman Catholics, including Franciscan fathers from Quebec, followed in later years. The Canadian missionaries came as teachers, evangelists, and medical workers. They founded churches, schools, hospitals, or contributed to church institutions that were not distinctly Canadian, such as the YMCA and YWCA, doing their work in prefectures and cities all over Japan.

Among Canada's many missionaries in Japan was the Reverend Dan Norman, a Methodist Minister who reached Japan in 1897 at age 33. He was the father of E. Herbert Norman, who would be a Canadian diplomat and Japanologist, and of W. Howard Norman, who was later to be a clergyman, teacher and educational administrator in Japan. Dan Norman studied Japanese in Tokyo and later worked in Kanazawa, in Tokyo, and finally in Nagano, the capital of Nagano prefecture. There he continued as a missionary and preacher until 1934, when he retired. His tireless zeal earned him the respect and affection of thousands of Japanese, because he showed by his actions that he was sincere in his beliefs, and he set an example for his sons, who were to make their own significant contributions to the Canadian impact on Japan.[18]

The first branch of the YWCA in Japan was opened in Tokyo in 1903 by A. Caroline Macdonald. The Canadian Methodist Church opened the Canadian Methodist Academy of Kobe in 1913, originally as a school for missionary children. D. R. McKenzie, secretary of the Japan Methodist Mission, had suggested to the Methodist Mission Board in Canada in 1911 that a full school program from Grade 1 through high school be established in Japan to meet the needs of the children of Canadian Methodist missionaries of school age. This eventually led to grants being made for land and buildings, and in 1912 Ethel Misener and Lucy Norman were sent to Japan to be principal and matron of the academy in Kobe. Land was bought at Aotanicho, and the school opened its doors in 1913. By 1923 the enrollment had risen to 244. The name was changed to Canadian Academy, and donations from a variety of sources made possible the purchase of additional land and buildings, as the institution acquired a fine reputation for the quality of its academic program and the intellectual caliber of its students. Among its graduates from the prewar years are two prominent Canadian diplomats, the late E. Herbert Norman, former ambassador to Egypt, and Arthur R. Menzies, former Canadian ambassador to the People's Republic of China, and also the Reverend W. Howard Norman, later to be principal of the Canadian Academy, James Stewart, former director of the Japan Society of New York, and a long list of distinguished professionals.[19]

The Reverend Davidson Macdonald had founded the first Methodist church in Japan in Shizuoka and also served as an adviser and practicing physician in the Shizuoka hospital. By the beginning of World War I there were 120 or more Canadian missionaries in Japan contributing to charitable and educational work. Canadian Methodists directly or indirectly developed the following schools: Toyo Eiwa Gakko,[20] Azabu Middle School, Kwansei Gakuin, Aoyama Gakuin, Toyo Eiwa Jogakuin, Shizuoka Eiwa Jogakuin, and Yamanashi Eiwa Jogakuin.[21]

Beginning in the late 1890s, some twenty years after the arrival of Manzo Nagano, a number of prominent Japanese visitors made brief appearances in Canada, reflecting, perhaps, the increasing awareness of and interest in Canada felt in Japan, though in a number of cases it seems that traveling by way of Canada to Europe or back from Europe was primarily a way of saving travel time, since the CPR and the excellent Canadian Pacific steamship service on the Empress liners was preferable to the Europe-to-Asia steamship services by way of the Suez Canal. Among the most prominent of these visitors were Ito Hirobumi, the father of the Meiji Constitution; Prince Iwakura Tomosada, son of the leader of the Iwakura mission to the United States; Prime Minister Hara Kei; Prince Fushimi; and Admiral Togo, the victor of the Battle of Tsushima.

It is against this background of a variety of interrelationships between Canada and Japan, dating back to the 1870s, that in 1928 King announced the Canadian government's intention to open a Canadian legation in Japan. The matter was considered as early as November 1927.

The matter was discussed with the British government in London, and Sir Austen Chamberlain declared his readiness to aid Canada in securing an exchange of ministers between Canada and Japan. Since the renegotiated Gentlemen's Agreement stipulated the involvement of Canadian representatives in Japan in issuing the passports of prospective Japanese immigrants to Canada, it was now proposed that the Canadian minister in Japan would be entrusted with that task. The British foreign office carried this proposal to the Tokyo government through its ambassador, Sir John Tilley.

According to a handwritten report on file in the Diplomatic Records Office in Tokyo, the British ambassador to Japan had an interview with the Japanese foreign minister, Baron Giichi Tanaka, on January 10, 1928, and inquired about the posting of a Canadian Minister in Japan.

> In reply to a question by the foreign minister, the ambassador explained the differences in competence between the British ambassador and the Canadian minister and the position of Canada with regard to the conclusion of treaties and stated that if the Japanese government were to receive a Canadian minister, relations between the two countries would become increasingly good.
>
> (Note) Moreover, the ambassador, before departing told me (Yamagata) that there were no major problems between Canada and Japan apart from immigration and that he did not think that the Japanese government had any objection to the posting of a minister. That he had discussed the matter with Vice Minister Debuchi and was unable to learn the Japanese government's intention from him, and he repeated that since his telegraphic instructions had been brief, he regretted that he could not give detailed explanations to the minister.[22]

It appears from this memorandum that the matter was clearly a Canadian initiative, with certain overtones in Canadian politics, and that the Japanese government, if not reluctant on the issue, was at the very least cautious and perceived no great urgency.

Finally, on January 19, 1928, the Dominions Office notified the Canadian government that "today His Majesty's Ambassador at Tokyo has telegraphed that he was informed by the Japanese Minister of Foreign Affairs last night that the Government of Japan will be happy to receive a Canadian Minister in Japan and to send a Minister to Canada."[23] During 1928 a sum of $50,000 was voted for the proposed new legation but was not used during that fiscal year. There was a delay in the appointment of the first minister, who was to be Herbert M. Marler, a former cabinet minister. Since

Marler could not reach Japan before September 1929, the Canadian government decided to open the legation in May 1929 under Keenleyside, the first secretary and chargé d'affaires. James A. Langley, the Canadian government trade commissioner in Kobe, was appointed as commercial secretary. Notifications of the acceptance of Marler from the Japanese government came on June 25, 1929. Marler presented his letters of credence to Emperor Hirohito on September 18, 1929, thereby becoming Canada's first accredited diplomatic envoy in Japan.

NOTES

1. This chapter is based largely on such pioneering works as Charles J. Woodsworth, *Canada and the Orient*; A.R.M. Lower, *Canada and the Far East, 1940*; Charles H. Young, *The Japanese Canadians*; Forbes E. La Violette, *The Canadian Japanese and World War II*; and Ken Adachi, *The Enemy That Never Was*. Unless otherwise noted, these have been my principal sources.

2. E. V. Warriner, *Voyage to Destiny*; H. Kaneko, *Manjiro—The Man Who Discovered America*.

3. Keitaro Yamashita, *Kanada Fugen*, pp. 108ff.

4. Ibid., pp. 368ff. Sugimura was Japan's consul general in Vancouver in 1889.

5. Canada, *Report of the Royal Commission on Chinese and Japanese Immigration*, 1902.

6. Named after an act passed by the state of Natal in the Union of South Africa, which sought to prevent immigration by requiring prospective immigrants to pass an examination in a European language.

7. Jinshiro Nakayama, *Kanada no Hōko*, pp. 1447ff.

8. Ibid., pp. 860-61.

9. Ken Adachi, *The Enemy That Never Was*, pp. 32-33.

10. The Treaty of Portsmouth was signed September 5, 1905, and ratified November 25, 1905.

11. Public Archives of Canada, *Laurier papers*, pp. 127879-82.

12. Woodsworth, *Canada and the Orient*, p. 80.

13. Interview with Dr. Keenleyside, April 13, 1977.

14. G. N. Tucker, *The Naval Service of Canada*, pp. 261-302.

15. Charles H. Young, *The Japanese Canadians*, p. 13.

16. See J. B. Brebner, "Canada, The Anglo-Japanese Alliance and The Washington Conference," *Political Science Quarterly* 50 (March 1935): 45-58.

17. Japan's sudden need for great quantities of Canadian lumber was occasioned in the aftermath of the great earthquake of 1923, which left millions of Japanese homeless and the cities of Tokyo and Yokohama in burned-out ruins.

18. Rui Watanabe and Tae Mizuno, *Witnesses of the Way in Japan*, pp. 3–17.

19. Data on the Canadian Academy are taken from a mimeographed paper by Gwen R. P. Norman (wife of the Reverend W. Howard Norman), entitled *A Brief History of the Canadian Academy* (Toronto: 1977), 10 pp.

20. Founded in 1884 by Martha Cartmell of the Women's Missionary Society of the Canadian Methodist Mission.

21. Nobuya Bamba, "Nippon, Kanada Kankei no Tenkai" (The Development of Japanese–Canadian Relations), *Kokusai Mondai*, no. 203 (February 1977), p. 3.

22. Records of Meetings with the Foreign Minister, no. 43, visit of the Ambassador of Great Britain, Sir John Tilley to Foreign Minister Tanaka, afternoon of January 10, 1928, Diplomatic Records Office, Ministry of Foreign Affairs, Tokyo. Author's translation.

23. Canada, Department of External Affairs (DEA), file 901–B27, January 19, 1928.

2

The New Legation, 1921–1941: Canadian-Japanese Relations up to the Outbreak of World War II

The establishment of a Canadian legation in Tokyo, soon after the setting up of similar missions in Washington and Paris, came when the Department of External Affairs (DEA) in Ottawa was still in its infancy. Prime Minister King appears to have seen the establishment of these missions merely as initial steps, which would eventually lead to the establishment of missions in several countries. The ministers in Paris and Tokyo were perceived as ministers-at-large, each with a whole continent as his field of activity, since they were Canada's only representatives in Europe and Asia, respectively.[1] Japan was seen as Canada's nearest neighbor in Asia, and the minister to Japan was also to develop friendly relations and trade with China. King thought that Canada should have its representatives in the capitals of the four great powers that controlled the affairs of the world, that is, in Washington, London, Paris, and Tokyo.[2] These representatives would also lend diplomatic authority and support to Canada's trade representatives and commercial negotiators, so that they would not be at a status disadvantage vis-à-vis the representatives of other countries.[3]

The Conservative Opposition in Parliament not only begrudged the expense involved ("It is idle boasting to talk about our position in a foreign country because some representative over there can

wear gold and lace and a uniform. That does not advance the interests of the country a single sou.''[4]), but it also saw a threat to the
unity of the commonwealth in this action. R. B. Bennett, who later
became prime minister, believed that all that Canada needed was
the trade commissioners "to carry forward Canada's trade," but
King forged resolutely ahead in establishing Canadian independence
in foreign affairs. He pointed out to Bennett that the Gentlemen's
Agreement, which had proved so effective in reducing the inflow of
Japanese immigrants, had been concluded by a Canadian minister
(Lemieux, who meanwhile had become the speaker in the House of
Commons) and might not have been achieved otherwise.[5]

Marler, who had been a member of King's cabinet in 1925 and
was chosen as Canada's first minister to Japan, had been elected to
the House of Commons in 1921 for the constituency of St. Lawrence–St. George (Montreal). Defeated in the general election of
1925, he resigned from the cabinet. Marler's appointment by King
was political, at a time when the Canadian diplomatic service was
still too young to provide senior career officers for diplomatic
postings.

Keenleyside, who preceded Marler to Japan in May 1929 in order
to establish the new legation, had been a lecturer in history at the
University of British Columbia and at Syracuse University before
joining the Department of External Affairs. That he was from British Columbia and could therefore represent Western Canadian
views in the legation appears to have been a consideration in his appointment. Langley,[6] who was to become the first commercial secretary in Tokyo, had for five years served in Kobe as Canadian
trade commissioner and thus brought experience in Japanese affairs that would be of great value to the mission.

Keenleyside recalls that he entered the first open examination for
DEA in July 1928, with Lester B. Pearson and many others in the
same room. Pearson joined the department in July 1928, and Keenleyside joined on September 1. Keenleyside worked in Ottawa for
the first eight months, and on May 20, 1929, he presented himself
to the Japanese government as the chargé d'affaires of the new Canadian legation. He had practically no previous experience or
knowledge of Japan, and he was not quite sure how one started a
new mission. He had, in fact, been given few instructions in that respect. Langley soon joined Keenleyside in Tokyo, where they were

to work together for the next seven years. Since there was no legation as yet, Keenleyside stayed at the Imperial Hotel until he found a house in the Nagai compound near Shibuya, where he set up an office on the ground floor and the residence on the upper floor. He was thirty years old at the time.[7]

The Canadian flag was raised for the first time in the Orient on July 1, 1929, at the Dominion Day celebration at the Tokyo legation, with Keenleyside as chargé d'affaires. D. R. McKenzie, the oldest Canadian resident in Japan at the time, delivered an address on that occasion.

Meanwhile, Baron Tanaka, the Japanese prime minister, who also acted as foreign minister, had notified the British ambassador on June 25 that "the Imperial Government accepts with pleasure the appointment of Mr. Marler." Marler sailed from Vancouver on the *Empress of France* on August 29 and arrived in Tokyo on September 9. Nine days later, on September 18, he presented his credentials to Emperor Hirohito, who was at that time in the fourth year of his reign.

Diplomatic procedure in the imperial capital of Tokyo was highly formal and required strict observance of a series of steps, beginning with the presentation of credentials and continuing with post-presentation calls and later attendances at imperial banquets, receptions, and various other festive occasions. Since a newly arrived minister is not officially confirmed in his position until the presentation of his credentials to the emperor, he was instructed that he might make no official appearance at any public function, nor might he accept any invitation tendered to him in his official capacity, for example, to formal dinners. He was permitted only informal private luncheons or teas. It was, however, expected that the new minister would make two informal calls, one on the foreign minister of Japan and the other on the senior member of the diplomatic corps. Then there were calls on other diplomats, visits to shrines and temples, imperial receptions and banquets, the imperial military review, the imperial duck hunting party, the imperial chrysanthemum and cherry parties, cormorant fishing at Gifu, the New Year's reception, the annual opening of Parliament, funerals of imperial relatives, New Year's Day calls, diplomatic funerals, and other social and cultural engagements. For all these diplomatic procedures, rigid protocol was prescribed.[8]

Chancery quarters for the new legation were originally set up in the Imperial Life Building in Marunouchi, close to Tokyo Station, the Imperial Palace, and most government offices. The commercial office was also established there. Meanwhile the minister rented, as a temporary official residence, a house formerly occupied by the Romanian legation and obtained permission to build an annex to it as a library.

Marler soon began the task of building a new Canadian legation, which was completed in 1933. As Keenleyside recalls, Marler went back to Canada, and in spite of the previously negative attitude of the Conservative prime minister, Bennett, Marler was able to obtain his agreement to the building of a Canadian legation in Tokyo.

Upon his return to Tokyo he was able to purchase an exceptionally well situated three-acre lot in Akasaka, facing the Akasaka Detached Palace (the residence of Prince Chichibu, the eldest brother of Emperor Hirohito) and within easy commuting distance of Tokyo's most important shopping, transportation, business, and governmental districts, yet well away from the noise and congestion of the downtown streets. Since the money for the building of the legation was not immediately available from Ottawa, which then faced the stringencies of the economic depression, Marler offered to advance the money himself (at 6 percent interest during construction and 5 percent thereafter). This meant that the legation could be built at a considerable savings to the government, since labor costs and land prices were then depressed in Japan. Marler stated that the government might save close to a quarter of a million dollars by building at that time. The government agreed, and five years later, in June 1935, Parliament approved an expenditure of $200,000 and repaid Marler the full amount.

Meanwhile Marler had borrowed the money, purchased the land, and built the legation. He personally planned and supervised the construction, helped to design the building, working with three architects (a Canadian from Montreal, a Czech-American living in Japan, and a Japanese), and saw to it that the buildings, a chancery and a residence, were earthquake resistant. As the result of Marler's labors, Canada today has one of the finest diplomatic residences in Tokyo, a large, handsome, impressive structure, more than equal to the task of representing Canada. The grounds were landscaped anew, a Japanese garden was retained, and spacious lawns provided. Lady Beatrice Isabel Marler personally supervised the interior decoration, traveling to Canada and England to buy furniture and seeking the help of a Montreal interior decorator to buy additional furniture, material for curtains, china, glass, silver, and linens. The Marler carpets, purchased in China, remained in all the rooms and halls into the 1970s, as did most of the furniture, re-upholstered from time to time. The final cost of construction was $200,549.21, of which $549.21 was paid by Marler himself, since he had undertaken to keep the cost within $200,000. Herbert O. Moran, Canada's ambassador to Japan from 1966 to 1972, decided to honor the memory of Marler by having the residence formally named Marler House.

In 1952 Canada's chargé d'affaires in Tokyo, Menzies, gave a dinner in honor of Prime Minister Shigeru Yoshida at the legation. Yoshida related to him that he had played an intermediary role in the acquisition of the Canadian embassy property. When Yoshida was vice-minister, Marler had been looking for a piece of property on which to build a legation. Yoshida was acquainted with a Japanese family that was having difficulty selling a well-situated property because it was alleged to be haunted by the ghosts of two suicides. It had come to him in a flash that the property could be sold to the Canadians, since Westerners apprehended the presence of ghosts only when they heard the thud of heavy feet. Japanese ghosts, however, make no heavy footfalls but move silently on a wisp of smoke. He had therefore concluded that Canadians would not be troubled by Japanese ghosts, and arranged to sell the property to Marler. He capped the story by asking Menzies if he had ever been aware of a ghost in the residence.[9]

Prime Minister Bennett, who had opposed the establishment of a legation in Tokyo while in the opposition and who could have replaced King's appointee when he came to power, did not do so. In fact, he spoke warmly of Marler in the House of Commons, declaring:

> The Minister to Japan, entering upon his duties with enthu-siasm, after having addressed a considerable number of pub-lic meetings in various parts of Canada, has zealously and with great toil continued to discharge the duties of his office. He has made sacrifices, not only financially but of his own

personal comfort. His hospitality so generously extended in the Far East, the excellent reputation Canada has gained through the sympathetic consideration which has been given by Mr. and Mrs. Marler to every matter engaging the attention of the people in the city in which they reside, has done much to raise the name of Canada among the people among whom they have lived.[10]

A different assessment of Marler comes from Keenleyside, who recalls that

he was a man without humour, and in consequence without the sense of proportion that humour can provide. He was overly impressed and misled, by a feeling of the dignity of his position, which resulted in a very rigid interpretation of the rules of protocol, which was sometimes unwise. But at base he was an honourable, decent, and a kindly man and I was very fond of him.[11]

Emperoro Hirohito first received Marler on September 18, 1929. A. Takahashi, master of the imperial household, came to escort the Canadian minister from the Imperial Hotel, which was decorated with Canadian and Japanese flags for the occasion. Count Tadasu Hayashi, a former ambassador to London, and Baron Kijuro Shidehara, the foreign minister, greeted Marler at the palace, where he exchanged greetings with the emperor, wished felicity to members of the imperial household, and expressed the intention of extending the bonds of trade and friendship between the two countries. Marler subsequently traveled around Japan expounding the advantages of mutual trade and explaining Canada's position in the British Commonwealth.[12]

As minister in Tokyo, Marler had been constantly concerned about being placed on an equal level with the British ambassador, to manifest Canada's equality in the empire and reinforce his own prestige as a diplomat in Japan. Accordingly, on the recommendation of Prime Minister Bennett, Marler was created a Knight Commander of the Order of St. Michael and St. George, so that in 1935 he became Sir Herbert Marler, K.C.M.G. The recognition extended to him by the Crown apparently came at a moment when his confidence had been somewhat impaired by a trade dispute between Canada and Japan and served partly to restore his prestige in Japan. Marler was recalled from Tokyo on July 3, 1936.

Meanwhile, the first Japanese minister to Canada, Prince Iyemasa Tokugawa, had arrived in Victoria, B.C., on October 12, 1929, and was greeted enthusiastically by large numbers of Japanese residents of British Columbia. Prince Tokugawa had been born in Tokyo in 1884, the eldest son of Prince Iyesato Tokugawa, then the senior member of the Tokugawa family, who had ruled Japan from 1603 to 1868. The new minister was a graduate in political studies from Tokyo Imperial University, had entered the Japanese Foreign Service, and served as consul general in Sidney, Australia, before becoming minister to Canada. During his early days in Canada, Tokugawa exhorted "the nations bordering on the Pacific to co-operate for Peace." He proceeded to Ottawa and was received at a public dinner by Prime Minister King on October 21, 1929. During the months that followed, Tokugawa spoke to Canadian clubs in Ottawa, Montreal, Toronto, Quebec City, Saskatoon, Edmonton, Vancouver, and Victoria.[13] He served in Ottawa until 1934, when he was posted as ambassador to Turkey.

Just prior to the establishment of the Canadian legation in Tokyo, Japanese immigrants, operating under the successive revisions of the Gentlemen's Agreement, were still coming into Canada at the rate of roughly 500 persons per year. (During the ten-year period from 1920 to 1929, the exact average was 485 a year.) Exclusionists in British Columbia continued to regard this as an excessive influx and kept demanding total exclusion of the Japanese. Meanwhile, the desire of Japanese citizens to come to Canada had diminished for various reasons, but the Tokyo government was nevertheless insistent that the indignity of excluding Japanese by name be avoided. However, the British Columbia legislature reacted to the news that Canada and Japan were about to exchange ministers with the demand that the dominion government ask Japan and China to repatriate Orientals in British Columbia, "so that the proportion of Orientals in Canada to the Canadian population shall not exceed the proportion of Canadians in China and Japan respectively to the population of China and Japan."[14] In actuality the immigration question had effectively been brought under control by 1929-30, with 150 passports issued annually by the Japanese government, after endorsement by a Japanese consular official in Canada, and visas being affixed to these passports by the Tokyo legation, provided they had passed the scrutiny of the Canadian immigration authorities in Vancouver, Victoria, or Ottawa.

The major differences between Canada and Japan during the thirties were political disagreements and suspicions generated by the Japanese takeover of Manchuria in 1931 and its subsequent series of political, military, and economic encroachments on the Chinese mainland.

On September 18, 1931, when a mysterious explosion damaged the railroad at Peitaying, the Japanese Kwangtung army blamed Nationalist soldiers for the explosion and killed three Chinese soldiers from a nearby barracks. By the following morning the Japanese army had taken over the nearby city of Mukden. Military operations continued apace, and by the end of the year Japan had taken over all of Southern Manchuria.

Keenleyside was reporting to Ottawa in the absence of Marler and was strongly critical of Japan's actions, which he regarded not as a case of self-defense against Chinese provocation but as part of a deliberate effort by the Japanese military to pursue its preference for a military takeover.[15]

The Chinese government immediately appealed to the League of Nations, which responded four days later, advising both sides to withdraw their troops. Japan refused withdrawal and contended that it would solve the dispute directly with China. Canada, following the lead of both Britain and the United States, showed little inclination to become directly involved in the matter at the league in Geneva.[16]

When Marler returned to the legation in November, he found himself largely disagreeing with his first secretary, whose reports he regarded as misleading. To redress the balance, on December 1, 1931, Marler sent off to Ottawa a forty-one-page memorandum in which he called Japan's military actions "self-defence," unpremeditated, and not in the nature of intentional aggression. As for the actions of the great powers in the league, he called it "a gigantic game of bluff."[17] O. D. Skelton, the Under Secretary of State for External Affairs (USSEA), replied to Marler in a brief note, concluding that "you have given Japan rather too clean a bill of health."[18]

In November 1931 the league accepted a Japanese proposal to

send a commission of inquiry to the Far East to conduct a fact-finding investigation. Lord Victor A.G.R. Lytton headed the commission, which produced its report in October 1932. The Lytton Commission found that Japan's actions in Manchuria were not in self-defense and that the creation of the "independent state of Manchukuo" was not the work of the Manchurians themselves.[19] It moreover recommended that an autonomous government be established in Manchuria under the sovereignty of China. The new government was then to reestablish order in the area and pledge to protect Japan's rights and interests.

Marler appears to have been generally in tune with the government in wishing to maintain a relatively low posture, in not believing in the efficacy of sanctions against Japan, and in hoping that a peaceful negotiated settlement could be brought about by moral suasion rather than by forceful action. Since Canada lacked substantial armed forces of her own and was essentially concerned with the maintenance of good trade relations with Japan, apparently it seemed to Marler that Canada could not really act differently.[20] On March 1, 1932, after the Japanese had attacked Shanghai, Marler cabled Ottawa that he did not believe that invoking sanctions would serve any useful purpose and ended his despatch as follows: "I am reluctantly obliged to say that the action of Japan at Shanghai should be censured. . . . If Canada takes part in [a] vote of censure [at the League of Nations], however, there is no doubt that our trade with Japan will suffer."[21]

In March 1932 Sir George Perley was appointed the Canadian delegate to the League of Nations assembly session, and in a speech on March 8 he spoke moderately of averting further bloodshed but also indicated that Canada took the U.S. position that the establishment of Manchukuo could not be recognized, since it had been brought about by force.

When the Lytton Report was, in fact, discussed by the assembly of the League of Nations on December 6, 1932, C. H. Cahan, the secretary of state, was sent to Geneva to speak for Canada. Cahan's speech was later perceived in Geneva, Canada, China, and Japan as having been, in effect, pro-Japanese, or at the very least not very critical of Japan, and not supportive of strong league action against Japan. In fairness, it should be remembered that neither King nor Prime Minister Bennett could be seen during the thirties as champions of strong action against Japan. Cahan rejected sanctions as out of place at this stage and wound up by saying:

> It appears to my government very desirable, as a lifelong friend of Japan, that the Government of that country should not take up irrevocably a position of isolation and hostility to the League, and I trust that, with reasonable patience, it will be possible for the League to work out a settlement which Japan can see its way to accept.[22]

F. H. Soward of the University of British Columbia has described the speech as the "Cahan Blunder,"[23] and Keenleyside has called it a "very silly speech."[24] The Americans were shocked at what they regarded as a viewpoint sharply at variance with their own, and top officials at DEA in Ottawa felt Cahan had seriously disregarded the instructions given to him prior to his statement before the assembly. But Marler cabled DEA in Ottawa that he agreed with Cahan "when he says 'All methods of conciliation should be exhausted and there should be no idea of imposing sanctions.' "[25]

We know from Skelton that the Japanese minister in Ottawa, Prince Tokugawa, warmly thanked him for the attitude the Canadian government had taken at Geneva. Skelton remarked in a dispatch to W. D. Herridge, the Canadian minister in Washington, that he had not refused to accept Tokugawa's thanks, thinking Canada had better keep at least one friend for the time being.[26] Apparently Prime Minister Bennett, whom Cahan met in London after the assembly meeting, was initially pleased with Cahan's remarks. However, after a discussion with Skelton back in Ottawa, the prime minister changed his views somewhat, though he decided not to repudiate Cahan publicly.[27]

Ultimately the Cahan statement had no decisive influence on the course of events, for on February 24, 1933, the assembly of the League of Nations unanimously approved the Lytton Report. The Committee of Nineteen, which had been created to study the recommendations of the Lytton Report, had reported on February 17, 1933. It found China blameless for the events since September 18, 1931, endorsed the recommendations of the Lytton Report, and urged nonrecognition of the Japanese puppet state of Manchukuo.

Japan and China were given three months to consider what they wished to do under the circumstances.

The Canadian government eventually took its stand in the assembly of the League of Nations on February 24, 1933, when W. A. Riddell, representing Canada, announced:

> [We] . . . have learned with regret that the efforts to effect a settlement of the Sino-Japanese dispute . . . have not been successful. . . . The Canadian Government have scrupulously refrained from word or deed that might have jeopardized the prospects of peaceful settlement. . . . The faith of the world in the possibility of peaceful settlement has been shaken; if it is destroyed, the structure of security . . . will be undermined. . . . For these reasons we must vote for the adoption of the report.[28]

Japan walked out of the League of Nations that day, and a month later, on March 27, 1933, an imperial rescript was issued in Tokyo declaring Japan's resignation from the league. Yet two years later, in January 1935, the council of the league ruled that Japan was entitled to continue to exercise its mandate over the former German territories north of the equator, which it had held under a league mandate since the end of World War I. The league was too weak to act, and the Japanese knew it. No sanctions were ever imposed, and the Japanese Imperial Army marched on. Seeing itself abandoned by the international community, China was eventually forced to sign the Tangku Truce with Japan on May 31, 1933, leaving Japan in control of all the territory north of the Great Wall. The league slapped Japan's wrists by sending out a circular letter to all governments, asking them to refuse diplomatic recognition to Manchukuo and to boycott Manchukuo's currency and postage. The ultimate inability of the league to act decisively and forcefully in this matter, as well as in the Italian invasion of Ethiopia, which followed, marked the failure of the collective security system in the post–World War I era. The failure to stop Japan in Manchuria opened the floodgates that eventually led to World War II, in Europe as well as in Asia.

After Canada had taken her February 1933 stand at the league against Japanese aggression, the Canadian government took no further action to involve itself actively in the Far Eastern situation. In the mid-thirties correct, cordial relations were maintained with Japan, and every indication pointed to a Canadian wish to maintain neutrality in the ongoing troubles between Japan and China. Yet the majority of the Canadian public was definitely supportive of the league's efforts to curb Japan, and when the Japanese army launched its attack on China proper on July 7, 1937, the anti-Japanese chorus grew ever louder and virtually unanimous.

Newspapers such as the *Toronto Globe*, the *Toronto Star*, and the *Winnipeg Free Press* were all stoutly proleague and anti-Japanese and condemned Britain as well as Canada for condoning Japanese aggression.[29] Yet in spite of the moralizing and righteous indignation manifested, some editorialists spoke of a need for the kind of realism reflected in Cahan's words in Parliament, when he said that he "did not believe that under the then existing conditions the Parliament of Canada would appropriate a single dollar toward maintaining a single company of troops in the Far East."[30]

Canadian trade with Japan was another factor that counseled realism to the Canadian government. Canada's two-way trade with Japan reached a peak volume of $55 million in 1929, which it was not to surpass until after World War II. Yet Marler had gone to Japan in that year, hoping to expand the trade with Japan as well as with China significantly. Japan had enjoyed a steady trade surplus until 1922, with silk and tea as the principal commodities determining that advantage, but the balance had shifted in 1923, and Canada has enjoyed a trade surplus ever since. Increasing exports of lumber, wheat, lead, zinc, aluminum, fish, wood pulp, and logs helped to bring about this turnaround. As Japan became increasingly involved on the Chinese mainland, the proportion of the trade occupied by strategic mineral exports from Canada rose dramatically. (See Appendix, Table 6.) It may be significant that the low point in Canada's trade with Japan was reached after the Manchurian incident, in 1933 for exports, and in 1934 for imports. (See Appendix, Table 5.) However, there was no significant movement to boycott Japanese imports until 1937.

In the years between the end of World War I and the arrival of Marler in Tokyo, Canadian-Japanese trade had in fact trebled, and Japan had become one of Canada's three or four most important trading partners after the United States and Great Britain. Marler was convinced of the possibility of even greater trade with Japan and promoted it with great zeal. In September 1929 he requested that Langley, who had been in Japan since 1923, be transferred from his post in Kobe (as trade commissioner) to Tokyo, to be the new commercial secretary of the legation. Under this arrangement the Department of Trade and Commerce paid Langley's salary, while External Affairs paid his living allowance.[31] Marler's zeal in the area of trade promotion sometimes involved him in controversy with the Department of Trade and Commerce, since he sought to function as supervisor-coordinator not only of the trade commissioners in Japan, but of those in China as well. He repeatedly visited China, usually taking Langley with him, and generally urged greater efforts to develop the China market, particularly for wheat, by the establishment of trade commissioners' offices in Dairen and Tientsin in addition to those already existing in Hong Kong and Shanghai. Marler hoped that the Tokyo legation would thereby become the coordinating headquarters and clearinghouse for the entire Far Eastern Trade Commissioner Service.

In spite of Marler's vigorous efforts at trade promotion, Canadian exports steadily declined in the early thirties, going from $30 million in 1930 to $10 million in 1933 and recovering only slightly in the years that followed. (See Appendix, Table 5.)

During the last year of the Bennett administration, Canada became involved in a short tariff war with Japan, which may also have adversely affected the trade. Tariffs applied to Japanese goods had been steadily on the rise since the beginning of the Bennett regime, leading to a drop by two-thirds of Canadian imports from Japan. At the same time, the trade balance was more than three to one in Canada's favor. When the Japanese government depreciated the yen early in 1932, Canada applied a special exchange compensation duty, on the assumption that a depreciated currency enjoys a competitive advantage equivalent to the amount of depreciation. In addition, there was the device of customs valuation for assessment of duties on goods entering Canada, constituting an arbitrarily fixed dumping duty.

The Japanese government contended that the cumulative effect of these duties, which moreover, in the Japanese view, were being unfairly applied to Japanese goods alone, was the cause of both the trade gap and the net drop in Canadian imports from Japan. The resulting exchanges between Tokyo and Ottawa showed no sign that Bennett was prepared to make substantial concessions to the Japanese viewpoint, and as a result, Japan applied a surtax of 50 percent ad valorem on all Canadian exports, such as wheat, lumber, pulp, and paper, as of July 1935. The Canadian government retaliated in August 1935 with a surtax of 33⅓ percent on all Japanese goods imported to Canada.

There is no doubt that the temper of the times contributed its share to this unfortunate turn in Canadian-Japanese trade relations. Anti-Japanese sentiment in Canada made it difficult for the Bennett government to appear too conciliatory toward Japan. Meanwhile, the Japanese press lambasted Canada for unfair and discriminatory practices directed specifically against Japan. Marler, in a dispatch to Prime Minister King of June 1, 1935, voiced his frustration:

> As matters now stand I would deprecate any settlement even if it is possible to make. . . . If we now give way we will be held up as giving way to this aggressive and bullying attitude of Japan, an attitude she is adopting in respect to everything she desires to achieve and without regard to Treaty rights existing. . . . If on the other hand we stand firm and tell the world that we intend to make no special exceptions for Japan but will treat the world alike, while we may lose a few million dollars of trade for a few years we will retain our respect and will gain from every small nation in the world its gratitude and additional respect.[32]

Marler had clearly come a long way since 1929, and the causes are not hard to identify. The internal political process in Japan had moved from Shidehara's compromises to a succession of attempts at military takeover of the governmental decision-making machinery. There were assassinations of top politicians, as groups of young army radicals pursued the Showa Restoration Movement, which was rightist, chauvinistic, imperialistic, determined to drive the white man out of Asia and to punish the financial clique (zaibatsu) and the corrupt politicians within Japan. Three prime ministers were assassinated, and at least a dozen senior officials, many of them themselves senior army or navy officers, were killed by the extreme activists.[33] In this kind of atmosphere, selling a few more dollars' worth of Canadian goods in Japan would seem of less than quintessential importance.

When the Conservative government fell in October 1935, it was not long before the new prime minister, King, entered into negotiations with Japan's new minister, Sotomatsu Kato, a career foreign service officer. Canada offered to cancel its former valuation practices and return to pre-1930 practice in the classification of goods, as well as to accept the yen at the current rate of exchange for computing duties. In addition, the 33⅓ percent surtax on Japanese goods was to be withdrawn. These measures met all the objections previously raised by the Japanese, and accordingly the Japanese government withdrew its 50 percent ad valorem surtax on Canadian exports as of January 1, 1936.[34]

On January 15, 1936, Marler reported to Ottawa that he had ascertained from Saburo Kurusu, chief of the commercial bureau of the Foreign Office, that the Japanese-Canadian trade agreement reached by the exchange of notes in December 1935 was satisfactory to the commercial interests in Japan. The Canadian government later made refunds of the 33⅓ percent surtax collected in certain cases.[35] An increase by one-third in the total volume of Canadian-Japanese trade occurred for two years, 1937 and 1938.

On July 3, 1936, Marler, having spent seven years in Japan, left to become the Canadian minister to Washington.[36] His replacement as minister to Japan was R. Randolph Bruce, a former lieutenant-governor of British Columbia, who presented his credentials to the Emperor on November 7, 1939. Bruce was a distinguished and wealthy Liberal, well-known to King. He was 73 years old at the time of his appointment and was partially blind as the result of an explosion of acid in a laboratory experiment. When King appointed Bruce as minister to Japan, he felt that neither his age nor his impaired vision would affect his ability to function as minister. His familiarity with conditions in the Far East and in British Columbia, as well as his immediate availability, were among the considerations in his appointment. King said of him that "he possesses some qualifications as diplomat, which, I imagine, are not excelled by any man in any post anywhere."[37]

With the renewed outbreak of hostilities between Japan and China, on July 7, 1937, the battle for northern China began in earnest. Fighting later spread to Shanghai and eventually to central and southern China. In short order the Japanese army took Nanking, Shanghai, and later Soochow, Kaifeng, Anking, Canton, Hankow, Wuchang, and Hanyang, thus controlling virtually all major Chinese population centers and the entire Chinese coast. The sadistic behavior of the Japanese troops, in Nanking in particular, created a worldwide uproar of anti-Japanese resentment, which was also reflected in Canada.

The possibility of a war between the United States and Japan was now seriously discussed, along with the role Canada would play in such an eventuality. As far as defense was concerned, the Canadian government's assumption continued to be that the United States would protect Canada from any possible threat of invasion or attack by Japanese naval forces in the Pacific. President Franklin D. Roosevelt had repeatedly given that assurance, for instance at Kingston on August 18, 1938, when he said, "The United States will not stand idly by if domination of Canadian soil is threatened by any other empire." Yet Canada intended to remain neutral in the case of an outbreak of hostilities and was mainly concerned about having the military capacity to defend her neutrality. A report to the government by the Canadian general staff expressed particular concern about what Canada might have to do to preserve its neutrality in case the Japanese navy were to enter Canadian waters in the Juan de Fuca Strait and eventually proceed to attack the U.S. naval base in Bremerton, Wash., from neutral Canadian waters.[38]

At the same time there were increasing demands for a boycott of Japanese goods and for an embargo on munitions, nickel, and other war supplies. In 1934 in the House of Commons, J. S. Woodsworth, a member of Parliament from Winnipeg, had proposed an embargo on nickel but had eventually withdrawn his proposal.[39] While boycott demonstrations in Vancouver and elsewhere may have caused some people to stop buying Japanese goods, the trade in both directions continued to register moderate growth between 1936 and 1938. Although an embargo on war supplies going to Spain was imposed in 1937, no similar measures were undertaken against Japan.

The Canadian government's attitude was perhaps best demonstrated by Prime Minister King after he had been urged to restrict the export of war materials to Japan so that Canada would not help kill men, women, and children in China. He replied that the government would not prohibit the export of munitions to Japan until the governments of other countries did likewise.[40] In a later speech in the House of Commons, he pointed out that Canada, as a member of the Far Eastern Advisory Committee of the League of Nations, had supported the adoption of two reports, one condemning Japan's action in China as a breach of her treaty obligations and the other expressing moral support of China and recommending that members consider giving aid to China.[41]

Canada was not alone in her reluctance to act forcefully against Japan but reflected a similar reluctance on the part of both the United States and Britain. In a confidential cable from King to British Prime Minister Neville Chamberlain dated October 27, 1937, the policy considerations are clearly spelled out.

> My colleagues and myself, after full deliberation, are unable to discover any grounds that would justify us in considering the responsibility of committing the people of Canada to a course of sanctions or of seeking or giving the military and territorial guarantees in question, a responsibility in effect involving a readiness in the end to ask them to participate in a war against Japan.[42]

Therefore, when the Brussels Conference was called to discuss the Sino-Japanese conflict in November 1937, attended by nineteen countries including the United States, Great Britain, and Canada,[43] the results were a foregone conclusion. Japan was invited to attend but refused. The final declaration of the conference, which Canada supported, once again condemned Japan for its resort to force and enjoined it to seek a peaceful resolution of its differences with China. King said of Canada's action at the conference: "Canada concurred in the action taken. It did not think less could be done; it did not urge the great powers represented to do more."[44]

Meanwhile, Canada's new minister to Japan, Bruce, had been quoted in the *Toronto Daily Star* to the effect that

> Japan's invasion of China is seen as simply an attempt to put her neighbour country into decent shape, as she has already done for Manchuria. Conditions in China are very bad. They lack constitutional government and their rulers are just self-

appointed warlords. Japan's improvement of Manchuria is causing many Chinese from other parts to flock there for protection under some form of constituted government.[45]

Opposition leader Bennett was shocked that the Canadian minister would take sides against China in this conflict, bearing in mind that China had been attacked and that Japan was openly violating the Kellogg-Briand Pact, which obliged Japan to renounce war as an instrument of national policy. "Has the thought of trade dulled our sense of honour?" he protested.[46]

The prime minister in due course replied that Bruce felt he had been misquoted, having in fact elaborated the Japanese view rather than his own. King nevertheless regretted Bruce's remarks, which he thought might as well have been left unsaid. He also defended the minister, saying he had done exceedingly well in Tokyo and that the reports received from him had been extremely helpful to the government. He finally indicated that Bruce would be resigning his post, as indeed he did in December 1938.[47]

With the departure of the Canadian minister, E. D'Arcy McGreer, first secretary of the legation, became chargé d'affaires and thus the last Canadian head of mission in Tokyo before the outbreak of the Pacific war. On August 5, 1941, word came to Ottawa from British Foreign Minister Anthony Eden and U.S. Secretary of State Cordell Hull that they both hoped Canada would defer the appointment of a new minister.[48] What tipped the balance toward postponement of an appointment was an accusation made against the Canadian chargé d'affaires, McGreer, on the very same day, August 5, 1941, alleging that McGreer had importuned the Reverend Marcel Fournier, a Dominican father in Hokkaido, to furnish information concerning Japanese military secrets. The accusation was based on a letter allegedly written by McGreer to Father Fournier requesting military information. McGreer maintained that the letter was a forgery, and the Canadian government demanded that the charge against McGreer be withdrawn and an apology extended to him. Father Fournier was convicted and sentenced to three years in prison, but no withdrawal of charges against McGreer nor apology was received before the outbreak of the war.[49]

While the political relationship suffered during the thirties, the matter of Japanese immigration to Canada had ceased to be a major issue between the two countries after 1929. Careful monitoring by both governments of the Gentlemen's Agreement was restricting the number of Japanese immigrants to Canada to 150 per year. The actual average of Japanese immigrants during the thirteen-year period from 1929 to 1941 was 107. (See Appendix, Table 8.) In spite of this fact, a number of people in British Columbia continued to campaign for total exclusion of the Japanese, claiming either that the total number entering was larger than 150 or that thousands of Japanese were entering Canada illegally, being secretly smuggled into the country. After the Japanese invasion of China proper in July 1937, these exclusionists sought to take advantage of the rising anti-Japanese sentiment in the country to pass new legislation in the Federal Parliament that would accomplish the total exclusion of the Japanese. A. W. Neill, independent member for Comox-Alberni, B.C., was the principal proponent of a series of measures along this line and repeatedly made his case in the House of Commons with considerable propagandistic skill and oratorical flourish.

Prime Minister King, a man long experienced in the matter of Oriental immigration, gave the issue his personal attention, insisting that total exclusion was an undesirable measure and that it had indeed been harmful to Canada's reputation in the case of China. He preferred regulation to exclusion and pointed out that no more than a hundred Japanese per year had been coming into Canada. "This parliament of Canada should not contemplate for one minute placing an exclusion act upon its statutes, especially an act directed against Japan, where we have before us the evidence that, so far as Japan is concerned, she has been perfectly loyal to the agreement that now exists and has more than carried out its terms."[50]

During the debate on the matter, the government agreed to the establishment of an interdepartmental committee and a board of review to look into the contention that large-scale illegal immigration of Japanese was taking place in British Columbia. A thorough examination of all the evidence in the hands of both civilian and military intelligence in British Columbia revealed not a single piece of corroborated evidence that the charges of illegal entry and military espionage were actually true.[51] Neill's exclusion bill was voted down on May 24, 1938, with seventy-nine nays and forty-two ayes, causing Neill to state that he had "been sacrificed to appease the Japanese Government."[52] A week later Neill introduced yet another bill, this time proposing that Japanese be excluded unless they could speak English. This was voted down by the even greater margin of eighty-seven to thirty-nine, but not before Neill, a West Coast parliamentarian, had recorded the following remarks:

> We dare not deal with the strict domestic matter of our own immigration for fear—and fear is an ugly word Mr. Speaker— that an alien heathen nation, that has no claim whatever to a grievance, might not like it, a nation whose best claim to fame at the present moment is the fact that it is raping and ravaging a friendly nation, whose territory it swore a few short years ago to protect and maintain. . . . For the first time in nearly half a century I have occasion to be ashamed of my adopted country.[53]

Yet although the law remained unchanged and the Gentlemen's Agreement remained in force, it may be noted that during the four-year period from 1938 to 1941 only 149 Japanese immigrants entered Canada. (See Appendix, Table 8.)

In the wake of Japan's aggressive action in East Asia and her conclusion of the Three Power Pact with Nazi Germany and Fascist Italy, relations between Canada and Japan were now rapidly deteriorating. The emergence of the Rome-Berlin-Tokyo Axis made it increasingly apparent to Canadians that their hopes of remaining neutral in the emerging worldwide struggle were doomed to disappointment. There was no doubt in anyone's mind on which side Canada would take her place; in the European war that was now widely predicted, Canada would surely rally to the side of Great Britain. If a Pacific war were to occur, Canadians, particularly in British Columbia, were more than ready to rally to the side of the United States in joint defense of the West Coast of North America. The Canadian contribution could not be massive, since Canada had neither navy nor air force units of any significance, but it could be expected to repel small Japanese naval raids on Prince Rupert or Vancouver with coastal batteries or mines in strategic areas, and it could afford the U.S. Navy and Air Force the necessary communications and supply facilities to turn back a Japanese invasion force approaching the Aleutians or Alaska. Speculation about a Pacific war was widespread from the middle thirties on and naturally contributed to an increasing sense of panic, in British Columbia in particular.

This new hostility accelerated demands for a boycott of Japanese goods in Canada and an embargo on the shipment of war material to Japan. As shown in Table 6 of the Appendix, Canadian exports of strategic minerals had in fact dramatically increased after 1936.

Agitation in the Canadian press and parliament during 1937, 1938, and 1939 calling for an effective boycott of Japanese goods and for an embargo on the shipment of war material to Japan was at times intense, yet ultimately without noticeable effect. The outbreak of the European war in September 1939, which resulted in a Canadian declaration of war upon Germany on September 10, 1939, provided a new economic situation in Canada, putting the Canadian economy on a war footing, with resulting greater utilization of strategic metals by Canada and her European Allies. Even during 1940, however, Canadian exports to Japan were the same as in 1938. Nevertheless, public sentiment was increasingly anti-Japanese, and the Canadian government was by this time well aware that war with Japan had become a strong possibility. Consultations on the defense of the Pacific Coast were conducted with the United States, pursuant to the Ogdensburg Agreement of August 17, 1940, which established the Permanent Joint Board of Defense (PJBD) between the United States and Canada. While the King government still maintained an attitude of neutrality toward Japan—the Japanese were watched carefully and given few favors—it was becoming increasingly clear that when the war came, Canada would be on the British and American side rather than attempting to maintain neutrality.

Meanwhile, hostility to the Japanese Canadians in British Columbia was becoming increasingly difficult to ignore. On October 1, 1940, the Cabinet War Committee appointed a special committee on Orientals in British Columbia, chaired by Lt. Col. A. W. Sparling of the Department of National Defence, with Assistant Commissioner F. J. Mead of the Royal Canadian Mounted Police (RCMP) and Keenleyside of DEA as members. Sir George Sansom, Britain's renowned historian of Japan, was added to the committee on October 17. The guidelines of the committee enjoined it to in-

vestigate the existence and causes of problems involving Orientals
in British Columbia, whether these constituted a danger to national
security or national defense, and what measures should be taken to
meet whatever threats there might be to national security or the
civil security of British Columbians. The committee was also asked
to make a recommendation about application of the draft to Oriental Canadians. The committee brought in its report by December
1940, recommending the voluntary registration of all persons of
Japanese race. On January 7, 1941, a standing committee on Orientals was appointed to supervise registration, to be carried out under
the supervision of the RCMP. No recommendation was made on
conscription, which meant that Orientals remained exempt from
the draft though they were permitted to enlist; very few Orientals
were accepted into the forces, however, for fear that incidents
might arise between white and Oriental conscripts and because, in
the case of the Japanese, there were those who had doubts as to
their loyalty should war with Japan break out. The twenty-two
thousand Japanese Canadians,[54] whether Canadian-born, naturalized, alien immigrants, or Japanese nationals, had not really
enjoyed equal status as Canadian citizens in British Columbia any-
way. They could not vote in municipal, provincial, or federal elections, nor could they become school trustees, perform jury service,
enter the legal or pharmaceutical professions, obtain a hand-
logger's license, or be employed on Crown timber leases or in public works. They also could not join the boards of trade or chambers
of commerce. To this second-class citizenship was now added the
implication that, being Japanese, they could probably not be
trusted to serve in the armed forces in a war with Japan. In spite of
this, Japanese Canadians were in fact loyal citizens of Canada, and
many were eager to serve their country to prove their loyalty.

On July 25, 1941, the Canadian government acted simultaneously
with the governments of Great Britain and the United States to
freeze all Japanese assets in the three countries, thereby blocking
bank balances and bringing trade between Japan and Canada to a
halt.[55] The commercial treaty between Canada and Japan was terminated at the same time. Shipments of strategic metals such as
iron, steel, nickel, zinc, aluminum, and cobalt had been terminated
toward the end of 1940. At that time, however, Canada's export restrictions had become more extensive than those of the United

States and Great Britain.[56] No more Japanese orders for wheat were accepted after February 13, 1941, when an order in council was passed requiring permits for wheat exports.[57]

Meanwhile, Japanese diplomatic representation in Canada had undergone a series of changes. The first Japanese minister, Prince Tokugawa, had served from October 1929 until January 1935. Kato became the Japanese minister on June 13, 1935, and served until April 1938, when he was transferred to Manchuria. The new minister to Ottawa, appointed on May 23, 1938, was Baron Shu Tomii, who had served in Ottawa previously. Born in Tokyo in 1890, Tomii was a graduate of the Tokyo Imperial University faculty of law, which has supplied most of Japan's envoys to Canada. Tomii was called home to Tokyo in September 1940 when Yōsuke Matsuoka, the new foreign minister, revamped the Japanese foreign service in the wake of the conclusion of the Tripartite Pact of Mutual Assistance in the case of war.[58]

During the farewell visit to Under Secretary Skelton at DEA in August 1940, Baron Tomii brought up the question of Canada's export policy toward Japan. Noting that Canada's policy was somewhat more restrictive than that of Great Britain, Tomii wondered if that was due "to some extent to the hostile attitude of certain groups in Canada towards Japan in connection with the present conflict in China." Skelton wrote:

> I told Baron Tomii that the decisive factor in our policy was of course the present and prospective needs of ourselves and our Allies. . . . At the same time I would readily agree that there was a vigorous demand for restricting shipments of munitions to Japan from a good many quarters on the grounds (1) of sympathy with China as the victim of aggression, and (2) because of the extraordinary open and unrestrained anti-British attitude of the leaders of Japanese army and political opinion in recent months.[59]

During his farewell call on Skelton, Baron Tomii touched on possible difficulties that might arise through what he called the unfriendly treatment of persons of Japanese race in British Columbia. Skelton replied that he would not say that in every respect treatment of the people of Oriental races in Canada was beyond reproach but that he was sure Tomii would agree that it would not be possible to admit that Germany or Italy or France had any right to intervene to protect Canadians who happened to be of German or Italian or French ancestry.[60]

Baron Tomii was replaced on October 16, 1940, by a new minister, Seijiro Yoshizawa, who was to be the last Japanese envoy before the outbreak of the war.[61]

Prime Minister King was convinced by 1940 that Japan would enter the war on the Axis side. He feared that if war between Britain and Japan broke out without U.S. involvement, this would leave Britain and Canada highly vulnerable to joint attacks by the Axis powers. It was for this reason that King resisted excessive actions against the Japanese in British Columbia, which were being urged upon him by the anti-Oriental elements there.

King, moreover, maintained some degree of social contact with Japanese ministers in Ottawa, seeking to inform them of Canada's correct attitude and to dissuade them from war with Britain. He had dinner alone with Baron Tomii on September 7, 1940, who asked him if Canada would intervene in hostilities in Asia. King replied that Canada would not have entered the war over Czechoslovakia, but that after the invasion of Poland the feeling was that there was an effort to destroy the British Empire and that therefore the British everywhere would not stop fighting until the Nazi regime and what it stood for was wiped out. Canada was prepared to fight wherever the British Empire was threatened. When Tomii appeared to be probing to find out how free Japan might be to pursue aggression in the Far East, King stated that the United States would fight to preserve democracy and that Canada and the United States would be drawn closer together in matters of common concern.[67]

On September 26, King informed the War Committee that it would be unwise to have firearms in the hands of Japanese Canadians at a moment when war with Japan was possible. On September 27, 1940, Germany, Italy, and Japan concluded the Tripartite Pact, and King felt that as a result the United States would not allow Japan to get control of Asia and the Pacific, that it would go to war first. He was relieved, for he believed that a U.S.-British alliance was now guaranteed and would prevail in the end.

When the government decided in January 1941 to carry out compulsory registration of all Japanese, fears about future Japanese subversion overpowered anxieties about Japan's possible reaction. Mackenzie King saw the new Japanese minister, Yoshizawa,[63] on January 8, 1941, and showed him a statement that had been prepared for the press announcing registration. Later that month Canada refused a British request to remove contraband cargo from Japanese ships in the Pacific because, once again, King did not wish to provoke war with Japan.[64]

On March 26, 1941, King had a long, confidential talk with the Japanese minister, who informed him that if the Germans should invade Britain, Japan would seek to extend her territory in the Far East. If Britain were to lose that fight, he thought the United States would not continue it. King contradicted the minister, saying he thought the United States would see to it that Hitler was defeated.[65]

As Japan became increasingly pro-German and Foreign Minister Matsuoka visited Rome and Berlin, anti-Japanese sentiment in British Columbia rose again, leading to strong demands for the stoppage of wheat and timber shipments to Japan, and King complied, agreeing that only shipments already ordered should be delivered.[66]

On April 29 Mackenzie King called the British Columbia members of the House to his office and pleaded with them to accept the government's action (in permitting contracts with Japan to be carried out) without criticism in order to help the British government. Except for Howard Green, all accepted King's view. On April 30 King called on Yoshizawa to discuss his meeting with the British Columbia members and their agreement to withhold criticism. Yoshizawa asked if he could now apply for the permits for previously placed orders and was given an affirmative answer. "I then said that I hoped he fully understood that, while I felt the United States was anxious to keep out of the war, I also believed that nothing would as quickly bring the States into the war as any attack by Japan on Britain, . . . that while U.S. sentiment might be divided as to active participation in war on the Atlantic, once war started on the Pacific, the story would, I was perfectly sure, be different. Yoshizawa said he was inclined to agree."[67]

When Japanese assets were frozen late in July in response to Japan's invasion of French Indochina, Yoshizawa called on King to protest, saying he thought the step was out of proportion to any step Japan had taken. King replied that "when warships were brought into use and troops were moved, that nothing could be considered as excessive as a means of defense on the part of either Britain or the United States. Yoshizawa finally asked if Canada had acted on her own or at the behest of Britain and was told that while different governments of the Empire were in constant consultation, . . . our action was taken independently and on our own."[68]

While the Canadian government remained correct and cautious in its attitude toward Japan right up to the attack on Pearl Harbor, there was a series of incidents in Japan's sphere of influence that were regarded as unfriendly or provocative by Canadian officials. After 1939 the operations of the Japanese army in China and Manchuria led to a series of cases of damage, looting and burning of Canadian property and injury or death to Canadian citizens, particularly missionaries. The Tokyo legation from time to time lodged protests with the Ministry of Foreign Affairs in Tokyo to demand compensation but received little if any satisfaction from Japanese officials. By April 1940 four Canadian missionaries had been killed by the Japanese military. There had been twenty bombings of Canadian missions and a number of attacks by Japanese-led mobs.[69]

The Tokyo legation, meanwhile, was urging Canadians (women and children in particular) throughout the Japanese Empire to evacuate, in view of the increasing danger of war and the uncertainty of what might happen to them if they waited too long.[70] Missionaries, however, Catholics especially, had a tendency to ignore evacuation notices, preferring not to leave until they were forced to do so. By February 1941 there were still close to two hundred Canadians in Japan and Korea, some 86 percent of them being priests, nuns, and missionaries. Father Fournier, the Dominican priest arrested in December 1940, was convicted by a Japanese court in September 1941. There was no further mention of any role played by the legation or by Chargé D'Affaires McGreer in the judgment.[71]

Another incident was the bombing on September 14, 1940, of the Canadian Pacific liner *Empress of Asia*, which was attacked by Japanese naval aircraft north of Oshima Island on her way from Nagasaki to Yokohama. The Japanese naval authorities agreed to pay compensation for damages and injuries inflicted, causing speculation that the attack had been a message from Japanese naval aviation to the U.S. and British navies.[72]

Japan's last pre-war Minister to Ottawa, Seijiro Yoshizawa, was a career foreign service officer, who had joined Gaimusho (The Japanese Ministry of Foreign Affairs) in 1917. Foreign Minister

Yōsuke Matsuoka appointed Yoshizawa minister to Canada as of October 16, 1940.

Yoshizawa recalls that coming to Ottawa proved to be a lonely assignment, since there were only five ministers in Ottawa at the time. The others were those of the United States, France (Vichy), Belgium, and Holland. Japan, as a member of the Rome-Berlin-Tokyo Axis, was naturally in bad repute. Yoshizawa therefore did not find himself invited to speak at any luncheon clubs, as might have been the case in "friendly times." He felt like an "almost enemy representative."

Nevertheless, he enjoyed what one might describe as a "special relationship" with Prime Minister King. He frequently met with King, who called on him, as well as inviting him to Kingsmere or his office. The exchanges between them reported by King were often matters of mutual disagreement, but the tone that prevailed between these men was never bitter nor one of mutual recrimination. They frequently agreed in their appraisals of situations, and King showed an obviously high regard for Yoshizawa and feelings of friendliness and sympathy, not for Japan or its policies, but for Yoshizawa as a human being. When it became clear that Canada and Japan were drifting toward war, both men seemed to display more sadness than anger at the turn of events.[73]

During a visit in Mackenzie King's office on April 28, 1941, Yoshizawa expressed his appreciation for the granting of certain permits for the shipment of wheat and wood to Japan and added that his government still desired the appointment of a Canadian minister to Tokyo, so that friendly relations between Japan and Canada might be maintained. King spoke of the difficulty of finding a wholly qualified person and finally asked Yoshizawa to suggest someone. Yoshizawa suggested Keenleyside, bringing the response from King that Keenleyside, especially since the death of Skelton (January 28, 1941), was very much needed at headquarters to assist Norman Robertson.[74]

Once war broke out in December 1941, Yoshizawa and the legation staff were confined to their respective residences while awaiting repatriation to Japan. Yoshizawa recalls that he "was treated most leniently" by Canadian officials in Ottawa. "The Canadian authorities treated us in such a friendly manner that we left Canada with the most favorable impression possible."[75]

Yoshizawa was evacuated from Ottawa on May 8, 1942, being allowed to proceed to the Swedish exchange ship *Gripsholm* in New York. When King heard that Yoshizawa had left Ottawa, he

> felt a great pain in my heart that I should have left him and his wife to go without a word. . . . I was not interested in protocol, was thinking of my heart and what was right to do. . . . Must remember that when all this war is over, we may wish to bind together the different countries and Yoshizawa might be helpful in that way, if his faith in me were not destroyed. Luckily, they were to stay over in Montreal for some time.

King thereupon telephoned Yoshizawa saying he had been sorry not to have known about the arrangements for his departure.

> I wanted him to know that during all the time he had been here as Minister, in his relations with me, I felt he had been wholly honourable, also that our personal relations had been very pleasant. . . . Yoshizawa spoke very feelingly, saying he thanked me very much for this word of good-bye; that the friendly relations which we had shared and my friendship while they were here would be among the memories he would cherish through all his life; that he had valued my friendship and thanked me particularly for saying what I had about his honourable conduct—that he was very grateful for that.[76]

The eighty-four-year-old Yoshizawa told me this story with tears in his eyes in June 1977. As King anticipated, he contributed to binding Canada and Japan together during the many years in which he served as president of the Japan-Canada Society in Tokyo after the war was over.[77]

On November 15, 1941, the Canadian government announced the arrival in Hong Kong of two battalions of Canadian infantry troops, in response to an appeal made by the British government on September 19, 1941, for Canadian reinforcements. The troops were the Winnipeg Grenadiers and the Royal Rifles of Canada, 1,975 officers and men who sailed from Vancouver in October under the command of Brig. J. K. Lawson in the *Awatea* under the naval escort of H.M.C.S. *Prince Robert*. Some 555 of the men who sailed on *Awatea* were never to return to Canada.[78]

When they sailed, war with Japan did not yet seem a real prospect to many, in that the United States, Canada, Great Britain, and many others still hoped to avoid a clash with Japan, or at least to postpone it. Eleven weeks before the Pearl Harbor attack, the Japanese government (through a former ambassador to London, Mamoru Shigemitsu) sought to create the impression that Japan was cooling in her enthusiasm for the Axis alliance and that she was genuinely interested in a negotiated settlement of her differences with the United States and Great Britain. The suggestion was made that in return for Britain's closing of the Burma Road, which would have terminated the flow of military and other supplies to the forces and supporters of Generalissimo Chiang Kai-shek, Japan might be prepared to withdraw her troops from Southern Indochina.[79] There were further suggestions that a relaxation of the trade embargo against Japan might lead to other concessions and would be helpful to the "peace party" in Tokyo.

When asked to comment on these signals, Keenleyside, who had become Assistant Under-Secretary of State for External Affairs in the summer of 1941 (and thereby Canada's top advisor on Far Eastern affairs), delivered a blistering memorandum to the prime minister, in which he eloquently counseled rejection of the Japanese démarche. Keenleyside, gentle, scholarly, restrained diplomat-historian that he was, did not usually write in violent or colorful phrases. But after a decade of dealing with the political gyrations of successive Tokyo governments, he had had his fill and he spoke his mind. In the first paragraph of his telegram (1.) Keenleyside sees no harm in having Japan loosen her ties with the Axis, but warns that the Allies should not fall into the "obvious Japanese trap" by promising economic benefits without "very concrete proof" of a change in Japanese policy. The telegram continues:

2. Throughout the early years of renewed Japanese aggression (1931–35) Japanese official and unofficial representatives abroad, at the instigation of their government, argued over and over again: "Just leave us alone, avoid all evidence of outside pressure, and sooner or later our liberal elements will regain control from the extremists and then we can re-

sume policies of international cooperation.'' By accepting this argument Britain and America were hamstrung for years, during which time the Japanese, laughing heartily up their kimono-sleeves, went on from aggression to aggression. Now this booby-trap is being tried again.

3. It is probably true that the Japanese are beginning to fear that they picked the wrong side, and that they do not like the manners of the German army of occupation in Tokyo. And it is natural that they should try to persuade Britain and America to pay them for deserting their present allies.

. . . . .

5. Ambassador Shigemitsu's proposal that Japan abandon Indo-China in return for the closing of the Burma Road by Great Britain, is, in effect, the promise of a homicidal criminal that he will drop one of the weapons that he intends to use against an intended victim if that victim will assist in the murder of an innocent third party. This proposal illustrates the dishonesty of Tokyo's new effort to get London and Washington to revert to a policy of appeasement. It is a very encouraging sign that the British Government will have none of it.[80]

Events in Japan now entered the decisive stage. On October 16, 1941, the third cabinet of Prince Fumimaro Konoe resigned en masse and Gen. Hideki Tōjō, former war minister, was asked to form the new cabinet. In Tokyo, Tōjō's elevation to the premiership was taken as a sign that negotiations with the Americans had failed and that the Japanese army and navy would be on the move again. Keenleyside commented cautiously but most appropriately to the prime minister:

The external dangers of any action are enormous, but they are probably equalled if not surpassed by the internal difficulties of inaction. The conflict is still unsolved and perhaps the only safe prediction is that General Tōjō is much more likely than was Prince Konoye to seek a solution by positive action. That this may mean involvement in war against Britain and America is not likely to be so great a deterrent to the tough and essentially uneducated General as it was to the more supple and more politically experienced Prince who has now resigned.[81]

While ambassadors Saburō Kurusu and Kichisaburō Nomura in Washington proceeded to go through the motions of continuing the negotiations with Secretary of State Hull, by this time there were few who believed that a negotiated settlement could be achieved. The United States was playing for time in order to reinforce its position in the Philippines, but both London and Washington, and indeed Ottawa, knew that it was merely a matter now of waiting to see where and when Japan would strike. That the U.S. high command did not foresee that the blow would fall upon Pearl Harbor is still a source of wonderment to many who lived through those times.

In Washington, meanwhile, there had been a meeting of representatives of Pacific powers attended by Great Britain, China, the Netherlands, Indies, Australia, and the United States. Hull had somehow forgotten to invite the minister of Canada. The discussions dealt with various Japanese proposals, none of which were found to be acceptable. Meanwhile, it had become known that a substantial Japanese convoy of troop and warships was on the high seas steaming toward Southeast Asia. It was widely assumed that the target was either the Isthmus of Kra or Thailand. When President Roosevelt asked Ambassador Kurusu the purpose of these troop movements, Kurusu replied that the danger of Chinese attack necessitated the sending of reinforcements to Indochina.

Two days later, on December 7, 1941, the blow finally fell upon Pearl Harbor, disabling most of the U.S. Pacific fleet. Japanese attacks on the Philippines, Malaya, Hong Kong, and other British territories in the Far East followed shortly thereafter.

Canada moved very quickly to declare her solidarity with Great Britain and the United States. On December 8, 1941, Prime Minister King cabled Canada's chargé d'affaires in Tokyo, McGreer, as follows:

Make following communication immediately to Japanese Government.

I am instructed by my Government to inform you that news of the wanton and treacherous attack by Japanese Armed Forces on British territory and British Forces and also on

United States territory and United States Forces reached Canada on December 7th, and that Japan's actions are a threat to the defence and freedom of Canada and the other nations of the British Commonwealth. Consequently I have the honour to inform the Imperial Japanese Government, in the name of His Majesty's Government in Canada, that a state of war exists between Canada and Japan as from the seventh day of December, 1941.[82]

This terminated normal diplomatic relations between Canada and Japan for the duration of the war. Argentina was designated as Canada's protecting power in Japan. And thus the friendly relations so hopefully established between Canada and Japan only twelve years earlier came to a halt and were not fully restored until some eleven years later, in 1952.

NOTES

1. H. Gordon Skilling, *Canadian Representation Abroad: From Agency to Embassy*, p. 236.
2. Ibid., p. 237.
3. Ibid., p. 237.
4. House of Commons, *Debates*, January 31, 1928, p. 29.
5. Ibid., p. 61.
6. The father of James Langley, a senior Canadian diplomat.
7. Interview with Hugh L. Keenleyside on April 13, 1977, in Victoria, B.C.
8. "Diplomatic Procedure in Japan," files of the Canadian Embassy, Tokyo, courtesy of Minister R. V. Gorham.
9. Ambassador A. R. Menzies contributed this anecdote in response to a series of questions posed to him in December 1977.
10. House of Commons, *Debates*, July 30, 1931, p. 4344.
11. Interview with Keenleyside, April 13, 1977.
12. *Canadian Annual Review*, 1930, p. 130.
13. In February 1930 Sentaro Yedo was appointed Japanese consul for Western Canada, succeeding Toyoichi Fukuma.
14. There are now more than forty thousand Japanese in Canada and fewer than two thousand Canadians in Japan. Creating equal proportions of residents in both countries would have been unrealistic, but it is worth remembering that Japan's immigration policy has been, if anything, more

exclusionist than Canada's policy. It is virtually impossible to immigrate to Japan, even as it is hard to find Canadians who would want to.

15. Despatch no. 178, from Keenleyside to the Secretary of State for External Affairs (SSEA), Canada, September 25, 1931.

16. Despatch No. 192, Keenleyside to External Affairs, October 9, 1931.

17. Despatch No. 258, Herbert Marler to External Affairs, December 1, 1931.

18. Letter, O. D. Skelton (who effectively ran the department during the prewar years) to Marler, January 23, 1932.

19. On February 18, 1932, Japan had announced the establishment of the independent state of Manchukuo, installing Henry Pu-yi, China's last Manchu ruler, as regent of the new state shortly thereafter. See M. E. Cameron, *China, Japan, and the Powers*, pp. 446–61.

20. Canada, DEA, *Documents on Canadian External Relations* (hereafter cited as *DCER*), Vol. 5, 1931–35, p. 304.

21. Ibid., p. 308.

22. League of Nations, *Verbatim Record of the Special Session of the Assembly*, December 8, 1932, pp. 3–5.

23. See F. H. Soward, "Forty Years On: The Cahan Blunder Reexamined," *BC Studies*, no. 32 (Winter 1976–77), pp. 126–38.

24. Interview with Keenleyside, April 13, 1977.

25. *DCER*, Vol. 5, 1931–35, p. 323.

26. Ibid., p. 321.

27. Ibid., p. 328.

28. Cited in Canada, House of Commons, *Debates*, 1933, pp. 2430–31.

29. A.R.M. Lower, *Canada and the Far East—1940*, pp. 33–41.

30. Canada, House of Commons, *Debates*, 1932–33, pp. 5059–69.

31. O. Mary Hill, *Canada's Salesman to the World*, pp. 496–501.

32. *DCER*, Despatch 138, Vol. 5, 1931–35, p. 722.

33. Interview with Keenleyside, April 13, 1977.

34. *DCER*, Vol. 5, 1931–35, pp. 750–52.

35. *DCER*, Vol. 6, 1936–39, pp. 773–74.

36. Keenleyside had left Tokyo six months earlier to serve with DEA in Ottawa.

37. Canada, House of Commons, *Debates*, February 9, 1937, p. 698.

38. *DCER*, Vol. 6, 1936–39, pp. 88–99.

39. Canada, House of Commons, *Debates*, 1934, pp. 1690–1710.

40. Canada, House of Commons, *Debates*, 1938, pp. 377–81, as quoted in Charles J. Woodsworth, *Canada and the Orient*, pp. 203–4.

41. Ibid., p. 205.

42. *DCER*, Vol. 6, 1936–39, p. 1031.

43. The Canadian representative at the Brussels Conference was Sen. Raoul Dandurand.

44. Canada, House of Commons, *Debates*, Vol. 3, 1938, p. 3186.
45. Canada, House of Commons, *Debates*, Vol. 1, 1938, p. 37.
46. Ibid., p. 38.
47. Canada, House of Commons, *Debates*, Vol. 1, 1938, p. 65. R. Randolph Bruce died four years later, in February 1942, at the age of seventy-nine.
48. *DCER*, Vol. 8, 1939–41, Part 1, pp. 97–104.
49. *DCER*, Vol. 8, 1939–41, Part 2, pp. 1147–71.
50. Canada, House of Commons, *Debates*, 1938, Vol. 1, p. 574.
51. Interview with Keenleyside, April 13, 1977
52. Canada, House of Commons, *Debates*, 1938, vol. 3, p. 3199.
53. Ibid., Vol. 4, p. 3410.
54. See Appendix, Table 9, for a breakdown of the Japanese residents in Canada by area of residence, sex, and citizenship status. It should be noted that, once restrictive measures were applied to Japanese Canadians, citizenship status was disregarded and the citizenship rights of all persons of Japanese race were uniformly violated, in that they were all treated as enemy aliens, though 75 percent of them were in fact Canadian citizens.
55. R. M. Dawson, *Canada in World Affairs*, Vol. 2, p. 278.
56. James Eayrs, *In Defence of Canada*, Vol. 2, pp. 165–66.
57. R. M. Dawson, *Canada in World Affairs*, Vol. 2, p. 277.
58. Data on Japanese diplomats are taken from *Gaimushō Nenkan*, (Ministry of Foreign Affairs Yearbook), published by Japan's Ministry of Foreign Affairs in Tokyo, for the applicable years.
59. Memorandum by Skelton, 28 August 1940, King papers, as quoted in Eayrs, *In Defence of Canada*, Vol. 2, pp. 166–67.
60. *DCER*, Vol. 8, 1939–41, Part 2, pp. 1302–3.
61. *Gaimushō Nenkan*.
62. All data on King's views on Japan are taken from J. W. Pickersgill, *The Mackenzie King Record*, Vol. 1, pp. 149–52.
63. Ibid., p. 151. I assume it was Yoshizawa. Pickersgill says "the Japanese Minister."
64. Ibid., pp. 152–53.
65. Ibid.
66. Ibid., p. 206.
67. Ibid., p. 207.
68. Ibid., p. 208.
69. Memorandum by Keenleyside, April 11, 1940, *DCER*, Vol. 8, 1939–41, Part 2, pp. 1141–42.
70. October 14, 1940, ibid., p. 1143.
71. Ibid., pp. 1148–60.
72. Ibid., pp. 1171–78.

73. Interview with Seijiro Yoshizawa in Tokyo, June 6, 1977.

74. *DCER*, Vol. 8, 1939–41, Part 2, p. 1399.

75. Interview with Yoshizawa, June 6, 1977.

76. Pickersgill, *The Mackenzie King Record*, Vol. 1, pp. 412–13.

77. Interview with Yoshizawa, June 6, 1977. Yoshizawa retired from the Japanese foreign service in 1958; his last post was as ambassador to India. He died in 1978.

78. Cecil Lingard and Reginald Trotter, *Canada in World Affairs 1941–44*, Vol. 3, pp. 47–48.

79. *DCER*, Vol. 8, 1939–41, Part 2, pp. 1487–89.

80. Ibid., pp. 1491–92.

81. Ibid., p. 1498.

82. Ibid., p. 1557.

3

From War to Peace, 1941–1952

Prime Minister King had anticipated that Canada would eventually be at war with Japan, though that was not his wish. He hoped it would not happen before the United States was ready to participate, thereby providing the vital element of security that Canada could not hope to furnish by itself. Specifically, King did not wish to see Great Britain or the Netherlands Indies at war with Japan while the United States remained neutral. These fears were swept away when the Japanese finally attacked Pearl Harbor. When Germany and Italy declared war on the United States on December 11, 1941, the massive power of the United States was ranged against the European Axis partners as well as against Japan, thereby, it was hoped, assuring the final defeat of all of Canada's enemies in this war.

On the fateful day, December 7, 1941, USSEA Norman A. Robertson called the prime minister at his farm house in the Gatineau Hills at 4:30 P.M. and informed him that the Japanese had attacked Hawaii and Manila. King then summoned the War Cabinet for 7 P.M. and eventually the entire cabinet for 7:30. President Roosevelt's cabinet met an hour later. At the Canadian cabinet meeting King said that war should be declared on Japan at once and the cabinet agreed to proceed without summoning Parliament, on the basis of the previous decision that Canada would stand at the side of Britain in case of an attack. King recalled, "When our troops were landed at Hong Kong, I gave a statement to the press which made clear that we regarded as part of the defence of Canada and of freedom any attack which might be made by the Japanese against British Territory or Forces in the Orient."[1]

It was exactly 9:15 P.M. when Mackenzie King signed the order in council recommending submission to the king of the declaration of war. As a result of the prime minister's quick action, Canada preceded both the United States and Great Britain in declaring war on Japan.

His cabinet also discussed measures to be taken immediately. It was suggested that the public must be enjoined to avoid anti-Japanese demonstrations in British Columbia and that the government should express its belief in the loyalty of Japanese nationals and Canadian-born Japanese in that province. After the results of Japan's Pearl Harbor raid became known (19 warships sunk or damaged, 177 planes destroyed, thousands of trained personnel killed), the fear of bombings, raids, or even landings by Japanese forces on Canadian territory was quite strong.

Varying degrees of racial tension, mutual distrust, and hostility had traditionally existed between the white and Oriental populations in British Columbia, where the greatest concentration of Japanese residents in Canada (96 percent) had been established. These tensions were generally exacerbated by perceptions of economic competition, of undue Oriental population increases through immigration or childbirth, or of a danger to military security generated by international events. Japan's program of military expansion in East Asia also aggravated the fear of Japanese aggression towards North America and the province of British Columbia in particular. This had led to gradually increasing anti-Japanese feelings in British Columbia during the thirties, beginning with anxieties about betrayal or sabotage by Japanese Canadians and culminating in near hysteria during the first three months after Canada and Japan entered a state of war on December 7, 1941.

While in hindsight it can legitimately be asserted that the fears and hysteria were completely unjustified, there being no instance of actually disloyal or treacherous behavior by Japanese Canadians, the feelings and tensions generated in British Columbia at the time were nevertheless real. Japanese Canadians who lived in British Columbia during those days know and remember what it was to be called a "goddamned Jap" in public places or to see their children chased and pelted with sticks and stones by other children. This situation put extreme, I would say irresistible, pressure on the federal as well as the provincial politicians involved to undertake drastic action, to wit, the total evacuation of all Japanese nationals from those areas in British Columbia where the supposed Japanese threat was most keenly felt.

The King government resisted the pressures from its British Columbia constituents to evacuate the Japanese for almost three months. This was partly because it was not convinced such action was necessary and partly because it wished to avoid possible retaliation by the Japanese government against Canadian prisoners of war. Canada's two battalions at Hong Kong were in combat with the Japanese army some three weeks after their arrival in the Crown Colony on November 15. Japan knocked out the British airfield and the half-dozen British combat aircraft on December 8. Two days later the battleship *Prince of Wales* and the battle cruiser *Repulse* were sunk by Japanese torpedo planes off the coast of Malaya. Deprived of air cover and with no hope of naval support or evacuation, the tiny British force fought bravely against overwhelming odds, first withdrawing to the island of Hong Kong on December 13 and finally surrendering to the Japanese on Christmas Day 1941. By the end of the fighting, 290 of the Canadians were dead and 1,685 had been taken prisoner.

It is clear that the Canadian federal government acted most reluctantly and only when it seemed that racial violence or riots could not be prevented if it failed to act. The fears of British Columbians were intensified by the startling series of quick victories by the Japanese forces in the Pacific theater of war. The virtual elimination of the U.S. Pacific fleet at Pearl Harbor, the quick fall of Hong Kong, the elimination of *Repulse* and *Prince of Wales*, the siege of Singapore, and the assault on the Philippines, with attendant reports of Japanese fifth column activities at the scenes of some of these victories, were like successive demoralizing hammer blows. Thus in the early days of 1942 it was not unreasonable to suggest that the imperial forces might land on Vancouver Island or at Prince Rupert. Some suspicious, worried white British Columbians were therefore quick to assume that Japanese nationals, as well as Japanese Canadians, living in British Columbia might indeed give aid and comfort to the enemy. The same assumption was quick to be made in the United States; however, there is no evidence that the Canadian government was directly pressured by the United States to take specific actions.

What now happened in Canada was determined by Canadian politicians and government officials, acting under extreme pressure from their non-Japanese constituents in British Columbia; there is little doubt that some people may have welcomed this opportunity to get rid of the Japanese once and for all. The Canadians of Japanese ancestry had given no cause to be distrusted in this way. It was the actions of the imperial government of Japan and the at times unspeakable behavior of the Japanese army that provided impetus and plausibility for the fears of the British Columbians. More than twenty-three thousand Japanese Canadians and Japanese nationals suffered grievously because of the measures that were then taken, but it is highly doubtful that Prime Minister King could have acted differently than he did without the gravest risk to the internal tranquillity and security of Canada.[2]

Given the fact that Canada was now at war with Japan, the Standing Committee on Orientals, appointed in January 1941, which had supervised the voluntary registration of Japanese Canadians during the early months of 1941, now advised the government to take a series of measures in the interest of national security and "for the protection of the Japanese-Canadians."[3]

As of December 7, 1941, Defence of Canada Regulations 24, 25, and 26 were extended to Japanese nationals, making their registration as enemy aliens compulsory. On December 16, 1941, compulsory registration was applied to all Japanese in Canada, including the Canadian born and naturalized citizens. Right after Pearl Harbor the government had arrested thirty-eight Japanese nationals who were regarded as threats to Canada's national security and impounded some 1,100 fishing boats belonging to persons of Japanese ancestry. At the suggestion of the RCMP, fifty-nine Japanese-language schools and three Japanese-language newspapers were also closed down, though the English-language *The New Canadian* was allowed to continue to publish. Yet public opinion in British Columbia felt that much more would have to be done, to wit, the total evacuation of all Japanese from British Columbia. In late December Maj. R. P. Alexander, the commanding officer of the Pacific command, wrote to the chief of the general staff to recommend the internment of Japanese males and their removal from coastal areas.[4]

The government responded to these pressures by convening a closed meeting in Ottawa on the Japanese problem on January 8 and 9, 1942. The conference was chaired by Ian Mackenzie, federal minister of pensions and member of Parliament for Vancouver Centre, and included representatives from various government departments.[5] There were substantial differences of opinion in the conference, particularly with regard to the evacuation of Japanese nationals, with the British Columbia representatives tending to favor the immediate evacuation of all Japanese. Mackenzie submitted both a majority and a minority report to the prime minister. Mackenzie personally favored immediate evacuation and disagreed with the conference recommendation that Japanese Canadians be permitted to volunteer for the Canadian army or be called up under the National Mobilization Act.[6]

The policy announced by the prime minister on January 14, 1942, initially spelled out the principles on which all government policy with regard to the Japanese problem was to be based.

A. National defence and victory are the first and overriding considerations.

B. Canadians of Japanese racial origin and Japanese nationals resident in Canada will be justly treated.

C. Every feasible step should be taken to maintain a calm and reasonable attitude by Canadian citizens generally.

D. No action will be taken or permitted which would give any excuse to the Government of Japan for mistreating Canadians under Japanese control.

E. Canada will collaborate with Great Britain and the United States to coordinate policies with respect to persons of Japanese racial origin.

In accordance with these principles the following measures were to be implemented. Japanese, for the duration of the war, were prohibited from fishing or serving on fishing vessels or other ships operated by Japanese off the coast of British Columbia. Sales of gasoline and explosives to Japanese were to be controlled by the RCMP. Japanese were to be forbidden to possess shortwave radio receivers and transmitters, and cameras. A civilian corps of Canadian Japanese was to be organized to accommodate those who desired to serve Canada. (This was not implemented.) A "protected area" was to be defined and all Japanese nationals, as well as other enemy aliens, not possessing permits from the RCMP were to be required to move from the protected area. Fishing boats heretofore owned by persons of Japanese race were to be sold, leased, or chartered to white fishermen or canners so that there would be no reduction in the fish catch. Work camps for adult male Japanese nationals were to be established outside the protected areas.[7]

In implementing these measures the government hoped that it would satisfy the demands of public opinion in British Columbia. On February 9, 1942, the Standing Committee on Orientals was dissolved and supervision of the new policy was turned over to a committee of the cabinet, including Mackenzie and the ministers of labor and agriculture.[8]

But the politicians and anti-Japanese agitators in British Columbia were not to be denied. Eight of British Columbia's members of Parliament, backed by resolutions of political party organizations, veterans associations, trade unions, and the Vancouver Citizens' Defence Committee, peppered Ottawa with demands for stronger action. The government, meanwhile, had not been able to get started even with its moderate program of partial evacuation of Japanese nationals, and it was February 23 before the first group was moved out of the protected area, which had been defined as a strip 100 miles wide from the Pacific Ocean to the Cascade Mountains, running from the U.S. border to the south to the Yukon in the north and including all the offshore islands. An additional protected area was later established around Trail, B.C., where the most important copper/zinc smelting works in Canada were located.

On February 19 King noted, "There is every possibility of riots. Once that occurs, there will be repercussions in the Far East against our own prisoners. Public prejudice is so strong in B.C. that it is going to be difficult to control the situation; also moving men to camps at this time of year is very difficult indeed."[9] A week later, on February 26, 1942, the government gave in to the pressures from British Columbia and announced a policy of complete evacuation of all persons of Japanese race, irrespective of citizenship, from the protected areas in British Columbia. This action was taken under the provisions of the War Measures Act, Chapter 206 of the Revised Statutes of Canada, 1927, and empowered the minister of justice to control individuals of Japanese origin with respect to certain protected areas. This meant they could be evacuated; prohibited from entering, leaving, or returning; restricted in their employment of communications with others; and deprived of their possessions. In other words, the Japanese Canadians had, with one stroke of the pen, been deprived of all their rights as citizens and were completely at the mercy of the government. The War Measures Act had never been successfully challenged and was not challenged in this case either. On March 4, 1942, Order in Council P.C. 1665 created the British Columbia Security Commission (BCSC), to which was entrusted the task of carrying out the evacuation.[10] The commission was to plan, supervise, and direct all matters relating to the evacuation from the protected areas of British Columbia of all persons of Japanese race and to provide for the housing, feeding, care, and protection of the evacuees. Finally, it was to decide who was to be evacuated, when, and how. The property of Japanese Canadians in British Columbia that was turned over to the custodian of enemy property by its owners or that the owners, on being evacuated, were unable to take with them was to be vested in and subject to the control and management of the custodian.[11] The "Custodian of Enemy Alien Property" was a government agency under the Exchequer Court in Ottawa.

The first measure pursuant to these regulations was the imposition of a sunset to sunrise curfew on all Japanese, effective on the night of February 28, 1942. The curfew order provided a considerable emotional shock to the Japanese community, which suddenly realized that it had lost its most basic civil rights. Yet some Japanese Canadians still believed that they could avoid the worst consequences of the regulations by exemption, postponement, or nonenforcement of the provisions of P.C. No. 1665. Others resorted to panic selling of their property, in a mad scramble to convert whatever they owned to cash, and in the process houses, automobiles, and other valuables were sold for a fraction of their real value, leaving the former owners with little or nothing to show for possessions accumulated in many years of hard work.[12]

The actual evacuation of 21,000 people from the British Columbia protected areas took nine months (February to October 1942) to accomplish, since an attempt was made to carry out the evacuation in a humane and orderly fashion. Road camps had to be organized, housing facilities prepared, and employment or work projects found for the prospective evacuees.

The Hastings Park Exhibition Grounds in East Vancouver were acquired by the BCSC, and the livestock building was converted into a giant dormitory so that Hastings Park would be able to serve as an assembly point for evacuees from all over British Columbia. Successive groups would pass through Hastings Park on their way to road camps in the interior of British Columbia; to sugar beet farms in Alberta, Manitoba, and Ontario; to detention camps in Ontario (Angler and Petawawa); or to the so-called interior housing projects in Tashme, Greenwood, Slocan City, Kaslo, Sandon, Roseberry, New Denver, and other places in British Columbia, usually referred to as ghost towns. The initial intention of the BCSC was to send as many as 4,000 able-bodied males between the ages of eighteen and forty-five to the road construction and logging camps. Security risks, troublemakers, and those who refused to work or be evacuated were sent to Angler, Ont., which was in fact a prison camp. Some 1,600 people who had independent or self-supporting work projects would be permitted to proceed to certain destinations outside the protected areas. The largest single group, however, some 12,000 women, children, and elderly or unemployable people, were to go to the various interior housing centers in central and eastern British Columbia. Sending the men only to the road camps meant that as a matter of policy the majority of the Japanese families were broken up.

The evacuees themselves, while initially docile and obedient, became increasingly unhappy, touchy, and rebellious as the enormity of their predicament and their total impotence to change anything became clear to them. Some evacuees were spared the indignity of being "herded like cattle" into Hastings Park by proceeding directly and as family units to farms in Alberta (Lethbridge) or in Manitoba or to employment at self-supporting projects elsewhere, but almost half of the evacuees did in fact go through Hastings Park. At the peak of the evacuation there were 3,866 people in the exhibition grounds.

The most serious traumas of most evacuees were psychological rather than physical. The breaking up of families was most bitterly resented, as was the sudden deprivation of all property, save 150 pounds of baggage per adult and 75 pounds for children under twelve. Many evacuees had no more than twenty-four hours' notice and were consequently unable to make arrangements to sell or secure property left behind. To this must have been added anxieties and uncertainties about the future and the realization, in seventy-five of a hundred cases, that though you were a Canadian citizen you were being treated as an enemy alien and potential saboteur.

An increasing number of incipient evacuees began to voice objections and protests and make demands for exemption, deferment, or improvement of their treatment. The evacuees also began to feud among themselves. Etsuji Morii, a first-generation, or immigrant, Japanese (*issei*) and two others, Arthur Nishiguchi and Ippei Nishio, also *issei*, were asked by the BCSC to form a liaison committee between the Japanese community and the BCSC. Since *issei* and *nisei* (second-generation Japanese) do not see eye to eye on very many issues, and since Morii had a somewhat murky reputation of being involved in gambling and the Black Dragon Society and as an informer to the RCMP, his appointment led to a confrontation between various groups within the Japanese community. While the BCSC attempted to work entirely through the Morii committee, three other groups were formed by naturalized Japanese and *nisei*, the Naturalized Citizens' Committee, the Japanese Canadian Citizens Council (JCCC), and the Nisei Mass Evacuation Group (NMEG), a militant faction that had split away from the JCCC.[13] The BCSC eventually worked with all of the Japanese-Canadian groups, since it became clear that Morii was not trusted by many of the evacuees. Accusations against Morii sent to Ottawa led to a judicial inquiry, which dismissed most of the charges made against him as unproven and sent him off to a self-supporting project at the end of May 1942.[14]

Conditions at Hastings Park, in the road camps, and in the interior housing projects were at first improvised, crowded, and inadequate but gradually improved as housing units were built and the evacuees themselves worked to make conditions more tolerable.

Many of the evacuees had to live in tents or ramshackle shelters for weeks or months in places like Tashme (the name was concocted from those of the three commissioners Austin *Ta*ylor, John *Shir*ras, and F. J. *Me*ad) but were moved into the two-family units (sharing a kitchen in the center) as quickly as the carpenters could build them. The food was tolerable where there were mess halls, while at Tashme the Japanese bought and cooked their own supplies and many people grew their own vegetables. Initially there was no schooling for the children, but they could work in the saw mills and other projects to earn a few cents. The male workers in the road camps could earn between $50.00 and $70.00 per month (25 cents per hour was their standard wage), working an eight-hour day, but had to pay $22.50 for room and board and $20.00 for their families, which did not leave them much for personal expenses. They were not permitted to buy liquor but were required to pay 88 cents a month unemployment insurance. Families could draw on their savings, consisting in many cases of the proceeds from the forced sale of their property by Order in Council P.C. 469, January 19, 1943, though the evacuees had initially been told that their property would be placed in safekeeping. Prior to that time only boats and automobiles had been subject to forced sale, but now all real estate and other property, from furniture to lawn mowers, was auctioned off without the owners' consent and at prices that most of them regarded as far too low.

By October 31, 1942, the task of mass evacuation had essentially been completed, resulting in the distribution of some twenty-one thousand Japanese Canadians from British Columbia as shown in Table 3.

Employment of Japanese workers outside the province of British Columbia was negotiated between the BCSC and the respective provincial governments, which sought guarantees at the time that the BCSC would thoroughly check and control the evacuees and make sure that they would move out once the emergency was over. As it turned out, however, many of the evacuees were later to re-settle in the provinces to which they had moved during the war.

It has been suggested that instead of acting to appease a vociferous minority of anti-Japanese extremists by evacuating the 21,000 Japanese Canadians, the government should have made it clear that it intended to protect the citizenship rights of Japanese Canadians against anyone who might threaten them.[15] To do so would have been noble and courageous and in accordance with democracy and justice; however, in all countries war tends to inhibit fair treatment for those who, even marginally or unjustly, can be perceived as enemies. King was a white Canadian politician leading a country at war with Japan, rather than a saint or a paragon of moral and legal rectitude. It is easy to say in hindsight that he should not have yielded to the pressures put upon him. Men like Keenleyside, H. F. Angus, and Escott Reid would have supported him had he done so. But public opinion and the British Columbia members of Parliament would have continued to complain and threaten, and a very damaging display of Canadian disunity before the enemy would have resulted. When confronted with a choice, King followed his political instincts in sacrificing the presumably compliant Japanese on the altar of national security. In so doing, he mangled the very principles Canada was supposedly defending in the war, his hand being forced almost equally by the Imperial Japanese Army and anti-Japanese politicians and civic groups in British Columbia.

Table 3
Distribution of Japanese Canadians from British Columbia,
October 31, 1942

Category	Number
At road camps in British Columbia	945
At sugar beet projects	3,991
In interior housing, British Columbia	12,029
Voluntarily self-supporting	1,161
Holding special permits	1,359
Repatriated to Japan (diplomats)	42
Voluntarily evacuated prior to March 1942	579
Exempted from evacuation (Japanese married to Occidentals and their children)	92
Interned at Angler and Petawawa, Ont.	699
Detained in Vancouver	111
In Hastings Park Hospital (tuberculosis, mental illness)	105
Total	21,113

Source: Canada, British Columbia Security Commission, *Report of the Removal of Japanese from Protected Areas*, pp. 28–29.

Japanese diplomats in Canada, as well as Canada's diplomats in Japan, were confined to their respective residences or quarters when the war broke out. Among the detainees at Marler House in Tokyo was E. Herbert Norman, third secretary there since 1940. During the seven months of house arrest in the legation, Norman, by his unexcelled wit and erudition, proved a most entertaining and pleasant companion to his fellow detainees, regaling them with his knowledge in such diverse fields as poetry, history, literature, and anthropology.[16]

It took some six months to complete arrangements for the Swedish passenger ship *Gripsholm* to pick up Japanese diplomats from all over the Western hemisphere from New York, to take them to Lourenço Marques in Portuguese East Africa, where they were to be exchanged for Canadian and other allied diplomats from Japan. A total of forty-two Japanese left Canada on May 8, 1942, going by way of Montreal to board the *Gripsholm*, which arrived in Lourenço Marques on July 21, 1942, one day before the *Asama Maru* and *Conte Verde* arrived from Japan with the Canadian diplomats from Tokyo. Seventy Canadians were transferred to the *Gripsholm*, nineteen being diplomats, the balance mostly missionaries.[17]

As E. Herbert Norman was about to board the *Gripsholm* for his trip to New York, he encountered a Japanese friend from the United States, Shigeto Tsuru, an economics scholar he had known at Harvard. Tsuru asked Norman to retrieve some papers for him that he had left behind in his apartment in Cambridge, Mass. As will be related later in this chapter, when Norman eventually acted to fulfill Tsuru's request, he may have taken the initial step in the drama that would finally lead to his death.[18]

The *Gripsholm* exchange was successfully concluded by the end of August 1942. Another exchange of civilians between Canada and Japan was effected, after long negotiations, in October 1943. On that occasion 61 Japanese nationals who had requested repatriation were exchanged for 210 Canadian civilians from various parts of the area under Japanese control.[19] Naturalized Canadians requesting repatriation to Japan were divested of their Canadian citizenship upon leaving for Japan.

A number of the repatriated Japanese gave the Tokyo government a report on what had happened to the Japanese Canadians and Japanese nationals living in British Columbia since the outbreak of the war. In October 1942 the Spanish consul general in Montreal, who represented Japanese interests in Canada, transmitted a Japanese protest to DEA over the treatment of Japanese residents in Canada. The note charged that Japanese were forced to do hard labor, that they were inadequately housed and fed in barren wastelands, that families were unnecessarily separated and their property left unprotected.[20] Robertson replied on behalf of the Canadian government that while some individual cases of hardship had occurred, the government was doing its best to reunite families and improve living conditions and also denied that compulsory labor had been imposed. Only those refusing to obey the evacuation order had been interned, and legitimate grievances would be adjusted as quickly as possible.[21]

The Japanese protest aroused some concern in Ottawa that the Japanese government might retaliate against Canadians in its custody on the basis of what it had learned about Canadian treatment of Japanese nationals from the *Gripsholm* returnees. USSEA Robertson responded with two specific actions: promotion of favorable publicity about the treatment of Japanese Canadians in the Canadian camps and encouragement to the BCSC and the Department of Justice to reexamine the cases of Japanese subjects interned in Ontario, to determine whether they could be released. Eventually some forty-two men who had indicated a willingness to work were released from internment and permitted to rejoin their families.[22] At the same time general conditions in the internment camps gradually improved.

Meanwhile, in the Far Eastern war zone, almost 1,700 Canadians had been taken prisoner by the Japanese forces in Hong Kong on Christmas Day 1941. A Canadian protest to Japan was lodged through the Canadian minister to Argentina in Buenos Aires, alleging that prisoners taken at Hong Kong by the Japanese forces were being held at Kowloon under atrocious conditions, without adequate food or water and without sanitation, so that many were sick. It was claimed they were receiving barbarous treatment at the hands of the Japanese and had not been allowed to communicate with anyone outside or with the Japanese commandant.[23] The Japanese government replied that it could not admit the truth of the accusations made but that the matter would be studied with attention.[24]

In a message conveyed by the International Red Cross Committee in Montreal two days earlier, the Canadian government had been given the following information about Japanese treatment of civilian internees.

> For the duration of present war Japanese Government will apply articles of 1929 prisoner of war convention to noncombatant internees of enemy countries provided belligerent countries do not compel them to physical labour against their will. . . .
>
> Japanese Legation in Berne assure us that enemy internees in Japan enjoy more favourable privileges than those of above mentioned convention, as in addition to provision by the authorities of bread, butter, eggs, meats, fuel oil, coal, internees may also receive food-stuffs, clothing. Possible to visit families in view of proximity of internment camps. Medical examinations and hospitalization for the sick. Possible for them to read Japanese newspapers, use radio, and to go out under certain required conditions.[25]

Lists of Canadian civilian internees in Japan were obtained by the Canadian government by April 1942. Lists of prisoners of war were delayed[26] and did not become available until November 1942.[27]

The evacuation of the Japanese Canadians having been essentially completed by the end of 1942, there remained the problem of disposal of their personal property left behind in the protected area. This property had then been placed under the control of the custodian of enemy property for "safekeeping," leading to the assumption by many of the evacuees that they would someday be enabled to reclaim their property or arrange for its sale.

The remaining property of the Japanese Canadians consisted of their houses, farms, and real estate and their furniture and personal belongings. On January 19, 1943, an order in council (P.C. 469) was issued by the government that placed all remaining property of "persons of the Japanese race" in the hands of the custodian.[28]

The government's decision to order the liquidation of Japanese property, treating Canadian citizens of Japanese birth on a par with Japanese nationals, was announced on February 6, 1943. The government also decided in March 1943 not to protest against the liquidation of Canadian property in Shanghai by the Japanese, since parallel action was being contemplated for Japanese property in Canada. In June 1942 the director of soldier settlements had been authorized to control Japanese farm land. The intention was to acquire the Japanese-owned farms for resettlement of veterans. Some 769 farms, grossly undervalued at $841,000, were acquired in this way without the consent of the former owners.

A large number of personal items were sent on request by the custodian to the original owners in the camps during 1942, but by January 1943 it was rarely possible to locate such chattels. It was therefore decided to auction off what remained.

The decision to liquidate Japanese property in the protected area of British Columbia foreshadows the later decision not to permit Japanese Canadians to return to British Columbia after the war. All but one of British Columbia's sixteen members of Parliament had regarded the evacuation and attendant measures as merely a first step, leading eventually to the complete eviction of the Japanese by deportation to Japan or possibly to some island in the Pacific to be purchased for that purpose.[29]

There was a small number of officials at DEA who attempted to moderate the new policy on property by pointing out its inequities, including Keenleyside and Angus, as well as the Reverend Howard Norman of St. George United Church, Vancouver. In a memorandum to the prime minister dated March 15, 1943, Angus called attention to protests received against the P.C. 469 provision for liquidation without consent. He pointed out the many injuries already suffered by the innocent internees because of their race, calling compulsory sale of their property unjust and suggesting that their consent to liquidation be required.[30]

The decision reached by the government in June 1943 was that, with the exception of articles of religious or sentimental value, all personal and real property be liquidated forthwith.

Relief was to be denied to able-bodied Japanese, for whom work was available. Others were to be required to expend capital assets before asking for relief, though depending on their family situations they might retain some reserve. Practical internment as well as compulsory employment were to be avoided, though policy might ban mass movement from essential jobs at work camps. Requests by Japanese for licenses to hold land were to be denied, and in answer to inquiries from the United States, persons of the Japanese race who were citizens of the United States were not to be admitted to Canada.[31]

Keenleyside, in a letter to the USSEA dated July 16, 1943, regretted that the American and Far Eastern Division of DEA had repeatedly been excluded from consultations where decisions on Orientals in Canada were discussed. He then pointed out "that the policy on relief is unjustifiable on any basis of decency or humanity unless it is assumed that all Japanese can obtain work if they want it."[32]

Since there continued to be protests about conditions in the camps through the International Red Cross Committee and the Spanish Consulate General, it was announced in December 1943 that a royal commission had been appointed to investigate the situation (P.C. No. 9498 of December 14, 1943). The commission, headed by J. W. Jackson of Manitoba, toured Vancouver and Steveston, B.C., as well as the camps, speaking to camp supervisors and camp committees.

The commission report[33] brings out the fact that the government regarded the interior settlements as a temporary means of meeting an emergency, "a step in the evacuation process and a training ground for employment in the prairies and the East." Food was found to be of average or better quality. The report recommended a 10 percent increase in the maintenance rates for unemployable and aged persons and their dependents. Housing was found generally adequate and thought to be at least equal to the housing the Japanese had lived in prior to the evacuation in Steveston and Vancouver. There was criticism of the British Columbia provincial government for failing to provide kindergarten and high school classes in the camps. The commission found medical, dental, and hospitalization services to be excellent at all the camps and concluded that the "medical care provided at the interior settlements for Japanese people exceeds that received by the average Canadian." The commission finally was "of the unanimous opinion that the provisions made by the Government of Canada through the Department of Labour for the welfare of the Japanese in the Interior Settlements in British Columbia are, as a wartime measure, reasonably fair and adequate."[34]

Administration of Japanese affairs had been taken over from the

BCSC by the commissioner of Japanese placement under the Department of Labour in February 1943, and it appears that this shift reflected a new phase in the evolution of government policy. The new concerns of the commissioner of Japanese placement were

1) to place all employable Japanese in useful work by relocating them, both singly and in family groups, where essential industries have urgent labour shortages;

2) to provide adequate welfare for the unemployables, aged, and infirm;

3) to insure for the children at least a minimum Canadian education.[35]

By March 1944 the Department of Labour reported that, while two-thirds of the evacuated Japanese (about 16,000) were still in the interior settlements, approximately one-third (about 7,500) had been moved east of the Rockies and were now living in Alberta, Manitoba, Ontario, or Quebec and were doing essential work in lumbering, farming, and factories. The commissioner of placement worked with employment and selective service offices in Lethbridge, Winnipeg, Fort William, Toronto, and Montreal to place as many of the employable Japanese as possible. Over half of the Japanese were supporting themselves by work; some 20 percent were on full maintenance; and another 20 percent were on partial maintenance. In the interior housing centers some three thousand children were being taught the regular curriculum in English, while those East of the Rockies attended regular provincial schools. Church groups tried to provide kindergarten and high school education, which was not provided in the camps. Teachers were scarce and inexperienced, but Japanese Canadians were given intensive educational training so that schooling could be provided as soon as possible. Some of the children lost between six and twelve months of schooling in the early days of the evacuation, while others in isolated areas had to take correspondence courses.[36]

What occasioned some problems was the uncertainty that surrounded future government policy with regard to the Japanese. The government had in effect turned the Japanese over to the Department of Labour, the custodian of enemy property, and DEA, and these agencies appeared to have difficulties in arriving at a common policy for the postwar period or even in coordinating their wartime policies.

In August 1944 King finally made a statement in the House of Commons that laid down the broad outline of what was to be the government's policy in the years to come. The outlines of this policy had first been suggested in a memorandum by Robertson in August 1943. Robertson had then commented that Canadian policy on the Japanese had been largely influenced by what Canada imperfectly understood United States policy to be. One difference was that Canada exempted Japanese from selective service and refused voluntary applications by Japanese for enlistment in the armed forces, whereas the United States had formed units from Japanese volunteers. Robertson looked ahead to the postwar situation and pointed out that "the communities from which the Japanese were evacuated are confident that they have gone for good and will probably resist their return."[37]

In his statement to Parliament on August 4, 1944, the prime minister made the following points.

1) that the matter of the Japanese was to be dealt with not only by British Columbia but by the whole of Canada as a Canadian problem;

2) that it would be unwise to permit all Japanese in Canada to concentrate in British Columbia again after the war;

3) that for the most part Japanese in Canada had remained loyal to Canada and refrained from acts of sabotage;

4) that those who had been disloyal, be they Japanese nationals or Canadian citizens by birth or naturalization, should not be permitted to remain in Canada after the war;

5) that no Japanese immigrants should be admitted to Canada after the war;

6) that the Japanese in Canada are persons who have been admitted here to settle and become citizens or have been born in Canada and that we cannot do less than to treat such persons fairly and justly. "It has not . . . been shown, that the presence of a few thousand persons of

Japanese race who have been guilty of no act of sabotage and who have manifested no disloyalty even during periods of utmost trial, constitutes a menace to a nation of almost twelve million people."

7) that the Canadian government in general outline would follow a policy similar to, though not identical with, that of the United States.

8) that a commission would be established fairly soon to determine who was and who was not disloyal among both Japanese nationals and Canadian nationals and those judged disloyal deported as soon as possible;

9) that those adjudged to have been loyal would be permitted to remain in Canada but would be encouraged to settle in provinces other than British Columbia, with the aim of achieving an even distribution of Japanese throughout Canada—"the sound and best policy for the Japanese Canadians themselves is to distribute their numbers as widely as possible throughout the country where they will not create feelings of racial hostility";

10) that "we must not permit in Canada the hateful doctrine of racialism, which is the basis of the nazi system everywhere. Our aim is to resolve a difficult problem in a manner which will protect the people of British Columbia and the interests of the country as a whole, and at the same time preserve, in whatever we do, principles of fairness and justice."[38]

The statement had the virtue of finally letting Japanese Canadians know what the future outlook was, though it was short on specifics and left in doubt how precisely the policies announced would be implemented.

Some six months later, in the spring of 1945, the commissioner of Japanese placement, T. B. Pickersgill, proceeded to have notices posted in the camps in English and Japanese inviting applications for voluntary repatriation to Japan. Regardless of citizenship, all persons of Japanese racial origin were informed by Minister of Labour Humphrey Mitchell that they could now make voluntary application to go to Japan after the war or sooner, where this could be arranged. They were promised free passage for themselves and their dependents, free transportation of their personal property, and permission to transfer the proceeds of their property that had been liquidated by the custodian. In a separate notice, those who wished to reamin in Canada were informed that they should now reestablish themselves east of the Rockies in order to show their intention to cooperate with the government policy of dispersal. Failure to accept employment east of the Rockies might be regarded at a later date as evidence of a lack of cooperation with the Canadian government in carrying out the policy of dispersal. A total of 6,903 forms were signed for voluntary repatriation to Japan, committing more than 10,295 Japanese to this program.[39]

These figures should not be interpreted as positive evidence that 43 percent of the Japanese in Canada wanted to go back to Japan. To begin, 3,392 were children under sixteen, who in many cases were not consulted on what they wished to do. A number of the wives may have been equally reluctant to return to Japan but may not have wished to be separated from their husbands. Finally, one must consider the circumstances under which the question was put to the evacuees. Already once uprooted from jobs, homes, and familiar surroundings and deprived of most of their property, they were now told: You must either move again to rather uncertain prospects in new and potentially hostile surroundings in eastern Canada, or you will be judged disloyal, deprived of your citizenship, and sent back to Japan even if born in Canada. The various restrictions imposed on Japanese Canadians, such as the travel restrictions,[40] the inability to buy homes and farms, and the ban on entering the city of Toronto, were not lifted until a year later. It is therefore likely that extreme frustrations, anxiety over future prospects, family circumstances, and the feeling that they would continue to face racism and discrimination so long as they remained in Canada all contributed to the high number of people signing to be voluntarily repatriated to Japan. A breakdown of the 6,903 signatories shows that 2,946 were Japanese nationals, 2,491 Canadian-born, and 1,466 naturalized Canadian citizens.

As it turned out, only one-third of the more than 10,000 people originally registered for repatriation were in fact shipped back to Japan in the postwar period. Many eventually changed their minds about wishing to go to Japan, and the government in due course changed its policy, deciding not to send people to Japan against their will.[41]

However, during 1945 the government was still intent upon implementing the segregation and deportation policy. The policy of dispersal was not succeeding to the extent the government hoped, and only small numbers of the Japanese in the British Columbia camps were accepting resettlement east of the Rockies. As of January 1945, two-thirds of the Japanese Canadians (15,610) were still in British Columbia and only one third (8,215) in the prairies and eastern Canada. Less than 1,000 moved east during 1945.[42] Public opinion in Canada, meanwhile, had shown little concern for the citizenship rights or the personal plight of the Japanese Canadians while Canada was still at war with Japan.

Canada's involvement in the military phases of the war against Japan was not on a scale or of an importance decisive to the outcome of the war. It started with the tragedy of the defeat and capture of the Canadian units at Hong Kong, which left almost 1,700 Canadian prisoners of war in the hands of the Japanese.

The necessities of continental defense led in August 1940 to the establishment of the PJBD, which both before and during the war advised on a number of Canada–United States cooperative projects, including the northwest staging route, the Alaska highway, and the Canol (Canada Oil) project.[43]

When in May 1942 Japan made its abortive attempt to take Midway, a diversionary Japanese task force had been sent to the Aleutian Islands, and during the second week of June these Japanese forces bombed Dutch Harbour and invaded and occupied three of the Aleutian Islands, Attu, Agattu, and Kiska, unopposed. In anticipation of this Japanese move, Canadian air units (No. 115 Fighter Squadron) had been moved into Alaska (Annette Island) in May 1942 and later participated in operations against Attu and Kiska from Yakutat, Umnak, Adak, and Amchitka, though only one Japanese aircraft was shot down in these operations. The seizure of the Aleutian Islands came at a time when Japanese military advances had reached their farthest points and caused some anxiety that the war was finally approaching Canada's Northwest. A degree of hysteria was briefly kindled in British Columbia when a Japanese submarine (I-26) surfaced off the coast of Vancouver

Island on June 20, 1942, and lobbed two dozen shells at the lighthouse and wireless station at Estevan Point, causing little damage in the process. This was to remain the only instance of Japanese armed forces directly attacking Canadian territory during the war. Some Japanese balloons carrying incendiary and explosive bombs drifted over Canada but did no damage.

The 8th Division for defense of the West Coast was authorized on June 17, 1942, in addition to the 6th Division mobilized a year earlier, so the Pacific Command had 35,000 troops available for the invasion that never came. The Air Force had seventeen squadrons in Western Air Command by the spring of 1943, of which four were in Alaska, two at Annette Island, one at Anchorage, and one at Kodiak.[44] Token numbers from the Canadian forces did serve against Japan in the British forces in Southeast Asia, and of these the most remarkable appears to have been Squadron Leader Leonard J. Birchall of St. Catharines, Ont., sometimes referred to as "the savior of Ceylon." On April 4, 1942, Birchall's squadron was on patrol 350 miles due south of Ceylon when it spotted a convoy of Japanese battleships, aircraft carriers, cruisers, destroyers, and troop carriers. Birchall's crew managed to code and transmit a message describing the convoy vessels, their speed, and their direction to Ceylon before his plane was shot down by carrier-based fighters. Birchall and some of his crew survived the crash into the Indian Ocean, were picked up by a Japanese destroyer, and later were taken back to Tokyo aboard the aircraft carrier *Akagi*. He found out only at the end of the war that his warning had enabled Ceylon to prepare for the Japanese attack, which came a few days later and was repulsed. Birchall was awarded the Distinguished Flying Cross, and Winston Churchill later referred to his action as "one of the most important single contributions to victory."[45]

The Japanese garrisons on Attu and Kiska in the Aleutians (2,500 men on Attu and 6,000 on Kiska) were under frequent bombardment by U.S. and Canadian air force units from the midsummer of 1942. The threat posed by these Japanese garrisons provided a rationale for keeping the Canadian 6th and 8th Divisions in readiness in British Columbia.

Yet after the battle of Midway, Japan was not expected to attack Alaska or British Columbia. In the spring of 1943 the U.S. military decided to evict the Japanese from their forward positions in the

Aleutians. After an official proposal was submitted to Prime Minister King by the U.S. government, he agreed to Canadian participation.[46]

In the battle of the Komandorski Islands on March 26, 1943, a Japanese convoy trying to reinforce Attu was repulsed by the U.S. Navy. The U.S. 7th Division finally landed on Attu on May 11, 1943. Some 2,350 Japanese soldiers were killed or committed suicide with their own grenades in wild *banzai* charges (cheering "may the Emperor live 10,000 years" as they charged), with only 24 being taken prisoner. In Tokyo it was announced that the entire Japanese garrison had died the death of honor (*gyokusai*) in defending the island. Both General Tōjō and Adm. Isoroku Yamamoto, commander in chief of the Japanese navy, apparently recognized that the tide of the war had turned both in Europe and Asia and that the battles at Midway, Guadalcanal, and the Aleutians and Germany's defeat in North Africa were the beginning of the end for the Axis powers.

After the fall of Attu, 6,000 Japanese soldiers remained on Kiska. Imperial Army headquarters decided to evacuate Kiska on May 19, using submarines at night to avoid detection. In the process of evacuating 830 men in this fashion, Japan lost four submarines to U.S. PT boat attacks. Because of this, the Japanese decided to try evacuation by surface vessels under the cover of fog. The almost 5,200 Japanese soldiers still remaining on Kiska were successfully evacuated by a flotilla of three Japanese cruisers and six destroyers in less than one hour on July 29, 1943.

During the two weeks between July 29 and August 13, a Canadian fighter squadron flew thirty-three individual sorties against Kiska and encountered little or no evidence of resistance from the island. The Japanese had left some timed explosives on the island to create the impression that it was still being defended, but the only living beings remaining on the island were three dogs the Japanese had left there. Accordingly, under Maj. Gen. G. R. Pearkes of Pacific Command, four Canadian infantry battalions, forming the 13th Infantry Brigade and the 1st Special Service Battalion, a total of 5,300 Canadians, joined over 29,000 U.S. soldiers, commanded by Maj. Gen. C. H. Corlett, in the assault on Kiska on the night of August 15, 1943. The landings were supported by three battleships, two cruisers, and nineteen destroyers. Although there was no opposition, four Canadians were killed, one officer stepping on a land mine and three others being killed by booby traps or exploding ammunition. The Canadian brigade stayed on Kiska for three months and was eventually withdrawn to British Columbia. A follow-up attack on the Kuriles was considered and endorsed by General Pearkes, but the idea was eventually dropped.[47]

While Canada did not substantially participate in the "island hopping" counteroffensive that ensued in the summer of 1943, about a hundred Canadian officers served with the U.S. forces in the Pacific area. Prime Minister King believed that Canada should participate in the final assault against Japan, but he was reluctant to see Canada involved in the South Pacific, where she might be perceived as engaging in the reconquest of former British colonial areas. The Canadian general staff recommended that Canada should be represented in the final assault on the Japanese homeland by one division. Also, the Royal Canadian Navy and Air Force would augment the Royal Navy and Air Force in the Pacific area. King stubbornly opposed both Canadian and British military commanders to keep the Canadian military commitment to a minimum level. The United States, meanwhile, remained quite content to win the war against Japan virtually by itself.[48]

On April 4, 1945, King announced in the House of Commons that the Canadian Army Pacific Force (CAPF) would be chosen from those who elected to serve in the Pacific theatre. It was to be an infantry division. Some seventy-eight thousand men and women of all ranks volunteered for the force. But meanwhile the war was rapidly drawing to a close.

On August 6, 1945, the U.S. Air Force dropped an atomic bomb on Hiroshima, totally devastating the city. Prime Minister King had learned of the nuclear bomb project in June 1942 because Canadian uranium was needed in developing the weapon. He learned on February 3, 1945, that the bomb might be used against Japan. After he heard on August 6 that the bomb had been dropped on Hiroshima, he noted in his diary:

> Naturally this word created mixed feelings in my mind and heart. We were now within sight of the end of the war with Japan. We now see what might have come to the British people had German scientists won the race. It is fortunate that

the use of the bomb should have been upon the Japanese rather than upon the white races of Europe.

(In Pickersgill's *The Mackenzie King Record*, that last sentence does not appear.)[49] Two days later the Soviet Union entered the war against Japan. On August 9 Nagasaki suffered the same fate as Hiroshima. Hostilities in the Pacific officially ended on August 14, 1945, and on September 1 the disbandment of the CAPF was announced.[50] A Canadian cabinet committee had meanwhile decided that Canadian forces would not participate in the occupation of Japan.

Finally, on September 2, 1945, Gen. Douglas MacArthur, Supreme Commander for the Allied Powers for the Occupation and Control of Japan (SCAP), accepted Japan's unconditional surrender. When the instruments of surrender were signed, Col. L. Moore Cosgrave signed sixth for Canada.[51] Thus the military hostilities between Canada and Japan, which had led to the death of 730 Canadians, mostly members of the Hong Kong force, finally came to a conclusion. Of some 96,456 casualties suffered by Canada during World War II, only 1.2 percent occurred in the war with Japan.[52] (See Table 4.)

Since the Japanese surrender ended the war for Canada, the settlement of the "Japanese problem" within Canada now became one of higher priority. The Canadian government moved to implement the policies it had decided on in the summer of 1944. Two weeks after the surrender, DEA advised Washington that it wished to repatriate or deport some ten thousand Japanese to Japan as

Table 4
Canadian Casualties in the War Against Japan

Area	Killed	Wounded	Total
Hong Kong	554	369	923
Far East–Pacific	5	5	10
At sea	171	56	227
Total	730	430	1,160[a]

Source: Adapted from C. P. Stacy, *Six Years of War*, p. 525.

[a] The table includes battle casualties as well as those suffered in prison camps through illness and other causes; 253 died of illness as prisoners.

soon as possible and inquired when it would be convenient for General MacArthur to receive them in Japan. A cabinet committee had been set up in Ottawa to deal with the whole Japanese problem, including relocation within Canada as well as deportation or repatriation to Japan.[53] While no reply was received from MacArthur until the end of October, the Canadian government was even slower in firming up its policies. The three orders in council to deal with the Japanese problem came out on December 15, 1945.[54]

In October 1945 the government, in Clause G of the National Emergency Transitional Powers Act, Bill 15, had sought the power to control deportations and the revocation of citizenship. This gave rise to widespread opposition in the press, and a flood of protests poured into Ottawa. The war was now over, and the mood had changed. A growing number of Canadians came to believe that the King government was arbitrarily pushing around Japanese Canadians whose only crime was that they were Japanese. Thus when Bill 15 was finally passed on December 7, 1945, the government had seen fit to omit Clause G. But those who favored deportation of as many Japanese as possible included Prime Minister King and at least two members of the Special Cabinet Committee on Repatriation and Relocation of Persons of Japanese Race in Canada, Labor Minister Mitchell, and Veterans Affairs Minister Mackenzie. Keenleyside and Angus were no longer among the top advisers on Japanese affairs. Thus when King tabled the three orders in council on December 17, 1945, Cooperative Commonwealth Federation (CCF) members Angus MacInnis (Vancouver) and H. W. Herridge (Kootenay West, B.C.) eloquently opposed the measures, whereas Liberal Tom Reid (Burnaby) and Progressive Conservative Green (Vancouver South) supported them, Green suggesting once again that all the Japanese evacuees be resettled, possibly on an island in the Pacific.[55]

Orders in Council 7355, 7356, and 7357 were immediately challenged in a lawsuit by the Cooperative Committee on Japanese Canadians (CCJC), with Toronto lawyer Andrew Brewin acting as their counsel. The Supreme Court of Canada and the Privy Council in London both upheld the validity of the orders in council, acting respectively in February and December of 1946.[56]

While awaiting the final decision of the Privy Council, the government carried out no "deportations" of Japanese. However, between May 31 and the end of the year, 3,964 "persons of Japanese race" who had signed up to go to Japan at the government's expense were "voluntarily repatriated." This group constituted 16.5 percent of all the Japanese in Canada; two-thirds of them were Canadian citizens, and a little over half were Canadian born. A number of them subsequently duly established their Canadian citizenship and were able to return to Canada, their real home, during the postwar years. The 20,558 Japanese remaining in Canada on New Year's Day 1947 were beginning to resettle in greater numbers in provinces other than British Columbia as the government began to close the detention camps in the British Columbia interior. There were 5,871 in the prairie provinces, 6,616 in Ontario, 6,776 in British Columbia, and 1,247 in Quebec.[57]

Meanwhile, public opinion in Canada no longer supported discriminatory measures against Japanese Canadians. The *Toronto Star*, the Toronto *Globe and Mail*, and even the *Vancouver Sun* were beginning to urge more liberal policies on the government, and a number of civic organizations, some formed by Japanese Canadians and others associated with religious or civil rights causes, were lobbying the government for fair treatment for the Japanese. These included the CCJC; the National Japanese-Canadian Citizens Association (NJCCA), formed in Toronto in September 1947; the Vancouver Consultative Council (VCC); and the Japanese Canadian Committee for Democracy (JCCD).

In light of these developments the cabinet committee on the Japanese problem reached a number of important decisions in January 1947. The most important of these was the withdrawal of Orders in Council 7355, 7356, and 7357, on deportation, revocation of citizenship, and the loyalty commission. The withdrawal was announced by Prime Minister King in Ottawa on January 24, 1947. The prime minister also stated that while the government believed that the Japanese Canadians whose property had been liquidated by the custodian had received a fair price, the government, to ensure fair treatment, was prepared to remedy injustices.[58]

In response to representations by the CCJC and the JCCD, a claims commission headed by Justice Henry I. Bird of the British Columbia Supreme Court was set up on July 18, 1947, to look into claims "by any person of Japanese race." The Bird commission received 1,300 claims for more than $4 million. At the conclusion of its hearings in April 1950, the Bird commission recommended payment of $1,222,929 in addition to what the claimants had initially received.[59] Attempts by the NJCCA to reopen the matter and press further claims were rejected by the government.

The prohibition to Japanese to move back to the protected area in British Columbia was not finally lifted until April 1, 1949. The last of the detention camps was not closed until the spring of 1948. What the Japanese Canadians suffered were insults to their dignity, deprivation of legal rights and property, injustice, and inequity— which is more than most people can bear. By Japan's ancient code, death with honor is preferable to survival in shame. It is evident that most Japanese Canadians did not adhere to this kind of tradition but preferred to suffer in silence and hope for better days. Those better days were now rapidly approaching. Bill 198, passed in June 1948, enfranchised Japanese Canadians in every province to vote in federal elections after March 31, 1949. On January 17, 1949, the Vancouver city council enfranchised Japanese Canadians to vote in municipal elections, and finally on March 7, 1949, Japanese Canadians obtained the right to vote in British Columbia's provincial elections.

Although more than 95 percent of all Japanese Canadians had at one time regarded British Columbia as their home, there was no big rush to move back into the former protected area when the travel restrictions were finally lifted in April 1949. Only a few hundred returned during the first year and about two thousand during the second year.[60] The Japanese were now dispersed all over Canada, roughly one-third in Ontario, one-third in British Columbia, and the remaining third mostly in the prairies and Quebec. No new Japanese ghettoes were created in the process, as the Japanese distributed themselves fairly evenly among the rest of the population in the new areas to which they moved. Two-thirds of the Japanese came to live in Canada's major urban centers, fully half in Toronto, Vancouver, and Montreal, in that order. Along with the dispersal came a branching out into new pursuits, a move into the professions, and a rise in living standards, which constituted the very positive response of most Japanese Canadians to what Barry Broadfoot has called their "years of sorrow, years of shame."[61]

Japan's surrender to the allies in September 1945 had been "unconditional," permitting the victors to determine the conditions that would be imposed upon the vanquished, and Gen. Douglas MacArthur had been appointed SCAP. Since Canada's military forces were needed in Europe and the CAPF had been disbanded, the Canadian government decided not to participate in the military phases of the occupation of Japan.[62] Given the preponderant role played by the United States in the Pacific war, it was natural that the United States would move to dominate both the occupation and the postwar policies to be enforced upon Japan. Like the United States, Canada wanted rapid restoration of normal economic activity in the area and demilitarization of Japan, to ensure that there would be no repetition of Japanese imperialism.

When the United States proposed the establishment of a Far Eastern Advisory Commission (FEAC) in Washington, D.C., in August 1945, it meant it to include representatives of the Big Four (the United States, the United Kingdom, the USSR, and China), as well as Canada, New Zealand, Australia, France, the Netherlands, and the Philippines. To meet certain Soviet objections, the commission was later renamed the Far Eastern Commission (FEC) and its function was redefined, calling for it to "formulate, the policies, principles and standards, in conformity with which the fulfillment by Japan of its obligations under the terms of the surrender may be accomplished." Canada was invited to membership, and Prime Minister King accepted on January 3, 1946.[63] Canada was represented on these bodies by Pearson, then Canadian ambassador to Washington, and also by E. Herbert Norman, who was sent to Washington for that purpose.

Norman, after his repatriation to Canada on the *Gripsholm*, had spent the remaining war years in Ottawa at DEA and also continued his work as a historian of Japan in his spare time. At the end of the war DEA sent Norman to the Philippines, to aid in the repatriation of Canadian prisoners of war, and later to Japan. Once in Japan, Norman had quickly gained the respect and confidence of General MacArthur and the occupation authorities, who asked the Canadian government to assign Norman to SCAP headquarters. There Norman proceeded to supervise the most important civilian intelligence operation of the occupation, the classification of Japan's elite into those to be banned because of their past political affiliations and those who would qualify to build a new democratic society. (In banning, the word used was "purged" and meant that the purgee would be ineligible to hold public office by election or appointment and unlikely to qualify for any significant role in the postwar reconstruction of Japan. Very few of those purged had their rights restored while the occupation continued.) It was a massive task, requiring research, interrogations, and the rendering of judgments on thousands of people. Norman was uniquely qualified to perform this function, as a brilliant linguist and historian and a sophisticated critic of Japanese society. Meanwhile, Norman was continuing his scholarly work and widening his contacts with Japanese scholars and intellectuals, gaining a high reputation for his works as they were translated and published in Japan.[64] In his work at SCAP headquarters, Norman was now in a unique position to nurture the democratic forces in Japan and suppress the influence of antidemocratic personalities, with the full backing of the occupation authorities. In the process Norman's views of Japanese society became Canadian policy, as manifested in the positions taken by the Canadian representative in the consultations of the FEC.

Meanwhile, the U.S. government proposed in early December 1945 that an Allied Council for Japan (ACJ) be established in Tokyo to advise SCAP on the implementation of the surrender terms and on matters of occupation policy. The ACJ was to have members representing the United States, the USSR, China, and the British Commonwealth. The British Commonwealth representative was to speak with a single voice for the United Kingdom, Australia, New Zealand, presumably Canada, and even India. The Canadian government declined to be represented in this collective fashion, believing that it was unlikely that the commonwealth representative could effectively reflect Canadian views. The United Kingdom, Australia, and New Zealand did agree to the scheme.[65] MacArthur, finding the Soviet propaganda posturing in the ACJ tiresome, increasingly ignored its recommendations, and in due course it ceased to have any great significance in the occupation's policies. The main policy-making body remained the FEC, and there Canada played an important role in influencing the policy directives forwarded to MacArthur.

H. Hume Wrong, as Acting USSEA, expressed Canadian policy concerns along the following lines. As a Pacific power, Canada wished to contribute to a settlement that would eliminate Japan as a threat to peace, to help form a stable and democratic government in Japan, and to provide for future peace and prosperity in East Asia. Because of her limited role in the war and occupation, Canada would not initiate proposals, but it would clarify Canadian interest and concern. Canada would favor a single U.S. military command over Japan and the laying down of policy by the FEC. In general Canada would support the announced initial postsurrender policy of the United States.[66]

Meanwhile, the question of representation of Canadian interests in Japan had to be faced. At the outset of the war, Argentina had been the protecting power for Canada, but in May 1942 the Canadian government had decided to transfer that task to Switzerland.[67] At the end of the war Canada dealt with the U.S. occupation authorities through the state department in Washington, but once the occupation was firmly in place, Canada felt the need to deal directly with various agencies and individuals in Japan. In May 1946 the U.S. State Department agreed to accept Canadian representation in Japan in the form of a civilian Canadian liaison mission, to be located in the Canadian legation.[68] About one month later Pearson, in his capacity as Canadian representative to the FEC, reported to the prime minister that he was somewhat discouraged with the performance of the FEC and felt that the U.S. representative devoted most of his efforts to shielding SCAP from pressure by the FEC to do anything he did not choose to do. MacArthur was evidently ignoring and overruling the FEC and running Japan the way he himself preferred, taking his cue from increasing tensions between the United States and the Soviet Union. Pearson foresaw that the projected Canadian liaison mission in Tokyo might prove a more effective instrument for influencing U.S. policy on Japan than the FEC.[69]

E. Herbert Norman, then 36, was chosen to be the head of the Canadian liaison mission. In December 1945 Norman had terminated his intelligence work for SCAP in order to serve as alternate Canadian delegate with the FEC.[70] The Canadian ambassador to Washington, Pearson, was Canada's chief delegate in the FEC; in December 1945 Norman was appointed the alternate delegate.[71] He appears to have played a very important role in the deliberations of the FEC, frequently acting as chairman and contributing his knowledge and powers of mediation in the disputes that naturally arose between the delegates of the eleven countries.

Norman took up his post as head of the liaison mission in Tokyo in August 1946, having been replaced by Ralph E. Collins at the FEC.[72] The liaison mission was accredited to SCAP and had all the functions of a regular diplomatic mission, and with its very limited staff it was soon overburdened with work. An economic attaché, J. E. Kenderdine, was appointed to prepare the way for the eventual resumption of Japanese-Canadian trade relations. The liaison mission looked after the interests of Canadians living in Japan, most of whom were Franciscan, Dominican, and Sulpiciens clergy in the process of reestablishing their missions and seeking restoration of their properties in Japan. There was also the matter of the Japanese Canadians who had been "voluntarily repatriated" during 1946, many of whom began to agitate for a return to Canada almost as soon as they arrived in Japan.[73]

Norman's influence with SCAP was apparently strongest in the early days of the occupation, when his memorandum on Prince Fumimaro Konoe may have led to Konoe's purge and classification as a war criminal. Norman also helped to bring about reductions in sentence for two former foreign ministers, Mamoru Shigemitsu and Shigenori Togo, but as the Cold War developed and the occupation became more conservative in its outlook, the influence of Norman and those sharing his attitudes notably declined.[74]

In the Potsdam Declaration of July 26, 1945, defining the terms for Japan's surrender, it was specified that stern justice would be meted out to all war criminals and just reparations exacted.[75] Accordingly, the Canadian government decided that it would request trial for persons charged with or suspected of having committed violations of the laws and usages of war or whose alleged criminality resulted in the death or permanent disability of Canadian nationals or members of the Canadian armed forces.[76] A crimes advisory committee was established to deal with the question of Far Eastern war crimes, and officers of national defense were engaged in the preliminary screening of reports from liberated prisoners of war. Canada's primary interest would be in the trials of those responsible for individual acts or atrocities. The Canadian army supplied ten officers for the court proceedings of interest to Canada carried out by British military authorities in Hong Kong and U.S. military authorities in Tokyo. In order to maximize allied participation in the International Military Tribunal, Far East (IMTFE), which tried major war criminals in Tokyo, a Canadian judge, E. S.

MacDougall, was appointed a judge of the IMTFE; no Canadian judge participated at Nuremberg, however. The lesser war criminals prosecuted in Tokyo and Hong Kong were camp commanders, staff officers, and guards who had been in charge of Canadian prisoners of war. All fifty-eight of the defendants identified by the Canadian division of the Legal Section Investigation Team were convicted and received sentences ranging from death by hanging to twenty years' imprisonment. The death sentences were commuted to prison terms by the reviewing authority. The trials of the lesser war criminals were concluded in April 1947, while those of the major war criminals were not concluded until November 1948.[77]

The matter of reparations was one of the problems taken up by the FEC. While the Canadian government was concerned about securing the payment of reparations as compensation for losses of Canadian property and to reduce Japanese war potential, this concern was balanced by the consideration that a viable economy for Japan was more important than the exaction of reparations. The Canadian Restitution and Reparations Team, responsible to SCAP and reporting to the Canadian government, was appointed on January 14, 1947. Kenderdine became chairman of the team. It was envisaged that reparations would be made in kind, with industrial plants or goods in stock that had been declared surplus to Japan's peacetime needs. Canadian interest was focused on an aluminum and a caustic soda plant. Negotiations on reparations in the FEC soon led to a stalemate, since the Soviet delegate insisted that the external assets of Japan, such as her industrial plants and materials in Manchuria, to which the Russians had already helped themselves, should not be included in the computation of reparations shares to be awarded to the nations of the FEC. Canada remained flexible on reparations questions and was agreeable to a modest 1.5 percent share of the reparations to be awarded in a final settlement. As the Cold War deepened, a change in U.S. policy finally terminated the exaction of reparations from Japan.[78]

Japan's new constitution, to which Canada had contributed significantly through the FEC, was promulgated in November 1946 and was to come into effect in May 1947. The new constitution reduced the emperor to the status of a symbol of the nation's unity, renounced war as an instrument of national policy, abolished the ministries of the army and navy, vested supreme political power in the National Diet (parliament), made membership in the Upper House (The House of Councilors) elective, granted women the right to vote, and called for the prime minister to be elected by the House of Representatives. In creating democratic rights and structures, this constitution, which because of its origin came to be known as the MacArthur constitution, created a solid basis for postwar political democracy in Japan. Social and economic reforms accompanied the political ones, encouraging the formation of labor unions, reducing land tenancy through radical land reform, and restructuring Japan's economy by breaking up the zaibatsu (financial cliques). All these reforms were in line with E. Herbert Norman's interpretation of what had been wrong with prewar Japan that had led it to the path of imperialism and aggression. Yet the dissolution of the zaibatsu, in particular, did not take hold, and by the early fifties the zaibatsu were well on the way back to power.

On March 17, 1947, General MacArthur called a press conference and suggested that a peace settlement with Japan was now timely. On July 11, 1947, the U.S. government invited the eleven FEC members to hold a preliminary conference on the drafting of a peace treaty. Meanwhile, in anticipation of the moves toward a peace settlement, a Canadian mission headed by Gen. H.D.G. Crerar had visited Japan from August 2 to August 20, 1947, partly to study the possibility of reviving trade with Japan and also to help formulate Canadian policy on the peace settlement. On the basis of his conversations with MacArthur, General Crerar concluded that Canada should support U.S. policy on the peace settlement.[79]

At a Commonwealth conference on the peace treaty in Canberra in September 1947, the Canadian minister of defense, Brooke Claxton, expressed his hope for an early restoration of peaceful commerce.[80]

Meanwhile, Washington no longer saw Japan as a threat, but rather thought of it as a potential ally in the coming struggle with communism. The Truman Doctrine, the Marshall Plan, and the rise of McCarthyism eventually had their reverberations in Japan.[81] The U.S. secretary of the army, Kenneth C. Royall, stated in January 1948 that Japan must become a bulwark against totalitarianism in Asia.[82] George Kennan of the U.S. State Department policy planning staff visited General MacArthur, urging him to go easy in his purge of the zaibatsu. Finally, the Draper-Johnston Mission to Japan in February 1948 urged far-reaching measures to rebuild the Japanese economy—"the first economic need of Japan is increased production"—including the exemption from the reparations allocation of industrial equipment vital to Japan's economic recovery.[83] The shift in policy, later called "Reverse Course," caused a split at general headquarters in Tokyo, with Gen. Courtney Whitney, head of Government Section, and his assistant, Col. Charles L. Kades, favoring a continuation of the "democratization" process, zaibatsu dissolution, and economic "demilitarization."

E. Herbert Norman was friend and mentor to this liberal wing at general headquarters, and as its influence declined, he became increasingly apprehensive about his own position in Japan. He suspected that he was under surveillance and that his own political connections were being investigated. According to Charles Taylor, Norman had become a member of the Communist Party at Cambridge University in the spring of 1935, following his close friend John Cornford.[84] How long Norman remained in the party and whether he ever acted as anything more than an intellectual supporter of communist causes is not clear, but Norman assured his brother and apparently convinced both Pearson and the RCMP that he had never betrayed his oath as an official of DEA, which had employed him since 1939.[85]

How or why Norman came under scrutiny has not been revealed, but an incident in 1942 might have started it all.[86] As was noted earlier, Norman had been asked by Tsuru, who was a fellow member of a Marxist study group at Harvard and whom he happened to encounter in Lorenzo Marques in 1942, to pick up some papers Tsuru had left behind in his apartment in Cambridge, Mass. When Norman did so he encountered agents of the FBI, and under questioning he initially stated that he was a Canadian foreign service officer acting on government business, but later retracted the statement. It is conceivable that Norman had been under suspicion from that moment on.[87]

The axe fell on October 21, 1950, when Pearson ordered Norman home to Ottawa on special duty, a euphemism for an RCMP investigation. Pearson himself wrote of the affair as follows:

When I was in Tokyo in [January] 1950 General MacArthur said of Herbert, . . . "He's the most valuable man we have.

We want to thank you for letting him help us." . . . [Ten months later in Ottawa] I invited [Norman] . . . to my office and told him, . . . "We're going to put you through the most exhaustive investigation that any Canadian civil servant can be put through. That's what we must do." He agreed. . . .

The enquiry went on for about six or seven weeks. The R.C.M.P. investigated in great detail and, I thought, in a very intelligent, sensible, and fair-minded way. The main charge against him was that as a student at Cambridge and Harvard he attended Marxist communist study groups. This was quite true, and he did not attempt to conceal it. The R.C.M.P. could not find anything to cast doubt on Herbert's loyalty. I went over the evidence with the Chief of the Security Branch and concluded that he had a clean bill of health.[88]

The investigation of Norman in Ottawa, which involved isolating him from his friends at DEA and subjecting him to a nerve-wracking series of repetitive interrogations, proved to be a severe emotional trauma for him, a trauma from which he may never quite have recovered. Anticommunist hysteria was running high at the time, in the aftermath of the Communist takeover of mainland China in October 1949, with charges made that fellow-travelers in the U.S. State Department had plotted to turn over China to the Communists. Worse yet, with the invasion of South Korea by the North Koreans in June 1950, the Japanese and MacArthur became legitimately concerned with the threat of Communist subversion in Japan itself. Now more than ever, MacArthur and the U.S. government wanted to boost the Japanese economy, speed up its full recovery, cement military and economic cooperation with Japan, and sign a peace treaty at the earliest possible moment.

Japan necessarily became a supply, reinforcement, and rest and recuperation (R & R) base for the U.S. armed forces engaged in the Korean War. This provided a tremendous boost to the Japanese economy, which furnished goods and services for the soldiers in transit to and from the battle zone as well as naval and air base facilities for actual operations. In the process Japan's conservative politicians gained ground; her industrialists made money; and the historic movement was initiated toward rearmament, the security alliance with the United States, and a peace treaty excluding what was now "Communist China" and the USSR.

Canada was an original member of the UN Temporary Commission on Korea, established in 1947. In April 1949 Canada had supported the admission of the Republic of Korea (ROK) to the United Nations, and three months later it indicated Canada's full recognition of the ROK government. When the Korean War started in June 1950, the Canadian government supported the UN police action in the name of collective security. E. Herbert Norman, then still in Japan, apparently was not opposed to the initial Canadian decision to participate in the Korean action, but he did counsel against a crossing of the 38th parallel, predicting correctly that the Chinese would intervene. General MacArthur and General Charles Willoughby believed differently, and MacArthur told Norman during his last meeting with him in October 1950 that the Chinese would never intervene. If they did, the U.S. Air Force would destroy their troops and reduce Mukden, Shanghai, and Peking to ashes.[89] On October 15, 1950, MacArthur spoke almost the same words to President Harry S Truman on Wake Island.[90]

It appears that General MacArthur held Norman in very high esteem during the years of their association in Tokyo, and before the "Reverse Course" ensued, the evidence is strong that he not only heard but took Norman's advice on occupation policy. When in 1947 Prince Mikasa (Mikasano Miya Takahito), the Emperor's brother, sought tutoring in English, it was apparently at MacArthur's insistence that Norman was permitted by Ottawa to tutor the prince in the reading and interpretation of historical texts. Norman's name had been suggested to the prince by the president of Tokyo University, and as the prince recalled thirty years later, he thought of him as a private English tutor, being unaware at the time of Norman's eminence as a historian of Japan.[91] In fact, Norman's major historical works on Japan were not published in Japanese-language editions until the late 1940s, beginning with *Japan's Emergence as a Modern State* in August 1947. Upon his return to Ottawa in October 1950, Norman was initially appointed head of the American and Far Eastern division of DEA and in July 1951 as alternate Canadian delegate to the UN.

On August 7, 1951, a month before the signing of the peace treaty, a former Communist, Dr. Karl August Wittfogel, had testified publicly before the U.S. Senate Internal Security Committee (under McCarran) that Norman had been a Communist in the 1930s. Pearson immediately came to Norman's defense, voicing his complete confidence in him and condemning the U.S. Senate for permitting the various charges to be made. Perhaps to demonstrate his complete trust in Norman's integrity, he also appointed him his chief adviser for the San Francisco Peace Conference (1951) and left him in charge of the DEA American and Far Eastern division, while publicly ridiculing the charges. In his memoirs, Pearson later wrote that he was not sure if he should not have published all that the government knew in 1951, but added that he had been urged by the security people not to do so.[92]

Meanwhile, in Tokyo, as of November 18, 1950, Norman had been replaced as head of the Canadian liaison mission by Menzies, who had preceded him as head of the American and Far Eastern division in Ottawa. Though born in China (1916), Menzies had attended three of the same schools as Norman (the Canadian Academy in Kobe, the University of Toronto, and Harvard University) and held an M.A. in Far Eastern history from Harvard. Menzies also shared Norman's missionary background, and the attitudes of both men toward Japan and the Japanese were in many ways similar.[93]

Meanwhile the war in Korea was at its height, and Canada had contributed three destroyers, a Canadian army special forces brigade with support and reinforcement troops (15,000 men), and a squadron of long-range air transport forces, including ground crews, to the UN Command. A first draft of the peace treaty was produced in March 1951, and Canada offered comments on the draft.

By July 1951 the United States had issued invitations to all countries that had been at war with Japan to attend a treaty-making conference in September in San Francisco. Communist China was not invited to the conference. On September 8, 1951, after signing the draft treaty for Canada, Pearson handed the gold pen to Norman, saying, "I'm giving this to the person who really did the work."[94]

Canadian concerns expressed during the treaty negotiations had centered on prevention of future aggression by Japan, acceptance by Japan of international fair trade practices, payment of reparations by retention of Japanese assets seized in Canada, and negotiation of an agreement curbing Japanese fishing activities after the peace.[95] The provisions of the treaty reduced Japan's territory essentially to the four main islands of Honshu, Kyushu, Shikoku, and Hokkaido. Japan agreed to pay reparations to the allied powers for damage and suffering caused, by making available the services of the Japanese people in production, salvaging, and other work. Japan declared its readiness to enter into negotiations for the conclusion of trade treaties according most-favored-nation treatment to each of the allied powers. It accepted the judgments of the IMTFE and other allied war crimes courts. Importantly, from the Canadian point of view, Japan agreed to enter into negotiations for bilateral or multilateral agreements providing for regulation of fishing and for conservation and development of fisheries on the high seas. The occupation was to end as soon as possible after the treaty came into force.[96]

Pearson had indicated at San Francisco that the Canadian government accepted the treaty and would sign it. He spoke in Parliament on April 8, 1952, recommending its ratification, and the instruments of ratification were deposited in Washington on April 17, 1952. The Treaty officially came into force April 28, 1952. In Pearson's words, "The Treaty is a generous one. It has been represented by one of its main architects as a treaty of reconciliation, and that, I think, is what it is."[97]

When the treaty became law on April 28, 1952, Menzies became the first postwar diplomat accredited to the Japanese government to represent Canada in Tokyo as temporary chargé d'affaires. At the same time the Canadian liaison mission became the Canadian embassy.[98] The Japanese government had established a Japanese overseas agency in Ottawa on June 5, 1951, headed by Katsushiro Narita, who held the rank of counsellor in the Japanese foreign service. Negotiations for the reestablishment of trade relations and related matters had in fact begun before the peace treaty entered into effect. As of April 28, 1952, the Japanese overseas agency in Ottawa became the Japanese embassy and Counsellor Narita the temporary chargé d'affaires.[99]

Prime Minister Louis St. Laurent of Canada, in a message to Prime Minister Yoshida of Japan, said in part,

> We . . . look to the new Japan to be an effective bastion of peace and freedom in an area afflicted by Communist aggression and oppression.[100]

It was left to Pearson to express the thoughts of those Canadians who might have had some reservations that the new Japan was not immune from a relapse into past patterns.

> It is [our] hope that . . . Japan will use its new power and developing economic strength not for those purposes which have caused so much damage, so much cruelty, and so much suffering in the past, but for the purpose of international cooperation, . . . which will lead not only to peace but to prosperity.[101]

Prime Minister Yoshida's reply to both of these included the following words:

> I desire to assure you that our nation, chastened and free and committed firmly to the ways of peace is resolved to follow the path of international conciliation, concord, and cooperation. May this day mark the beginning of a new era of friendly intercourse, commercial and cultural, between Japan and Canada.[102]

After more than ten years of war and occupation and many unhappy experiences for Canadians, Japanese, and Japanese Canadians, Canada and Japan were back to the hopeful beginnings of Keenleyside, Marler, and Tokugawa in 1929. The attempt to build a friendly and prosperous relationship between Canada and Japan could begin all over again, and this time it had a far better chance to succeed.

NOTES

1. J. W. Pickersgill, *The Mackenzie King Record*, Vol. 1, pp. 297–99.

2. W. Peter Ward, "British Columbia and the Japanese Evacuation," *Canadian Historical Review* 57, no. 3 (1976): 289–308.

3. A number of detailed accounts of the fate of the Japanese Canadians during World War II have been published. All of these were consulted, as well as the DEA files (DEAF), in compiling the account here rendered. For the viewpoint of the Japanese Canadians, the two most detailed accounts are Ken Adachi, *The Enemy That Never Was*, and Barry Broadfoot, *Years of Sorrow, Years of Shame*. A factual and sociological

view is given in Forrest E. La Violette, *The Canadian Japanese and World War II*, and a historical analysis is found in C. Cecil Lingard, *Canada in World Affairs*, Vol. 3, pp. 60–65.

4. *Public Archives of Canada, Ian Mackenzie papers*, File X-81, extracts from letters, December 27 and 30, 1941, as cited in J. L. Granatstein, "Defence Against the Imagined Internal Enemy: How the Japanese Canadians Were Treated," in *Canadian Defence Quarterly* 4, no. 3 (Winter 1974): 41–44.

5. The members of the standing committee were Lieutenant Colonel A. W. Sparling; Assistant Commissioner Mead, RCMP; Mayor Fred J. Hume of New Westminster, B.C.; the committee chairman, H. F. Angus, a professor at the University of British Columbia; and Lt. Col. MacGregor Macintosh, a member of the British Columbia legislature.

6. Letter to King by Mackenzie, dated January 10, 1942, DEAF. The Canadian army did not want Japanese Canadians in the forces. The Special Committee on Orientals recommended in December 1940 that neither Japanese nor Chinese be called up for service. While Keenleyside urged the use of Japanese Canadians as interpreters, Prime Minister King announced in January 1941 that Orientals would not be called. Thirty-six *nisei* (Canadians who are children of Japanese immigrants) had voluntarily enlisted during the early years of the war. A change of policy came in January 1945, when the Cabinet War Committee decided that up to 100 Japanese Canadians could be accepted for enlistment (six months later that figure was raised to 250). The intent was to loan the *nisei* as interpreters or translators to the British Imperial Forces in Southeast Asia. During World War II, 134 *nisei* served in the Canadian army; 2,300 would have been eligible to serve. The 1945 change in enlistment policy was kept secret until after V-J Day. Three *nisei* were in combat in Europe, one being captured at Dieppe and another wounded in the Rhine battle zone. Among *nisei* soldiers attending the S-20 Japanese language school in Vancouver were Thomas Shoyama, later to be deputy minister of finance in the Trudeau cabinet, and George Tanaka and Roger Obata, both prominent in the postwar Japanese Canadian Citizens Association. Japanese-Canadian veterans of both world wars were enfranchised by the British Columbia legislature early in 1945. See Adachi, *The Enemy That Never Was*, pp. 292–96.

7. Mimeographed press release, January 14, 1942. Also see House of Commons, *Debates*, February 9, 1942, p. 398. Not one newspaper in British Columbia saw fit to reprint the government's press release in its entirety.

8. Lingard, *Canada in World Affairs 1941–1944*, p. 63.

9. Pickersgill, *The Mackenzie King Record*, p. 354.

10. Forrest E. La Violette, *The Canadian Japanese and World War II*, pp. 56–63.

11. The only Japanese exempted from this order were those married to

Occidentals and their offspring, who were to be recognized as Canadian in the full sense of the word.

12. La Violette, *The Canadian Japanese and World War II*, pp. 50–63.

13. The NMEG wrote to Commissioner Austin Taylor on April 15, 1942, announcing its refusal to agree to the policy of breaking up families, while the JCCC advised everyone to comply with government orders. NMEG members, about 3 percent of the evacuees, were consequently sent to Angler for internment.

14. La Violette, *The Canadian Japanese and World War II*, pp. 63–87.

15. In his book *The Enemy That Never Was* (p. 211), Ken Adachi makes the case as follows:

> King's fear of reprisal against Canadians in Japanese-held territory was no doubt genuine. But to preclude the possibility of reprisal by evacuating those threatened with riots and placing them in detention camps was to replace the possibility of evil by an act of greater evil. The way to meet the threat of mob violence—and Japanese reprisal—was to have taken strong preventive measures against those who violated the law, not against those who might have suffered the violation.

16. Charles Taylor, *Six Journeys*, pp. 123–24.

17. Data for the period 1941 through 1948 are taken from *Department of External Affairs Records* (hereafter cited as *DEAR*), scheduled for publication in *DCER*, Vols. 9–11, unless otherwise footnoted.

18. Taylor, *Six Journeys*, p. 124.

19. The Canadian government wanted to send at least a hundred Japanese, but the Japanese government refused to accept more than sixty-one, possibly believing that Canada had planted spies among the repatriates.

20. *DEAR*, 3464-AD-40, Pedro E. Schwartz to Robertson, October 20, 1942, Canadian Pacific cable.

21. *DEAR*, 3464-AD-40, letter, File no. J95, USSEA Robertson to Consul General of Spain, Montreal, October 27, 1942.

22. *DEAR*, 3464-AD-40C, Cypher no. EX3116 SSEA, to Canadian Minister, Washington; *DEAR*, 3464-AD-40C, Associate Deputy Minister of Labour Arthur J. MacNamara to Robertson, October 30, 1942.

23. *DEAR*, 2998-40C, cable, SSEA, Ottawa, to Canadian minister to Argentina, Buenos Aires, February 16, 1942.

24. *DEAR*, 2998-40, cable, Canadian minister to Argentina to SSEA, Ottawa, February 22, 1942.

25. *DEAR*, 2998-40C, cable, International Red Cross Committee to SSEA, Ottawa, February 21, 1942.

26. *DEAR*, 2670-A40C, letter, USSEA Robertson to Deputy Minister of National Defence, August 17, 1942. As late as January 1943 the fate of fourteen Canadian soldiers, including two nursing sisters, remained unknown.

27. *DEAR*, 2670-A40C, cable, SSEA to International Red Cross Committee, Geneva, November 25, 1942.

28. *DEAR*, 4606-C-13-40, P.C. 469, signed by A.D.P. Heeney, clerk of the Privy Council.

29. La Violette, *The Canadian Japanese and World War II*, pp. 202–13.

30. *DEAR*, 4606-C-13-40, memorandum, Angus to Prime Minister, March 15, 1943.

31. *DEAR*, 3464-B-40, letter, USSEA to Deputy Minister of Labour, Ottawa, July 12, 1943.

32. *DEAR*, 3464-B-40, memorandum, Keenleyside to USSEA Robertson, July 16, 1943.

33. Canada, Department of Labour, *Report of the Royal Commission Appointed Pursuant to Order in Council, P.C. No. 9498 to Enquire into the Provisions Made for the Welfare and Maintenance of Persons of the Japanese Race Resident in Settlements in the Province of British Columbia* (Ottawa, 1944).

34. Ibid., as quoted in Canada, Department of Labour, *Report of the Department of Labour for the Calendar Year Ending March 31, 1944*, p. 65.

35. Ibid.

36. Ibid.

37. *DEAR*, 104 (5) (1), memorandum, USSEA Robertson to the Prime Minister, August 20, 1943, pp. 1–2.

38. House of Commons, *Debates*, August 4, 1944, Vol. 6 (1944), pp. 5915–17.

39. La Violette, *The Canadian Japanese and World War II*, p. 272.

40. *DEAR*, 104 (S)-1, note for file by Robertson, January 18, 1944. As of January 1944, under Department of Labour, Commissioner of Japanese Placement, Order no. 1 (new series), "Persons of Japanese Race" had to obtain RCMP permits in order to enter a protected area; cross any provincial boundary; travel more than fifty miles within British Columbia; change their places of residence; remain absent from residence for more than eight days, if living in British Columbia; or remain absent from residence for more than thirty days, if living outside British Columbia. When this order was discussed, Robertson expressed the view that it was desirable that travel restrictions on Canadian nationals outside British Columbia be lifted, since the original danger had now passed and such restrictions meant

discrimination against persons because of their race. This suggestion was
not acted on at the time.

41. La Violette, *The Canadian Japanese and World War II*, p. 272–73.

42. Canada, Department of Labour, *The Re-establishment of Japanese in Canada, 1944–1946.*

43. Lingard, *Canada in World Affairs 1941–1944*, pp. 24, 30–34, 65–66.

44. C. P. Stacey, *Arms, Men and Governments*, pp. 45–58, 388–90.

45. Reader's Digest, *The Canadians at War, 1939–45*, Vol. 1, p. 135.

46. Stacey, *Arms, Men and Governments*, pp. 388–92.

47. C. P. Stacey, *Six Years of War*, Vol. 1, pp. 492–505; R. H. Roy, *For Most Conspicuous Bravery*, pp. 185–98.

48. Pickersgill, *The Mackenzie King Record*, Vol. 2, pp. 64–78. See also Roy, *For Most Conspicuous Bravery*, pp. 203–39, 262–63, on some of the military policy disputes involving Major General Pearkes.

49. Quotation from James Eayrs, *In Defence of Canada*, Vol. 3, pp. 258–59, 274–76. See also John W. Holmes, *The Shaping of Peace*, Vol. 2, pp. 197–225; *Diary of W. L. Mackenzie King*, August 6, 1945, Public Archives of Canada, King Papers; Pickersgill, *The Mackenzie King Record*, Vol. 2, p. 451.

50. Stacey, *Six Years of War*, Vol. 1, pp. 519–21.

51. John Toland, *The Rising Sun*, p. 869. Colonel Cosgrave was Canadian military representative in Canberra.

52. Stacey, *Six Years of War*, p. 525.

53. *DEAR*, 104 (S)-2, teletype, SSEA, Ottawa, to Canadian Ambassador to the United States, Washington, D.C., September 17, 1945.

54. Order in Council re deportation of Japanese, P.C. 7355, December 15, 1945; Order in Council revoking naturalization of deportees (under P.C. 7355) P.C. 7356, December 15, 1945; Order in Council re commission to inquire into conduct of persons of Japanese race, P.C. 7357, December 15, 1945.

55. La Violette, *The Canadian Japanese and World War II*, pp. 247–56.

56. Ibid., pp. 263–69.

57. Adachi, *The Enemy That Never Was*, pp. 317–35.

58. "Japs Allowed to Remain," *Vancouver Sun*, January 24, 1947, p. 1.

59. Canada, Department of Justice, Henry I. Bird, *Report upon the Investigation into Claims of Persons of the Japanese Race. Pursuant to terms of the Order in Council, P.C. 1810, July 18, 1947, as Amended.*

60. Ken Adachi, *A History of the Japanese Canadians in British Columbia*, p. 39.

61. Broadfoot, *Years of Sorrow, Years of Shame.*

62. *DEAR*, 50061-40(1), top secret, Clement R. Attlee to King, August 15, 1945. Attlee had requested that a Canadian brigade group participate in the occupation. King cabled back: "We are not ready to undertake any further commitment of this nature, involving either Army or Air Force Units." He followed this up with another cable chastising Attlee for having mentioned the participation of Canadian units without first checking with Ottawa.

63. *DEAR*, 50061-40(2), letter, King to U.S. Ambassador in Ottawa, January 3, 1940.

64. Taylor, *Six Journeys*, pp. 126–28.

65. *DEAR*, 50061-40(1), top secret, Pearson to H. Hume Wrong, November 3, 1945.

66. *DEAR*, 50061-40(1), top secret, Wrong to Pearson, October 27, 1945.

67. *DEAR*, 1954-C-40(1), letter, Canadian minister to Argentina to Argentine minister of foreign affairs, May 6, 1942. The Swiss minister to Japan, Camille Gorge, eventually moved into the Canadian legation, renowned as Tokyo's finest, where he lived until the large-scale bombardment of Tokyo by the U.S. Air Force began.

68. *DEAR*, 8620-M-40, memorandum, G. S. Patterson to USSEA, Ottawa, May 10, 1946.

69. *DEAR*, 8364-40, dispatch, Pearson to SSEA, June 4, 1946.

70. *DEAR*, WLMK, Vol. 283, Robertson to King, March 6, 1946.

71. Keenleyside was also considered for the post but could not be spared.

72. Nobuya Bamba, "Senryoo to Nooman" (The Occupation and Norman), *Shisoo*, no. 634 (April 1977), special issue on the twentieth anniversary of the death of E. Herbert Norman, pp. 55–84. Bamba's study benefits from extensive use of both Canadian and Japanese sources, including official reports and correspondence.

73. *DEAR*, 4606-F-2-40, n.d. 1946, monthly report of the Canadian Liaison Mission in Japan, September 1946.

74. Interview with Norman's translator and biographer, Genji Ōkubō, Tokyo, June 1977. Ōkubō is the author of the four-volume Japanese-language edition of Norman's collected writings, *Haabaato Nooman Zenshu*, published in Tokyo in 1977–78.

75. U.S., Department of State, *Occupation of Japan: Policy and Progress*, pp. 54–55.

76. *DEAR*, 4060-C-40(1), December 31, 1945, note, E. R. Hopkins to Deputy Undersecretary of State for External Affairs.

77. *DEAR*, 4060-C-40(3), A. R. Crepault, Summary, Japanese Peace Settlement: War Criminals, August 18, 1947.

78. *DEAR*, MG 32-B5, Vol. 99, Japanese Peace Settlement: Repara-

tions. See also Holmes, *The Shaping of Peace*, pp. 124–36.

79. *DEAR*, 9770-A-40(3), secret, report on the visit of the Canadian mission to Japan, Gen. H. D. G. Crerar to SSEA, September 20, 1947.

80. R. A. Mackay, *Canadian Foreign Policy*, pp. 279–81.

81. Since the classified files and records of the DEA remain closed to public scrutiny for at least thirty years after the event, no reference is made in this book to classified material dated later than 1947. Classified material consulted for the period 1948–78, while reflected in my analysis, is not quoted or attributed except by special permission. All post-1947 references are to published materials or to interviews conducted by me in 1977 and 1978. On E. Herbert Norman, interviews with his brother, the Reverend W. Howard Norman; his translator and biographer, Okubo; and his former associates in DEA, such as Menzies, James McCardle, and Keenleyside, provided insights that did not necessarily emerge from the published sources.

82. Speech by Kenneth C. Royall, U.S. Secretary of the Army, at the Commonwealth Club, San Francisco, January 6, 1948.

83. Eleanor M. Hadley, *Anti Trust in Japan*, pp. 144–46.

84. Taylor, *Six Journeys*, p. 117.

85. Interview with the Reverend W. Howard Norman, Toronto, December 8, 1977.

86. The RCMP file on the Norman investigation is not available for public scrutiny.

87. Taylor, *Six Journeys*, pp. 124–25.

88. Lester B. Pearson, *Mike*, Vol. 3, pp. 168–69.

89. Taylor, *Six Journeys*, pp. 134–35.

90. Gen. Douglas MacArthur, *Reminiscences*, pp. 4–12.

91. Prince Mikasa, "Nooman Sensei no Omoide" (Recollections of Professor Norman), in *Iwanami Shoten Monthly Bulletin* 1, no. 1 (1977): 1–2.

92. See Pearson, *Mike*, Vol. 3, p. 172.

93. Letter from Menzies, the Canadian ambassador to the People's Republic of China, to the author, January 8, 1978, from Peking.

94. Taylor, *Six Journeys*, p. 139.

95. H. F. Angus, *Canada and the Far East*, p. 58.

96. Canada, DEA, *Canada Treaty Series*, 1952, no. 4.

97. Canada, House of Commons, *Debates*, April 8, 1952, p. 1298.

98. *External Affairs* 4, no. 5 (1952): 176.

99. Japan, *Gaimushō Nenkan*, 1965, p. 76.

100. *External Affairs* 4, no. 5 (1952): 176.

101. Ibid., p. 194. See also House of Commons, *Debates*, April 9, 1952, p. 1418.

102. *External Affairs* 4, no. 5 (1952): 176–77.

4

Building the Trade Partnership, 1952–1968

More than four years of war and almost seven years of occupation had left Canadian-Japanese relations in great need of repair and readjustment, which could not be accomplished by the simple signing of a peace treaty. The process of restoring smooth relations had begun during the occupation, within the limitations imposed by the fact that the Canadian liaison mission was accredited to SCAP rather than to the Japanese government. E. Herbert Norman's deep understanding and basic sympathy for Japan had done much to inform and enlighten Canadian policy toward Japan, a fact that was appreciated in Japan and augured well for the future of the relationship. Through Pearson as SSEA and Prime Minister St. Laurent, Canada's Japan policy continued to be imprinted with the insights of E. Herbert Norman, in addition to those of Menzies, Collins, Keenleyside, and others who had a basically positive attitude toward Japan.

A Japanese trade mission that came to Canada in January 1951 had stressed the fact that Japan was in great need of raw materials to help her produce manufactured goods and that it would be desirable to integrate the Japanese economy with the West so that Japan would be less tempted to be drawn into the Communist orbit. "We critically need nickel, pulp, and asbestos from Canada," said Ryuki Takeuchi, leader of the mission, and he also expressed Japan's desire to join the International Wheat Agreement and the General Agreement on Tariffs and Trade (GATT).

Canada, in turn, was more than eager that a prosperous trade relationship should now ensue. During the occupation, both in the FEC and in the peace treaty consultations, Canadian concern for military security matters vis-à-vis Japan had still played an important role. However, while Canada had joined the collective security action in Korea and fully supported UN policy there, once the Japanese peace treaty was signed and things were moving toward an armistice and eventual peace in Korea, Canada no longer focused primarily on security issues in her Far Eastern policy.

On September 8, 1951, within a few hours of the peace treaty signing, the United States also signed a provisional security treaty with Japan. The Security Treaty gave the United States the right to dispose U.S. air, land, and sea forces in and about Japan to maintain international peace in the Far East, to defend Japan from external attack, and at the express request of the Japanese government, to put down large-scale internal riots and disturbances in Japan caused by outside powers. Japan, meanwhile, obligated herself to give no military bases to other countries.

The United States also subsequently signed military agreements with the Philippines, Australia and New Zealand, the Republic of Korea, and the Nationalist government on Taiwan. In a sense this was part of the price the United States had to pay to obtain agreement on the peace treaty from countries in the Far East that were uneasy not only about Communist aggression, but also about the possibility of a recurrence of Japanese aggression. While there were discussions on the possibility of a Pacific Pact similar to the NATO alliance, disagreement between the United States and the United Kingdom on the China question terminated that plan, the United Kingdom having recognized the People's Republic, while the United States continued to recognize the Nationalist government in Taipei. The Canadian policy was articulated by Pearson in the House of Commons.

> As I see it there are three fundamental difficulties . . . in the way of the early realization of a Pacific pact on a multilateral basis. The first difficulty—and it is a basic one—is which Pacific states should be included and which should be left

out; the second is how to get the various countries which might participate to agree to team up with other potential members; and finally there is the lack of community of interest and purpose and policy among some of the potential members.

. . . . .

While we are not members of a Pacific security pact, . . . and while we are not now members of the A.N.Z.U.S. [Australia-New Zealand-U.S.] association, we are just as much concerned with security in the Pacific as we are with security in the Atlantic; because security, like peace itself, is indivisible. But that does not mean, as I see it, that the expression of this concern must be through the same type of collective security machinery everywhere.[1]

These rationalizations aside, Canadian interest in the Far East was in trade rather than in territory or military bases, and as had been the case during the Pacific war, the United States, while happy to have Canadian moral support, did not press for a Canadian military commitment, which the United States neither needed nor wanted. By the same token the United Kingdom did not join in the ANZUS treaty.[2] Angus went so far as to define the Far East as "an area of tertiary interest" for Canada and found it paradoxical that Canada should be waging active war there, pointing out that there was very little Canadian opinion on the Far East. "The primary interests of Canadians, even when they are extra-territorial in character, lie elsewhere."[3] The peace treaty with Japan had been generally accepted, though there were those who had reservations. B. S. Keirstead articulated these feelings as follows:

It would not be correct to say that the Japanese Treaty was unpopular. It did, however make some Canadians uneasy. . . . It was nonsense to pretend that in six short years she "had learned the democratic way of life" or could be a "bulwark for freedom" in Asia.[4]

And so Canada, leaving security matters to the United States, addressed herself realistically to building the trade relationship for which she had such great expectations.

One of the problems between Canada and Japan during the pre-war period had been the operation of floating Japanese canneries off the coasts of British Columbia and Alaska, which were believed to threaten the conservation of salmon, halibut, and herring stocks in the area. Accordingly, Article 9 of the peace treaty provided that Japan would promptly negotiate on fish conservation measures with the Allied powers so desiring. Tripartite negotiations between the United States, Canada, and Japan, on a basis of ad hoc sovereign equality for Japan, began on November 5, 1951, in Tokyo.

Under the terms of the agreement, Japan consented to abstain from fishing for salmon, halibut, and herring in the waters of the Eastern Pacific, while Canada agreed to abstain from fishing for red salmon in the East Bering Sea. A provisional line was drawn on the 175° W meridian of longitude, with Japan and Canada agreeing to abstain from fishing eastward of that line in the Bering Sea. An international commission was established, representing the United States, Canada, and Japan, which would promote and coordinate the scientific studies necessary in order to make recommendations for abstention. The treaty was to run for ten years and could not be signed until after the peace treaty restored full sovereignty to Japan. Stewart Bates, the deputy minister of fisheries for the government of Canada, and Menzies initialed the treaty for Canada on December 14, 1951, and W. C. Herrington of the Department of State initialed it for the United States. After the peace treaty went into effect, the fisheries treaty was signed in Tokyo on May 9, 1952, entering into force on June 12, 1953.[5] In retrospect it may be said that the fisheries treaty effectively enabled the United States and Canada to exclude the Japanese from taking fish east of the date-line and that the Japanese understood that they did not really have any choice about signing it.

Menzies, who became chargé d'affaires of the Canadian embassy as of April 28, 1952, recalls that as the occupation ended, the relationship between the Japanese and Canadians was quite good, Canada not having been involved in the military phase of the occupation and thereby lacking in the condescension that seemed to be an inevitable element in the behavior of the occupying power. Indeed, the changeover on April 28 was largely symbolic, since SCAP had begun back in 1951 to transfer responsibility to the Japanese government. The most notable change was perhaps in terms of diplomatic precedence, since during the occupation precedence had been determined by date of arrival. After the peace treaty, Menzies moved down to the bottom of the table as a mere chargé d'affaires.[6]

Meanwhile, the Japanese chargé d'affaires in Ottawa, Narita, was replaced on June 13, 1952, by Japan's first ambassador to Canada, Sadao Iguchi, a career officer in Gaimushō (the Japanese Ministry of Foreign Affairs). Iguchi was vice minister (under secretary) under Prime Minister Yoshida, who at that time also held the foreign affairs portfolio. Iguchi had worked with Yoshida and John Foster Dulles during the peace treaty negotiations and had been one of the Japanese negotiators of the fisheries treaty. He recalls that his two main tasks during his twenty-two-month tenure in Ottawa were to escort Crown Prince Akihito across Canada and to negotiate the Japan-Canada agreement on commerce. Iguchi initially perceived Canada as a "cross-breed" country that had adopted the best points of Britain and the United States, with some degree of French influence. Iguchi felt that Canadians did not treat him as the ambassador of a defeated nation and he consequently greatly enjoyed his stay in Canada. He wanted to purchase an embassy for Japan in the Rockcliffe section of Ottawa, but at the time the Japanese government was not prepared to appropriate the money. (The new embassy residence, which is in Rockcliffe and is one of the finest in Ottawa, was acquired in the late 1950s when Tohru Hagiwara was ambassador.) Iguchi believes that his appointment as vice minister to the Canadian post indicated Yoshida's great expectations for the future of Japanese-Canadian relations.[7]

By 1953 Japan had become Canada's fourth largest market, taking close to $120 million worth of Canadian goods while selling less than $14 million in Japanese goods to Canada. In Pearson's words, Japan had become

> one of our best customers. . . . We must aid Japan in her trade. . . . We look to Japan to adhere to a democratic way of life and to make a contribution to collective security in the Pacific. . . . On the other hand, I suppose Japan has the right to expect us to do our part . . . to show that her choice of friendly association with us is wise from the point of view of enlightened self-interest.[8]

This idea was to become a theme song not only for Canadian but also for U.S. policy in the decades to follow. Reasonable access and favorable trading conditions for Japanese goods in the Canadian and U.S. markets were regarded as vital to ensure Japan's continued adherence to a pro-Western and anticommunist political line as well as to the security arrangements put in place by Dulles in September 1951.

Since Japan had appointed a high-ranking diplomatic official as the first Japanese ambassador to Canada, the Canadian government more than reciprocated in appointing a cabinet minister, Robert W. Mayhew, the minister of fisheries (January 1948–November 1952), as the first Canadian ambassador to Japan. Mayhew had been in Japan briefly in November 1951 for the Japan–United States–Canada Fisheries Conference, which had led to the conclusion of the fisheries treaty. He was a businessman as well as a politician, serving originally as councilor and reeve and ultimately as the federal member of Parliament from Victoria, B.C.

All reports indicate that the Canada-Japan relationship moved smoothly and cordially, as both governments concurrently negotiated a series of bilateral agreements on commerce, airline traffic, war graves of Canadian servicemen in Japan, the waiving of visa fees, and administrative and financial matters related to the presence of Canadian members of the UN forces at a reinforcement base in Japan. In discussing the new trade agreement with Japan in Parliament, C. D. Howe, minister of trade and commerce, noted that

> Japan has already become our third largest customer. It seems probable that Japan will continue in the future to increase in importance as a market. . . . This new agreement provides . . . for the exchange of most-favoured-nation treatment. . . . We could not continue for much longer to withhold most-favoured-nation treatment from a country such as Japan; . . . in the new trade agreement we are now proposing to correct this anomaly. . . . There are three important ways in which this agreement will facilitate the access of Canadian goods to the Japanese market. . . . Our exports will be guaranteed most-favoured-nation treatment in Japan. . . . Ratification of our agreement should open a new

era of fruitful trade relations between Canada and Japan. . . .
We are happy to play our part in helping Japan to take her
place as a partner in the world trading community.[9]

The agreement on commerce between Canada and Japan was signed
in Ottawa on March 31, 1954, and upon ratification, entered into
effect on June 7, 1954.[10] The balance of trade had been better than
eight to one in Canada's favor during 1953; that dropped off to no
more than two to one by 1956, but throughout the 1950s and 1960s
Canada never once suffered an unfavorable balance of trade with
Japan. (See Appendix, Table 11.)

Shortly after the trade agreement was concluded, Japan established a consulate general in Toronto (May 24, 1954), the first consul to serve there being Kenzo Yoshida.[11] Meanwhile, Ambassador
Iguchi had been posted to Washington, the first of several Japanese
ambassadors to move to the United States by way of Ottawa. The
new Japanese ambassador, posted to Ottawa on March 25, 1954,
was Kōto Matsudaira.[12] A member of a wealthy cadet branch of the
Tokugawa family, Matsudaira was a graduate in French juris-
prudence from Tokyo University and had also attended the Sor-
bonne University in Paris. Ottawa was his first ambassadorial post,
and Prime Minister Shigeru Yoshida had specifically charged him
with the task of enlarging trade. Matsudaira later recalled:

When I came to Canada, the trade balance was thirteen to one
in Canada's favor and we imported around 500,000 tons of
wheat.[13] When I left three years later, the trade was more
nearly in balance and Japan was importing more than a million tons of wheat. Prime Minister Yoshida came to Canada
in the fall of 1954, and when he visited the Japanese embassy,
he once again lectured me that I should make the embassy a
showcase for the sale of Japanese commodities and that it was
my task as ambassador to make an all-out effort in trade promotion by traipsing around the country in straw sandals and
making a sales pitch. So I told Yoshida that in that case I
could no longer be the ambassador and would have to resign.
It is certainly necessary to promote trade, but the task of an
ambassador is not direct involvement in the advertising and
sale of products. The task of an ambassador is rather to pro-

tect the good reputation, the good name of his country. I saw my task not merely in raising Japan's export figures, but also in acting to help Canadian exporters so that Japan would be perceived as observing fair play in her trade relations. And so Yoshida and I had a really noisy row on this subject in Ottawa and I was all set to resign. Later . . . my secretary handed me a telegram from Yoshida. . . . It said simply: "Carry on resolutely with your good work. Yoshida." The embassy subsequently came to be well respected in Ottawa, and I had a long and intimate association with such people as Lester Pearson, Mitchell Sharp, Fred Bull, Prime Minister St. Laurent, and C. D. Howe.[14]

Matsudaira believes that there were no frictions or political problems between Japan and Canada in the middle 1950s, though there might have been some residual mistrust as to the quality and reliability of Japanese manufactured goods or the observance of fair trade practices.

A great many trade delegations came from Japan to Canada to try to develop new markets. When they arrived at the airport, during the welcoming speeches I would always insist that they must announce for everyone to hear: We will observe fair play in our dealings with Canadians.[15]

The Japanese consulate in Winnipeg was opened on December 30, 1956, by Consul Norihiko Yoshikawa.

Meanwhile official visits to Canada had been made by Prime Minister Shigeru Yoshida (September 1954) and Crown Prince Akihito (April 1953), and Canada's Prime Minister, Louis St. Laurent, visited Japan in April 1954.[16]

Ambassador Mayhew returned to Canada in the fall of 1954, and his replacement was appointed on September 11. The new ambassador, who arrived in Japan in December 1954, was Thomas C. Davis, a former puisne judge in Saskatchewan who had been brought into government service during the war. Davis had been deputy minister of national war services and high commissioner to Australia and had been appointed Canadian ambassador to China in October 1946. In 1950 he went to Germany as allied high commissioner, later becoming Canada's first postwar ambassador to West Germany. T.F.M. (Ted) Newton, a former director of information with the Atlantic Council, joined Davis as minister-counselor of the Canadian embassy that winter. Ambassador Davis reportedly was the closest thing Canada had to a Texas senator, a big, breezy, dynamic man who got along well with the Japanese.[17]

Apparently there were few problems between Canada and Japan at that time. The new trade treaty guaranteed the "orderly marketing" of Japanese products in Canada, and Canadian goods were more than welcome in Japan. Trade was in fact moving along well during 1954, with a two-way volume of $115 million and Canada enjoying a five-to-one advantage in the balance of payments. (See Appendix, Table 11.) It was also during this year that Japan became Canada's third most important trade partner, following the United States and the United Kingdom, a position it would continue to hold for the next twenty years.[18]

On January 12, 1955, a bilateral Canada-Japan air agreement was signed in Ottawa to regulate commercial airliner traffic between the two countries. Canadian Pacific Airlines inaugurated bi-weekly flights from Vancouver to Tokyo (and on to Hong Kong), thus considerably speeding up travel between Japan and Canada.[19] Japanese commercial flights to Canada did not commence until 1961, some six years later. Symptomatic of the developing good relations, another agreement was signed in Ottawa on June 13, 1955, waiving the visa fees for visitors to both countries who were not seeking employment or permanent residence.[20] Finally, on September 21, 1955, an agreement between the British Commonwealth and Japan on war graves was signed, establishing the status of the graves of Canadian soldiers who had died in Japan during the Pacific war and were buried in the foreign cemetery in Yokohama. Japan agreed that no taxes would be levied on these graves.[21]

During these early post-peace treaty years, Japan was deeply concerned with reestablishing her position as a respected member of the international community. She desired particularly to become a member of the United Nations and to join such organizations as GATT or participate in international aid programs such as the Colombo Plan. The Canadian government made particular efforts to help Japan achieve these aims. At the Colombo Plan Conference in Ottawa in October 1954, a motion by Canada brought Japan into the plan. The joint support of Canada and the United States led to Japanese accession to GATT in 1955. Finally, after protracted negotiations at the United Nations throughout 1955 and 1956, in which both SSEA Pearson and Paul Martin repeatedly intervened on behalf of Japan, it was on December 17, 1956, that Japan was finally admitted to the United Nations as its eightieth member.[22]

In response to the rising volume of trade (Canada exported $128 million worth of goods to Japan in 1956 and imported $61 million), the Japan Trade Center was opened in Toronto in March 1956. At the opening of this trade center, sponsored by Japan's Ministry of International Trade and Industry, Howe, Canada's minister of trade and commerce, commented:

> Japan is a good customer for Canadian goods and we believe it will be an even better customer in the future. . . . There are considerable possibilities for the further development of trade between Canada and Japan, to the benefit of both and on a basis which need do harm to neither country.[23]

However, as the volume of trade increased, difficulties also began to develop. The rapid increase in textile shipments from Japan began to cause problems for the Canadian textile industry in 1956. Japan, therefore, voluntarily agreed to place restrictions on textile exports. Moreover, a quota system was applied to certain other products, such as cotton tablecloths, cotton blouses, and sport shirts and eventually (1959) on stainless steel cutlery and elastic braids. Howe paid a two-week visit to Japan during October 1956 and was warmly received.[24]

Ambassador Davis, 67, returned to Canada in February 1957, leaving Minister Counsellor Newton in charge of the embassy as chargé d'affaires for eight months. The year 1957 marked the breaking of new ground in a number of ways for the Canada-Japan relationship, with the arrival of new ambassadors from both countries and the launching of new governments as well. In December 1953 in Japan, after more than seven years in office, Prime Minister Shigeru Yoshida had been replaced, initially by Ichiro Hatoyama for three years, and then for two months by Tanzan Ishibashi, who had narrowly defeated Nobusuke Kishi for the party presidency only to be forced to bow out of the premiership by illness on February 23, 1957.

During those first three post-Yoshida years, various conservative factions had united in the fall of 1955 to form the Liberal Democratic Party (LDP), which was to control the Japanese National Diet for the next two decades and beyond. A number of Socialist factions had also united, to form the Japan Socialist Party.

Hatoyama, a very different personality from the imperious Yoshida, had attempted to be more flexible in his domestic as well as foreign policy positions. He succeeded in negotiating the restoration of diplomatic relations with the USSR, though no peace treaty was signed and there was little real warmth in the newly established relationship. On December 18, 1956, just before Ishibashi became prime minister, Japan had been admitted to the United Nations, thus much strengthening Japan's international stature. On February 25, 1957, Kishi, a prewar politician who had been purged and imprisoned by the occupation authorities, having been a minister in Tōjō's cabinet, became the new prime minister.

In Canada, meanwhile, the nine-year ministry of St. Laurent was drawing to a close. The election was held on June 10, 1957, and quite unexpectedly brought to power the Progressive Conservatives, led by John C. Diefenbaker.

Two additional agreements were concluded by Canada and Japan, the first being the Interim Convention on Conservation of North Pacific Fur Seals, which called for management of the herds and restrictions on pelagic sealing by four countries: the United States, the Soviet Union, Canada, and Japan. The United States and the Soviet Union alone were to carry out an annual kill in the rookeries, with Canada and Japan each receiving a 15 percent share of the proceeds from the kill. The agreement, which was signed on February 9, 1957, also provided for a six-year research program and a joint commission on sealing.[25] In an exchange of notes of March 27, 1957, Canada and Japan also agreed to initiate a program of agricultural training in Canada for young Japanese farmers. Three Japanese farmers per year would come to Canada to work as farm hands on Canadian farms to learn contemporary Canadian farming techniques, especially in dairy farming and mixed farming.[26]

It was at this time (April 4, 1957) that the distinguished Canadian scholar-diplomat E. Herbert Norman was driven to suicide (in Cairo, where he was Canadian ambassador to Egypt and had rendered valued service during the Anglo-French invasion and its aftermath) by the Senate Internal Security Subcommittee hearings in the U.S. Congress. With an election in the offing in Canada and Pearson in line to become prime minister, Norman, with a sensibility appreciated in Japan, may have seen himself as having become a dangerous burden to the political fortunes of his friend and benefactor and may therefore have accepted the need for a noble gesture by which he would remove himself from the scene.

The tragic consequence of this persecution came as a great shock in Japan, where Norman was deeply mourned at a ceremony attended by many friends and notables, including Prince Mikasa and Chargé d'Affaires Newton. Eloquent tributes were also paid to Norman in Canada in the House of Commons by Pearson and Diefenbaker. Pearson mentioned that Norman had been overworking under great pressure in Cairo and had been distressed by the revival of the old charges, which had been disposed of years ago. "The combined effect of over-work, over-strain, and the feeling of renewed persecution on a sensitive mind and a not very robust body produced a nervous collapse, the tragic result of which has brought to me . . . both shock and grief and a sense of great loss."[27] Diefenbaker added: "This man was a devoted public servant—he is a victim of witch-hunting proclivities. . . . I suggest that parliament show its feelings by having the flag on this building flown at half-mast for one who served well and died in the service of his country."[28]

Genji Ōkubō, Norman's long-time friend and translator, still works for the Canadian embassy and has published the collected works of Norman in Japanese in four volumes, including a biography of Norman.[29] While the full story of the Norman tragedy will not be known until the RCMP files on the Norman investigation are made public, if indeed then, I regard it as unlikely that these files contain evidence of serious wrongdoing by Norman, an assumption that is widely shared in Japan. As a historian I can only call the matter unresolved. Finally, an exchange between Pearson and Diefenbaker in the House of Commons on April 12, 1957, hints that while Pearson was telling the truth in regard to this matter, he may not have been telling all that he knew.[30]

Not long after the Norman tragedy, toward the end of May, Japan's new ambassador to Canada, Hagiwara, 51, was sent to Ottawa. A graduate of the faculty of law at Tokyo University (1928), he was a Gaimusho career officer and had been ambassador to Switzerland prior to his posting in Ottawa. Arriving in Ottawa just before the federal election, he presented his credentials while Pearson was still at DEA.

Hagiwara recalls encountering complaints, particularly from Quebec, that Japan was selling too many textiles in Canada. It appeared to him that the Conservatives were more protectionist than the Liberals. He repeatedly met with the minister of finance, Donald Fleming, to discuss quota restrictions and self-restraint by Japan.

Aware that there were ministerial meetings between Japan and the United States, Hagiwara wanted a similar setup with Canada. When Prime Minister Kishi and Foreign Minister Aiichiro Fujiyama visited the United States and then came to Ottawa (January 1960), Hagiwara advanced his suggestion.

> I felt that while Japan in a sense was part of the West, this was a matter almost entirely of being in communication with the U.S. rather than being directly in communication with OECD, NATO, Canada, or Europe. So I wanted to multilateralize our relationships, breaking out of the pattern of merely talking to the U.S. and having Japan join a number of international groupings. So after that, the Japanese government began to move in that direction and the Canada-Japan Ministerial Committee was eventually established.

Hagiwara appreciated that in Ottawa you get to know the important people personally and intimately, so that when you go to the Rideau Club you recognize virtually everybody and everybody knows you.[31]

In spite of minor adjustments such as textile or flatware quotas, made necessary by competition between Japanese imports and Canada-made goods, the trade relationship began to hit its stride in 1957, with a total two-way trade of $200 million (more than two to one in Canada's favor) as Japan's postwar industrial boom got under way. Existing bilateral agreements were working well, though there were the beginnings of some problems with customs valuation. A steel mission from Japan visited Canada, and Japanese steel exports to Canada were on the rise, including pipe, structural steel, and casings. Among Canada's new exports were some $4 million in copper concentrate from British Columbia.

The issue of the composition of Canadian-Japanese trade, in which the export of Canadian raw materials and the import of Japanese manufactured goods predominated, began to be discussed at this time, with some Canadian businessmen feeling that more processing in Canada before export to Japan was a desirable goal. On June 27, 1957, a direct radio-telegraph circuit was established between Canada and Japan, improving the speed of communications between the two countries.

Canada's new ambassador to Japan was William F. (Fred) Bull, 53, appointed in August 1957, who arrived in Tokyo on September 5. Ambassador Bull had been deputy minister of trade and commerce under Howe for seven years, which got him the nickname of "C. D. Howe's work-horse." During the war Bull had taken two Japanese-Canadian boys into his home in Ottawa, enabling them to complete their education. One became a doctor and the other a minister. Moreover, Bull had dealt with Canada-Japan trade problems at DEA, and so Pearson suggested that he become the new ambassador.

> They sent me off to Japan . . . to see if we could work out some arrangement with industry and the Japanese government, whereby we would substitute components for complete articles coming into Canada so that our firms in Canada would be in a better position to compete with suppliers, say in the United States, but they would be making the product in Canada, and Japan would be getting part of the product but not all of it, and that they would not simply kill the textiles, or kill the other things that would come in, but they would be reasonable. I had a great big club all the time, which was valuation for duty purposes. We could put an arbitrary value for duty on products if people were dumping them. . . . I made it very clear . . . that if these regulations once got on, there would be a long time before they would be taken off. So they would meet me on this thing and would then proceed to

pass the word around, through an industry and through the Keidanren [the Federation of Economic Organizations], and this was more effective by far than regulation.

Canadians at this time—the government—felt that Japan had gone through the occupation, and coming into the middle fifties, they were just beginning to feel their oats a little bit and flex their muscles. They were very anxious to get into international acceptance as a country. I felt that it was very definitely one of my responsibilities to do what I could to help them. At that time the Japanese were very anxious to get into the World Bank and the Monetary Fund. They felt that they . . . had grown large enough as a world trader to do this. The Honourable Donald Fleming was the chairman of the World Bank Conference in Brussels, and Prime Minister [Hayato] Ikeda sent one of his protégés to the conference to speak about Japan, and the progress they had made, and how they would like to be members of the fund, and that they could make a contribution to the funds to be loaned. . . . When the Japanese delegate reported back to Prime Minister Ikeda, he dealt more with the courtesy shown to him by Fleming than with the results of the meeting. . . .

The Japanese knew about the continuing committee I'd been on in London where the deputy ministers met with their opposite numbers in England, which had gone on for seven or eight years, and they wanted to have a similar arrangement with Canada. Some of our people in the department felt that there were already enough committees, and why were the Japanese pushing ahead so fast. But Mr. Fleming was very keen on it, and at the last Ikeda-Diefenbaker meeting we had an arrangement with the Japanese that I would give them a signal if they should bring it up. So at the last moment they looked at me and I shook my head because I hadn't got clearance on it. So Mr. Diefenbaker said: "Now, is there anything else to discuss?" Mr. Ikeda said: "No, we've had a very fine series of meetings, and I think that's all!" Then Dief, who was a bit of a tease, said: "Well, I've been thinking," and he looked at me, while Prime Minister Ikeda must have been puzzling about my failure to advise him properly by nodding my head, "we really should get together more often. This has been very profitable. I think we should have a ministerial committee of Japanese and Canadian ministers who meet from time to time. I will ask our ambassador to work out something whereby we will have much closer contacts." Well, the Japanese were highly elated. Now they had the same kind of arrangement with us as we had with the U.S., the British, and with the Commonwealth.

This kind of thing of course gave me a lot of status in Japan with people like the prime minister. And then (Mr. Diefenbaker has certain critics) when he came on that trip to Japan, and we were with him, it was roses all the way. He did everything right, and so did Mrs. [Olive E.] Diefenbaker. At one point in talking with Prime Minister Ikeda, Mr. Diefenbaker looked at Ikeda over the top of his glasses in a funny way and said, "Mr. Prime Minister, I like you!" Ikeda seemed a little startled, and looked over to his ambassador [Hagiwara], who quickly whispered in his ear. Then a smile came over Ikeda's face and he replied, "I like you too, Mr. Prime Minister." No one had ever said that, one prime minister to another. You don't do these things, but Dief did.[32]

The ministerial committee established on the Diefenbaker-Ikeda initiative worked out very well, too, and I was proud of our Canadians.

My big negotiation in Japan was on coal. We got involved in the first shipment of coal from Canada to Japan. Japan had been buying coal from China. When the famous flag incident of May 1958 occurred,[33] coal shipments from China were cut off, and this nearly stopped the Japanese steel industry. They decided they had to have another string to their bow, and at this time the Canadian Pacific Railroad, who owned coal mines in the Crowsnest Pass area, had turned to diesel fuel and some of these places in the mountains were actually going to become ghost towns unless they could find a market for this coal. We had a coal board at that time and the Japanese were very keen on this and we worked on this with them and sent a shipment of coal out to Japan. A small steamerload brought it out and they sent it to the steel mill in Hokkaido, because they felt it would blend with Hokkaido coal as a good coking coal. Well, they found it would work and we got the price down to where the Japanese could handle it.

The first order was for a million tons at $10.00 a ton, and now, of course, the price has gone into the stratosphere.[34] What the Japanese wanted to do was to keep those mines open, because they were drawing coal from Virginia and now they're drawing coal from Australia—but they use an awful lot of coal. So that's how we started the coal trade there, which is now one of the biggest items in our trade.[35]

The late 1950s and early 1960s witnessed a series of positive and mutually beneficial developments in the Canada-Japan relationship, which made possible both a twofold increase in trade volume[36] and the close and cordial relations between the two governments, which ever since have enabled Canada and Japan to solve problems by diplomatic negotiations. By 1958 the Canadian Pacific Airlines jet-prop airliners provided the fastest trans-Pacific service, with a flying time of fourteen hours or less between Vancouver and Tokyo. Some twenty Japanese freighters per month were calling at the port of Vancouver to bring Japanese manufactured goods and carry back the ever-growing volume of Canadian exports, which included wheat, flaxseed, scrap iron and steel, aluminum, asbestos, lumber, copper, and coal. Canadian imports consisted mainly of cotton textiles, radios, plywood, toys, footwear, cameras, mandarin oranges, rubber products, and synthetic fabrics.[37]

Canadian-Japanese cooperation and trade in the field of nuclear energy also began to develop during this period. The vice-president of Atomic Energy of Canada Ltd. (AECL), Lorne Gray, had visited Tokyo in November 1957. Ten months later, in September 1958, four engineers of the AECL came to Japan for two weeks to advise on the design of the first Japanese research reactor. Canada had also offered a gift of three tons of natural uranium to the International Atomic Energy Agency for sale to Japan.[38] While Canada was evidently eager to become the supplier of uranium and nuclear technology to Japan, this desire was tempered by an awareness of the necessity for safeguards that nuclear energy would be used exclusively for peaceful purposes, and negotiations for a bilateral agreement were soon under way. On July 2, 1959, the Canada-Japan agreement for cooperation in the peaceful uses of atomic energy was signed in Ottawa.[39] The two countries stated that they would cooperate in the development and use of atomic energy and that the fissionable material supplied by either country to the other, pursuant to the agreement, would be used for peaceful purposes only. The agreement provided the basis for the development of a market for Canadian uranium in Japan.

While trade flourished and diplomatic relations were cordial and untroubled, the sudden flooding of the Canadian market by Japanese spun rayon textile products in 1959 led to difficult negotiations in the latter half of the year to maintain the "orderly marketing" of Japanese textiles in Canada. Nevertheless, Canada's image in Japan remained highly favorable and the trade outlook justified great optimism for the future.

Cultural relations were also beginning to warm up, as an increasing number of Canadian visitors found their way to Japan. The Royal Canadian Navy made several good will visits to Japanese ports, and large Canadian delegations attended the International Air Transport Association (IATA) and GATT conferences in Tokyo in 1959. Two Canadian rugby teams from British Columbia came to play several Japanese teams, and some twenty Canadian students were doing full-time research in Japan. A similar number of Japanese students were studying in Canadian universities.

Meanwhile, the Canadian community in Japan numbered close to 1,200, thus becoming the sixth-largest group of foreign residents in Japan.[40] Most of the Canadians residing in Japan were missionaries and missionary teachers, in missions from one end of the archipelago to the other, including Roman Catholic orders, the United and Anglican churches of Canada, and a number of other Protestant churches, many with histories of nearly a century of missionary and educational activity in Japan.

Some 120 Canadian *nisei* living in Japan, meanwhile, formed the Canadian Nisei Association on October 31, 1958, to coordinate *nisei* activities in Japan and also serve as a link between Japan and Canada, welcoming Canadian groups visiting Japan and generally promoting amity between the two countries.

While this organization limits its membership to Canadian-born second-generation Japanese, its aims and functions are similar to those of the Canada-Japan Society, which is an organization originally founded in 1934 that draws its membership largely from business and government circles in Japan. The Canada-Japan Society was suspended during World War II but reactivated on December 5, 1952, when Prince Iyemasa Tokugawa, Japan's first minister to Canada, was elected president of the society, a post he continued to hold by annual reelection until 1961. The constitution of the Canada-Japan Society provides that it will promote understanding and friendship between the peoples of Canada and Japan by strengthening the cultural and economic relations between the two countries. While the membership of the Canada-Japan Society is predominantly Japanese, the Canadian ambassador became its honorary president. Twelve directors and fifteen councilors were elected by the membership, most of whom were prominent Japanese businessmen or business firms. Among the society's major activities was the holding of dinners or banquets for prominent visiting Canadians, from the Prime Minister on down, and providing an opportunity for members of the society to meet and talk with the visiting Canadians, while giving the visitors a chance to get to know those Japanese who have special ties to or interest in Canada. It should be pointed out that while the Canadian ambassador is honorary president of the society, it is a private Japanese organization, in no sense either sponsored by or linked with the Canadian government.

It was also during 1959 that the *Muneshima Maru* of Iino Lines became the first Japanese ship to enter Toronto Harbor via the St. Lawrence Seaway, thirty-seven days out of the port of Yokohama, carrying a cargo of plywood, ceramic tile, toys, chinaware, cameras, smoked oysters, and 500 cases of sake (Japanese rice wine).[41]

In September 1959 Japan's finance minister, Eisaku Satō, who was to become prime minister in 1964, returned the visit of Fleming by coming to Ottawa. He was perhaps preparing the ground for the subsequent visit to Canada of his brother, Prime Minister Kishi, who arrived in Ottawa on January 2, 1960, on his way back from signing the revised U.S.-Japan security treaty in Washington, D.C. Kishi was accompanied by his foreign minister, Fujiyama, who had visited Canada sixteen months earlier.

Kishi's visit to Canada came at a time when Canadian-Japanese relations could hardly have been better at the political level. Prime Minister Diefenbaker and the SSEA Green certainly shared a dislike for communism with Prime Minister Kishi as well as a reliance upon the United States as the free world's leader. Japan and Canada had shared membership in the Security Council of the United Nations during 1958–59, and as middle powers with highly developed economies, they shared an interest in the maintenance of peace and stability.

In the area of trade, however, there were some irritants. While Japan had been Canada's third-best customer for six years and the two-way trade had more than doubled during the same period, Japan in turn had also become Canada's fifth largest supplier, and the Canadian textile industry claimed that its very existence was being threatened by Japanese competition.[42] There were difficult and extended negotiations in which Canada urged Japan to exercise self-restraint in the export of textiles, hardwood plywood, and steel flatware. The Japanese attitude tended to be that since Canada enjoyed a favorable balance of trade with Japan, Canada should not object to increases in Japanese shipments, whereas Canada maintained that if a serious deterioration in trade relations was to be avoided, Japan would have to act with discretion and restraint to avoid disrupting Canadian markets. These trade difficulties were eventually resolved, though it took a long time.

The Kishi government fell in July 1960 after the forced passage through the National Diet of the revised U.S.-Japan security treaty, which had led to violent anti-Kishi demonstrations in which a young girl student was killed. Kishi's handling of the treaty revision was considered high-handed and undemocratic, since he had not permitted the revision to be properly debated in the Diet. In the ensuing uproar, an invitation to President Eisenhower to visit Japan had to be cancelled for fear that his person might be threatened. An attempt to assassinate Kishi followed, and only his prompt resignation restored order in Japan. He was immediately replaced as LDP president and prime minister by Ikeda, a Yoshida protégé and a man with a friendly and outgoing personality, who consequently struck a responsive chord with the Japanese people. One of his early actions was his announcement of an economic program to double the income of the Japanese people during the decade of the 1960s. That program was more than achieved as the Japanese "miracle" of the 1960s began to unfold.

Prime Minister Ikeda's newly appointed foreign minister was

Zentaro Kosaka. Less than two months after his appointment, on September 14, 1960, Kosaka arrived in Ottawa and called on Prime Minister Diefenbaker to reassure him that Japan was taking measures to resolve the trade problems. Japan committed herself to limiting the increase in textile and radio shipments to 10 percent so as to preserve the principle of orderly marketing. Kosaka also predicted that the market for Canadian wheat in Japan would expand, which was welcome news at the time.

A month later, on October 18, 1960, Finance Minister Fleming addressed the annual convention of the Woolen and Knit Goods Manufacturer's Association, stating that

> the Canadian Government accepts the principle of orderly growth of Japanese exports to Canada. . . . By orderly growth we have in mind for individual products which are highly competitive with Canadian production and which already supply a significant part of the market, increases of about 5 to 10% in a year in which Canadian demand for the products is rising.[43]

The matter of Japan's adherence to the quotas of self-restraint requested by Canada continued to be an irritant in the years that followed, and there were doubts as to the effectiveness of the voluntary quota system. By the late seventies most of these problems were resolved and most of the quota items phased out, as Japan continued to produce and introduce new products that were not directly in competition with Canadian products. Canada did not invoke the clause in the 1954 trade agreement that gave her the right to apply fixed values for duty on certain goods being shipped in excessive volume.

The matter of Canadian immigration policy toward the Japanese was a sensitive one, since the Japanese government had always strongly objected to discriminatory legislation that specifically excluded the Japanese from Canada on the basis of race. On August 4, 1944, Prime Minister King had stated in the House of Commons that "as a guiding principle in the years after the war, it is felt that Japanese immigrants should not be admitted."[44] Three years later, on May 1, 1947, King reiterated his view, arguing that to admit a large number of Orientals would change the fundamental composition of the Canadian population, which "would be certain to give rise to social and economic problems."[45]

While this policy of totally excluding Japanese immigrants remained in effect until 1962, governmental policy was in fact evolving during the St. Laurent years, and *nisei* or other Canadian-born Japanese stranded in Japan or deported to Japan during or after the war were being admitted to Canada as individual cases. During the 1950s entry was granted to the wives, husbands, and unmarried children of Canadian citizens of Asiatic race legally admitted to and resident in Canada who were in a position to receive and care for their dependents, and later fathers over sixty-five and mothers over sixty were added to the list.[46]

Finally, on January 19, 1962, Ellen Fairclough, the minister of immigration, announced that the major criteria for the admission of unsponsored immigrants would be education, skill, and training, thus eliminating racial discrimination as a major factor in the admissibility of immigrants.[47] The numbers of Japanese immigrants coming into Canada during the postwar period have nevertheless remained quite small (see Appendix, Table 12), with 1,394 by 1962 and a cumulative total of 11,352 by the end of 1979.

On October 28, 1961, Diefenbaker, while on a visit to Japan, addressed a joint meeting of the Japan-Canada Trade Council and the Canada-Japan Society in Tokyo, during which he mentioned that 26,000 Japanese Canadians were making a valuable contribution to life in Canada. He also stressed the threat to freedom posed by world communism and Canada's solidarity with Japan in opposition to nuclear testing and in support of disarmament. Turning to bilateral problems, he pleaded for a continuation of the International North Pacific Fisheries Convention. On immigration he made the following announcement:

> Non-immigrant managerial, supervisory and technical personnel for specified Japanese-owned enterprises in Canada will be admitted to Canada for periods of three years each, subject to annual renewal of status which will be granted automatically if the original conditions of entry still exist. Permanent admission will be granted to limited numbers of key managerial, supervisory, or technical personnel of Japanese mining and manufacturing enterprises establishing in

Canada, provided such personnel are shown to be essential to the enterprise and needed on a long-term basis and that the enterprise will employ a majority of Canadian citizens or persons already resident in Canada.[48]

Turning to trade, Diefenbaker noted that a significant and mutually beneficial expansion of trade had taken place under the stimulus of the trade agreement, with Canadian exports showing an eightfold increase in less than eight years. He proceeded to argue the trade issues as follows:

> Concern has sometimes been expressed that trade between Japan and Canada is not in balance. I think the answer lies in the approach to international trade which is taken by both Canada and Japan. We believe in multilateral trade which has regard to overall balance and does not consider that the value of trade between two individual countries should be approximately equal.
>
> . . . . .
>
> I think it is generally agreed that Japanese goods enjoy freer access to the Canadian market than to the market of any other industrialized country in the world.
>
> . . . . .
>
> It is of interest that Canada, with a population of 18 million people buys more made-up textile products from Japan than does the whole of Western Europe with over 200 million people. When industrial nations maintain severe restrictions on imports from Japan, problems of market disruption are bound to arise in Canada and other countries that do not maintain such restrictions.

In concluding, Diefenbaker applauded Japan's plans for liberalization of imports and pleaded once again for orderly marketing.[49] In the late 1970s textile production in both Canada and Japan became a progressively less important element in their respective economies.

Three weeks earlier, on October 11, 1961, Japan's new ambassador, Nobuhiko Ushiba, 51, another Gaimusho career official, had arrived in Ottawa to succeed Ambassador Hagiwara.[50] Ushiba

recalls that there were no political problems between Canada and
Japan during his three years in Ottawa, and also few cultural contacts except in British Columbia. When Sumitomo Metals and Mining invested in the Bethlehem mine of British Columbia Copper,
this was the first major Japanese-Canadian joint venture. As to
future Japanese investment in Canada, Ushiba believes that the
strength of Canadian unions, the high wages of Canadian workers,
and the difficulties caused by Canadian environmentalists will be
severely inhibiting factors.[51]

The year 1962 saw the initiation of the oil seed business, involving principally the export to Japan of rapeseed, which has since
become one of Canada's biggest agricultural export items. Rapeseed is crushed for oil (*canola*), which provides the basis for salad
oil production. The seed itself can be used as an animal feed.[52]

In the area of cultural relations, the first twinning of a city in
Canada with a city in Japan took place in December 1962, when the
town of New Westminster, B.C., became the sister city of the town
of Moriguchi, in Osaka prefecture. Twinning involves the periodic
exchange of visits by civic and student groups between the two
sister cities and seeks to generate friendship and mutual understanding on a people-to-people basis. It provides opportunities for
Canadians and Japanese in all walks of life to get to know one
another, live in one another's homes, and share the social, cultural,
and material content of their lives.[53]

Ambassador Bull was in Tokyo for five and a half years, from
August 1957 to January 1963. One of the later ambassadors,
Moran, calls the period of Bull's ambassadorship the era of "laying
the foundation." He says, "The 57–63 period did in fact lay the
foundation, even for the trade that is going on today."[54] That
trade, meanwhile, had risen from a two-way total of $200 million
(1957) to a two-way total of $340 million (1962), retaining the
approximately two-to-one advantage in the balance of payments
enjoyed by Canada. In 1963 it was up to $426 million.

The first meeting of the Canada-Japan Ministerial Committee
was convened in Tokyo on January 11 and 12, 1963. Canada sent
over an eight-man delegation, including as its leader the minister of
justice, Fleming. Japan was represented by her foreign minister,
Masayoshi Ohira, and finance minister, Kakuei Tanaka, both later
to become prime ministers, and three other ministers. Japan was

concerned with the discussion of revisions of the North Pacific fisheries treaty, with the easing of restrictions on some of her exports to Canada, and with the development of Canadian support for Japan's membership in the Organization for Economic Cooperation and Development (OECD). The Canadian side was preoccupied with the trade composition ("we don't want to be mere hewers of wood and drawers of water") and orderly marketing issues. The meetings were described as successful by both sides.[55]

Ambassador Bull's successor in Tokyo was Richard P. Bower, appointed on December 4, 1962, who reached Japan in February 1963, shortly before the defeat of the Diefenbaker government. Ambassador Bower, 58, was a career civil servant in the Department of Trade and Commerce, persuaded by Howe to shift to DEA to become ambassador. After being posted to Tokyo, Bower also presented his credentials to President Park Chung-hee of the ROK and thereby became Canada's first ambassador to South Korea. Ambassador Bower presented Emperor Hirohito with Canadian maple trees for the imperial palace gardens and arranged for Prince Mikasa to learn square dancing at the Canadian embassy.

Bower thinks that Prime Minister Pearson gave only occasional and fleeting thought to Canadian-Japanese relations, and the only time he spoke to SSEA Martin (by phone) was when a Canadian Pacific airliner crashed with some of Martin's constituents aboard. He believes that the ministerial meetings "ensured that at least once a year Canadian ministers and the Japanese as well had to focus for a short period on Canadian-Japanese problems." He emphasizes the very important role played by the embassy in trade development because of the language barrier and the desire of Japanese businessmen to deal through the embassy. He also recalls many Japanese complaints about the balance of trade, which was heavily in Canada's favor at the time.[56] Ambassador Bower feels that Japanese dumping of manufactured goods in Canada could have been prevented if Canada had insisted on unrestricted access for Canadian manufactured goods to Japan, and he regrets that Ottawa did not take a tougher stand with Japan both on trade issues and in the negotiations on airline operations.[57]

Ambassador Ushiba was transferred back to Tokyo in June 1964 to become vice minister of foreign affairs. His replacement was Ambassador Hisanaga Shimazu, 48, a member of one of Japan's great noble families, a family that for centuries had included the feudal lords of Southern Kyushu (Satsuma). Shimazu had served as ambassador to New Zealand, Pakistan, Spain, and Thailand before coming to Ottawa in October 1964. He had also participated in the second meeting of the Canada-Japan Ministerial Committee, held in Ottawa on September 25–26, 1963.

A year later SSEA Martin reported to Parliament on the third Canada-Japan Ministerial Conference, held in Tokyo on September 4–5, 1964.

> We found that like ourselves, the Japanese were giving careful thought to the problem of Communist China. . . . There is every reason to believe that Canadian exports to Japan, which have risen so rapidly in recent years, will continue to expand at a good rate as a result both of expansion of the Japanese economy and further trade liberalization. . . . The Japanese ministers drew attention to the imbalance of trade with Canada, and to the inhibition of their sales to Canada represented by the restraints they observe on exports of certain of their products. The communique records our agreement that recourse to . . . restraints should be kept to a minimum. . . . We renewed our invitation to Japan to participate in Expo '67. . . . The Minister of Finance took advantage of his visit to Japan to sign on behalf of Canada an agreement for the avoidance of double taxation and the prevention of fiscal evasion with respect to taxes on income. . . . I signed on behalf of Canada an exchange of notes covering the mutual waiver of certain visa requirements between the two countries. . . . Japan, after the United States and Great Britain, is Canada's most important trading partner, and these ministerial meetings have provided a valuable opportunity for developing closer relations with this great Pacific nation as a neighbour and a friend.[58]

Ambassador Shimazu's first duty in Ottawa was to meet the trade mission of Yoshihiro Inayama, which had been organized by the Japanese government to generate contacts between business leaders in both countries.

Because of the importance of the personalities on this mission, headed by Yawata Steel's Y. Inayama and including representatives of Mitsui, Mitsubishi, Nissan, Nippon Kōkan, Hitachi, and the like, I as ambassador had to be in Ottawa to receive them when they arrived.

During my two years in Canada, I traveled throughout the country. . . . There was no great problems except for the annual negotiations my officials carried on in regard to certain commodities which came into Canada in excessive volume, such as textiles, chinaware, and the like.

My contacts in Ottawa were mostly with Paul Martin and Mitchell Sharp. I believe I may say that the associations between Canadian and Japanese officials in Ottawa were extremely friendly during my time.[59]

The Inayama trade mission spent almost four weeks in Canada during the month of October 1964, visiting Victoria and Vancouver, B.C.; Calgary and Lethbridge, Alberta; Regina, Saskatchewan; Winnipeg, Manitoba; Toronto and Ottawa, Ontario; and Montreal and Quebec City, Quebec, before disbanding. It was received by lieutenant governors, provincial premiers, and cabinet ministers, including members of the federal cabinet, as well as by top leaders of the business world in Canada. Inayama no doubt reflected both business and government attitudes in Japan in his address to the Ontario government luncheon in Toronto on October 23, 1964, when he said:

Growth of our heavy and chemical industries will necessitate expanding imports of raw materials including asbestos, iron ore, coking coal, copper ore, nickel ore, molybdenum ore, liquid petroleum gas to mention but a few. These are some of the natural resources with which your country is blessed in your treasure house of underground resources.

. . . . .

We find it refreshing to note that Canadian understanding of Japan has greatly increased in recent years. However, it seems that many Canadians still have an outdated image of

Japan. We fear that Japan is viewed as an overpopulated country with cheap labour, relying heavily upon the production and export of shabby goods. We are working hard to dispel this notion. . . . Japan's position as the world's largest shipbuilder was made possible, not by the use of cheap labour but by adoption of advanced welding techniques, prefabrication methods and other new processes. Japan's position as the world's third largest steel producer was made possible, not by the use of cheap labour, but by a 1.7 billion dollar modernization programme in our steel mills. . . .

Canada's 1963 exports to Japan provided jobs for well over 60,000 Canadian workers, farmers and miners. In 1962 Canada was Japan's seventh largest customer.[60]

Canada's trade with Japan rose to more than half a billion dollars in 1964. Three Canadian provinces, Alberta, Ontario, and Quebec, opened provincial trade and tourism promotion offices in Tokyo during the 1960s, and all Canadian chartered banks opened offices in Tokyo after 1964, though they were not allowed to provide banking services, since Japanese banks were not allowed to operate in Canada. Japan, meanwhile, announced that it would participate in Canada's centennial exposition Expo '67 in Montreal.[61] The buildup of Japan's industry, meanwhile, had developed to the point where less of the highly sensitive goods competing with Canadian manufactures were being sold to Canada, and this led to a lessening of the tensions generated by the "orderly marketing" problem.

The ambassadors in both capitals were recalled during 1966. Ambassador Bower was replaced by Ambassador Moran, 57, of DEA. A graduate of Osgoode Hall Law School and the University of Toronto, Moran had been a corporation lawyer during the 1930s. He had joined DEA in 1946 and had been seconded in 1960 to organize and head the External Aid Office, later to be redesignated the Canadian International Development Agency (CIDA). Ambassador Moran calls the years of his tenure in Japan (1966–72) a period of "progress and development in the Canada-Japan relationship."[62]

Japan was in the process of lifting itself out of the postwar doldrums of defeat, poverty, low posture, and humble acquiescence to the wishes of others into a new position that was self-assured, increasingly prosperous, self-conscious, and even self-assertive. The Olympic Games of 1964 had introduced a vigorously resurgent Japan to international society. Incomes, profits, and production were all rising. The Bonin (Ogasawara) Islands had been returned to Japan by the United States, and Japan's new premier, Satō, a deliberate and doggedly tenacious politician, had pledged himself to achieve the return of the Okinawa Islands as well. In 1965 Japan had become a member of the UN Security Council, and in that year a treaty normalizing relations between Japan and the ROK was concluded. The defeat of 1945 and the suffering that had followed seemed ever more like a forgettable nightmare, and the future outlook appeared most promising.

Canada, her economy thriving, the centennial celebrations and Expo '67 in the offing, untouched by the Vietnam war other than by a surge in exports to the United States, seemed equally buoyant and upward bound at this time, and the prospects for profitable trade with Japan appeared limitless.

In this atmosphere of prosperity, euphoria, and rising nationalism, unrealistic expectations for the future may have been generated in both Canada and Japan. Prime Minister Pearson, aging and ailing, was about to make room for a dynamic new leader of the Liberal Party. The trade between Canada and Japan in 1966 stood at an unprecedented $648 million and seemed headed for early attainment of the billion-dollar mark, which was in fact reached by 1968.

In September 1966 Jean Marchand, the minister of manpower and immigration, came to Tokyo to open a Canadian immigration office to help facilitate the immigration of new Japanese immigrants admissible under the revised immigration regulations. To encourage tourism to Canada, a Canadian Travel Bureau office was also opened, along with a representative office of the Canadian Wheat Board.

Ambassador Moran went to Korea a few times a year, when the demands of the Tokyo embassy permitted, but Canadian-Japanese relations had grown to such proportions that the ambassador and his staff were unable to devote to Canadian-Korean affairs the attention they deserved. It was agreed that an embassy in Korea would be opened when resources of finance and personnel would permit.[63]

Meanwhile the fourth Canada-Japan Ministerial Committee was convened in the west block of the Parliament buildings in Ottawa on October 5-6, 1966. The committee discussed the international situation. The continuing growth of trade between Canada and Japan, as well as the removal of a number of items from the voluntary export restraints list, were noted with satisfaction. Canada stated its desire to increase the proportion of processed and manufactured goods in its exports to Japan, pleading for easier access of these goods to the Japanese market and for relaxation of restrictions on Canadian investment in Japan. Canada announced the Canadian government's decision to participate in Expo '70 in Osaka, Japan. Prime Minister Pearson received and accepted in principle an invitation to visit Japan.[64]

As to the usefulness of the ministerial committee meetings, Ambassador Moran, who had attended the fourth, fifth, and sixth meetings,[65] commented that in 1966 the ministerial committee meeting had produced little of profit except for the benefits of personal contacts.

Meanwhile, Japan's new ambassador to Canada, Osamu Itagaki, 57, had arrived in Ottawa on September 9, 1966. A graduate in political studies at the faculty of law of Tokyo Imperial University in 1932, Itagaki had entered Gaimushō immediately and had had much overseas experience before being posted to Canada. Ambassador Itagaki recalls that there were "no hot issues" between Japan and Canada during his years in Ottawa except the usual negotiations over the voluntary export restraints. The principal topic of political discussions in 1966 and 1967 was Canada's plans with regard to the recognition of Communist China.

> Within Gaimusho there were two factions, one for and one against recognition. When I was appointed ambassador, official policy was still against recognition, since Eisaku Satō was Prime Minister and he was very conservative and absolutely opposed to recognition. A number of foreign ministers made different proposals, but Sato turned them all down. So the official position remained opposed. Therefore our policy was for me to deter as much as possible the movement towards recognition in the United States and Canada, which embarrassed me in the extreme. It was just the time when Prime

Minister Pearson had started to talk about recognition in Parliament in connection with Canada's grain exports to China. After Mr. Sharp became SSEA, Canada very clearly indicated its intention to recognize, and when I left Ottawa in 1969 the negotiations had begun in Stockholm and by that time finally my government gave up on the matter.

Mr. Takeo Miki, who was our foreign minister,[66] saw Mr. Sharp and propounded his favorite idea of a Pacific rim concept. This was not discussed at the ministerial conferences, since the Gaimusho authorities felt that the time for this was as yet premature, but Foreign Minister Miki was enthusiastic about it and raised it privately with Mr. Sharp to probe Canada's thinking on the subject. I was also asked to raise this matter and found that in Ottawa they were still mostly Atlantic-oriented and felt it was too soon for such an idea. But in the Canadian West, in Vancouver, in British Columbia, in Alberta they agreed with the concept of Pacific Area regional cooperation.

In the trade area we only had the usual problems. I feel that relations have developed very well, and with Expo '67 Japan became very Canada-conscious. People-to-people relations were much intensified and improved during this period. In Japan, meanwhile, Canada came to have a very high reputation as a good country, on a level with Switzerland, and with the establishment of an immigration office by Canada in Tokyo during 1966, an increasing number of Japanese technicians emigrated to Canada—between 600 and 800 a year during my time. But cultural relations were still insufficient. We have to use a little more money for that, but money alone won't do it either. You need people for that.

Basically I do not believe that a perfect balance of trade can be achieved between Canada and Japan, since Japan wants virtually all of Canada's resources while Canada in turn has a limited market for Japanese goods with her limited population and consumption. . . . When it comes to countries like Canada and Australia we don't really expect to strike a balance of trade, and shouldn't try to force the matter. Finally, on the upgrading and processing problem, there has been some progress, such as shifting from copper concentrates to pellets or from raw timber to cut lumber. So some increased processing is in fact taking place.

On the basis of my personal experience I have come to believe that between Canadians and Japanese we can bridge the Oriental-Occidental gap. In my view the feelings of racial discrimination against Orientals are very slight among Canadian whites. Part of the background may be that Canadians feel they can't afford to be discriminatory in that they need a labor force. If the Trudeau administration were to clearly follow this kind of policy on human intercourse, it would create an excellent potential for the future.[67]

Since 1967 was Canada's centennial year, the Japanese press and television presented many features on Canada, including films on the centennial and on Expo '67. A record number of Japanese (about 20,000) came to Canada, starting a boom of Japanese tourism to Canada that is still steadily increasing.

Ambassador Moran made a gesture of friendship that found great resonance among the Japanese public when he ordered the conversion of an undeveloped area in the grounds of the Canadian embassy in Tokyo into a baseball field for children attending the nearby Akasaka Primary School.[68]

During July 1967 Prince and Princess Takamatsu came to Expo '67 to represent the emperor and were accompanied by Ambassador Itagaki and Ambassador Moran during their highly successful visit.

As 1967 gave way to 1968 and Canada's centennial of confederation was replaced by Japan's centennial of the Meiji restoration, there was change in the wind for both countries that would significantly affect both their domestic and international positions. While the change occurred gradually and in different ways at different levels, the formation of the administration of Pierre Elliott Trudeau in Ottawa in June 1968 initiated a new phase in Canadian policies toward Japan. The Sato administration in Tokyo, meanwhile, was searching for new policies as well, as the postwar era drew to a close.

Because of the Vietnam tragedy, U.S. influence in the world was declining as Soviet troops invaded Czechoslovakia and Richard M. Nixon became the thirty-seventh president of the United States.

Meanwhile, for the first time in history, a Japanese novelist, Yasunari Kawabata, had been awarded the Nobel prize for literature. Japan was beginning to build the Expo '70 exhibition park in Osaka, where Japan would show the world what it was capable of, even as Canada had done at Expo '67. Canada and Japan did close to a billion dollars' worth of business in 1968, as Japan Airlines began to operate its direct service from Tokyo to Vancouver.

So as the Trudeau government came to power during the summer of 1968, Japan and Canada were headed for a broader, deeper, more complex, less euphoric, and perhaps more mature relationship.

NOTES

1. Canada, House of Commons, *Debates*, February 11, 1953, pp. 1853–54.

2. H. F. Angus, *Canada and the Far East*, p. 65.

3. Ibid., p. 101.

4. B. S. Keirstead, *Canada in World Affairs*, Vol. VII, 1951–52, pp. 127–128.

5. See International Convention for the High Seas Fisheries of the North Pacific Ocean, Canada, DEA, *Canada Treaty Series*, 1953, No. 3.

6. Letter, Menzies to author, January 8, 1978.

7. Letter, Sadao Iguchi to author, December 25, 1977.

8. *External Affairs* 5, no. 3 (1953): 88.

9. Canada, House of Commons, *Debates*, May 12, 1954, pp. 4648–50.

10. For text of the treaty see Canada, DEA, *Canada Treaty Series*, 1954, no. 3. The signatories in Ottawa were Pearson, Kōto Matsudaira, and Howe.

11. *Gaimushō Nenkan*, 1965, p. 79.

12. Ibid., p. 76.

13. The official Canadian trade figures make that eight to one. See Appendix, Table 11.

14. Tape-recorded interview with Kōto Matsudaira, Tokyo, May 24, 1977.

15. Ibid.

16. Nobuya Bamba, "Nippon, Kanada Kankei no Tenkai" (The Development of Japanese-Canadian Relations), *Kokusai Mondai*, no. 203 (February 1977), p. 10.

17. Letter, Arthur R. Menzies to author, January 8, 1978.

18. Japan Trade Center, *100 Years of Trade and Commerce Between Canada and Japan*, p. 12.

19. The agreement between Canada and Japan for air service entered into force on July 20, 1955. See Canada, DEA, *Canada Treaty Series*, 1955, no. 14.

20. The agreement between Canada and Japan on the waiving of visa fees entered into force on July 1, 1955. See Canada, DEA, *Canada Treaty Series*, 1955, no. 10.

21. The agreement between the British Commonwealth and Japan on war graves entered into force on June 22, 1956. See Canada, DEA, *Canada Treaty Series*, 1956, no. 8. There were 137 Canadian prisoners of war who had died in Japanese prison camps during the war; they were buried in the Canadian section of the British Commonwealth Military Cemetery in Yokohama.

22. James Eayrs, *Canada in World Affairs*, pp. 217–23.

23. Japan Trade Center, *100 Years of Trade and Commerce Between Canada and Japan*, p. 12.

24. Statement by C. D. Howe to the Women's Canadian Club, Montreal, December 3, 1956 (Extracts), quoted in Arthur E. Blanchette, *Canadian Foreign Policy*, pp. 329–30.

25. The fur seals convention entered into force on October 14, 1954. See Canada, DEA, *Canada Treaty Series*, 1957, No. 26.

26. *External Affairs* 9, nos. 6–7 (1957): 226. The agreement entered into force on March 28, 1957.

27. Canada, House of Commons, *Debates*, April 4, 1957, p. 3058–3059.

28. Ibid., p. 3059.

29. Genji Ōkubo, translator, *Haabaato Nooman Zenshu*.

30. Canada, House of Commons, *Debates*, April 12, 1957, pp. 3492–3502. Diefenbaker asked whether the allegations about Norman were untrue. Pearson replied that Norman was known to have been associated with Communists in university, that allegations about him were checked and the conclusion was reached that Norman was a loyal Canadian "in whom we could trust. I am not going to say at this moment whether any single statement made in a U.S. Subcommittee is accurate or not. I have not got the statement before me." Diefenbaker finally asserted that Pearson "has either spoken too much or too little," and that is where the matter was left hanging—where in fact it still hangs, slowly twisting in the wind. (See Canada, House of Commons, *Debates*, April 12, 1957, pp. 3493–95.)

31. Tape-recorded interview with Tohru Hagiwara, Tokyo, April 27, 1977.

32. Tape-recorded interview with William F. Bull, Ottawa, October 20, 1977.

33. In Japan a young Japanese radical tore down the flag of the People's Republic of China from an exhibit of postage stamps from all over the

world. The Chinese government chose to take offense and broke off trade relations immediately.

34. During 1980 Japan imported 11.5 million tons of coal from Canada at an average price of $51.21 per ton.

35. Interview with Bull, October 20, 1977.

36. Two-way trade stood at $200 million in 1957 and reached $426 million by 1963.

37. Japan Trade Center, *100 Years of Trade and Commerce Between Canada and Japan*, pp. 13–15.

38. Trevor Lloyd, *Canada in World Affairs*, p. 147.

39. Canada, DEA, *Canada Treaty Series*, 1960, no. 15, Agreement and Exchange of Notes Between the Government of Canada and the Government of Japan for Cooperation in the Peaceful Uses of Atomic Energy, Ottawa, July 2, 1959, and July 27, 1960. The agreement entered into force on July 27, 1960.

40. The largest group are the Koreans (600,000), followed by citizens of China, the United States, the United Kingdom, and Germany.

41. Japan Trade Center, *100 Years of Trade and Commerce Between Canada and Japan*, p. 15.

42. Richard A. Preston, *Canada in World Affairs*, p. 90.

43. *External Affairs* 13, no. 1 (January 1961): 15.

44. Canada, House of Commons, *Debates*, 1944, p. 5914.

45. Canada, House of Commons, *Debates*, 1947, pp. 2644–47.

46. Order in Council, P.C. 6229, December 28, 1950; Order in Council, P.C. 1957–1675, December 20, 1957.

47. "Persons in any country in the world who can satisfy the Immigration Department, that they have the education, training and skill or other special qualifications to get established successfully in Canada will be considered admissible." See *Globe and Mail*, January 20, 1962, pp. 1, 3.

48. Canada, DEA, *Statements and Speeches*, 1962/1.

49. Ibid., p. 6.

50. After his Ottawa posting Ushiba became Vice Minister for Foreign Affairs (1964), Ambassador to the U.S. (1970), Advisor to Gaimusho (1973), and Minister of State for External Economic Affairs, in the second Fukuda cabinet in 1977.

51. Tape-recorded interview with Nobuhiko Ushiba, Tokyo, April 21, 1977.

52. By 1976 oil seeds constituted 17.4 percent of Canada's total exports to Japan, worth $416 million.

53. For a list of sister cities, see Table 13.

54. Tape-recorded interview with Herbert O. Moran, Tequesta, Fla., December 13, 1977.

55. *Globe and Mail*, January 14, 1963, p. 26.

56. Canada's total trade with Japan in 1964 totaled more than $500 million, with Canadian exports amounting to $330 million. Japan's overall balance of trade (postwar) turned favorable in 1965 and stayed that way until the oil crisis of 1973. In 1976 Japan had $16.6 billion in foreign exchange and gold reserves.

57. Tape-recorded interview with Richard P. Bower, Alicante, Spain, December 8, 1977.

58. Canada, House of Commons, *Debates*, September 8, 1964, p. 7721–22. See Canada-Japan Agreement on Double Taxation, *Canada Treaty Series*, 1965, no. 13. The agreement entered into force on April 30, 1965. For the exchange of notes on visas, see *Canada Treaty Series*, 1964, no. 22. The agreement entered into force on September 20, 1964, providing that visitors to either country who were staying no longer than three months would not require visas.

59. Tape-recorded interview with Hisanaga Shimazu, Tokyo, May 17, 1977.

60. Hōkakeizai Shisetsudan Hōkokusho (Report of the Economic Mission to Canada), October 4–29, 1964 (Tokyo: January 1965), pp. 78–80.

61. *External Affairs* 16, no. 11 (1964): 550–52.

62. Tape-recorded interview with Moran, December 13–14, 1977.

63. Ibid.

64. *External Affairs* 18, no. 11 (1966): 488–92. The Pearson visit did not become a reality due to his illness and retirement.

65. The fifth meeting was in Tokyo in April 1969, and the sixth in Toronto in September 1971.

66. Former Prime Minister Miki was foreign minister from December 1966 to November 1968. He visited Canada in October 1966 as Minister of International Trade and Industry, attending the ministerial committee meeting, and again in November 1967 for talks on international affairs with SSEA Martin.

67. Tape-recorded interview with Osamu Itagaki, Tokyo, April 26, 1977.

68. *External Affairs* 19, no. 12 (1967): 514–16.

5

"Man Shall Not Thrive by Trade Alone": The Quest for a More Diverse Relationship in the Trudeau Years, 1968-1978

Trudeau became prime minister of Canada in April 1968. During the election campaign that followed in May and June, he served notice that a review of Canada's foreign policy would be undertaken. "We wish to take a fresh look at the fundamentals of Canadian foreign policy, to see whether there are ways in which we can serve more effectively Canada's current interests, objectives and priorities."[1] The review took almost two years and culminated in the publication in 1970 of six booklets collectively entitled *Foreign Policy for Canadians.*[2] Canada soon moved to negotiate the establishment of diplomatic relations with the People's Republic of China, to reduce by half Canada's military contribution to NATO, to broaden Canada's relations with Latin America and countries in the Pacific, to extend unilaterally Canadian control over Arctic waters, and to whittle down the Canadian commitment to the North American Air Defense Command Agreement (NORAD). *Foreign Policy for Canadians* provided a theoretical framework for most of the new foreign policy initiatives implemented by the Trudeau administration. Canada's role as a "helpful fixer" in international affairs was to be downgraded, and close identification with U.S. foreign policy (Vietnam), as well as excessive dependence on economic relations with the United States, were to be avoided. The emphasis would be on independence, nationalism, and the rational pursuit of Canadian interests. External activities were to be directly related to national policies pursued within Canada and were to foster economic growth, safeguard sovereignty and independence, pursue peace and security, promote social justice, enhance the quality of life, and ensure a harmonious natural environment.

The decision to give more emphasis to Pacific affairs that envisaged "expanding activities in the Pacific basin and Latin America" followed from the objective of safeguarding sovereignty and independence.[3] Moreover, the Pacific section of *Foreign Policy for Canadians* spoke of the search for a power balance among the United States, China, the Soviet Union, and Japan in the Pacific area and saw Japan surging ahead and playing a more active role in such fields as trade, aid, political influence, and possibly even security, particularly in Southeast Asia. Turning to Canada's role as a Pacific power, the following realistic statement was included. "In the Pacific, as elsewhere, Canada is not a great power, not a prime mover. At the present it does not appear to be in the Canadian interest to seek to participate in the various multilateral or bilateral security agreements in the Pacific."[4]

In the white paper on defense issued in August 1971, there is no mention of a Canadian military role in the Pacific area, though it is noted that "the emergence of the People's Republic of China as a nuclear power and the growing economic strength of Europe and Japan have resulted in a loosening of the bipolar international system."[5]

Peyton Lyon christened *Foreign Policy for Canadians* the "Trudeau Doctrine."[6] Noting the expansion of Canada-Japan trade and the preponderance of resource exports, it expressed Canada's desire for a lowering of nontariff barriers and barriers to investment in Japan and predicted that Japan would remain Canada's most important trading partner in the area and Canada's second most important one-country market in the world. Efforts for trade liberalization were to continue; meanwhile, there was to be an improvement of facilities for Asian studies in Canadian universities, with emphasis on contemporary Japan and China, and educational exchange agreements with Japan were to be pursued.[7] These formulations of Canada's policy toward the Pacific area and Japan were not new in 1970 but did stress the importance of Japan to Canada.

Canada's new SSEA, Sharp, traveled to Japan in April 1969 to head the Canadian delegation to the Fifth Canada-Japan Ministerial Conference. Sharp recalls:

At the outset of the Trudeau administration there was a very general idea which preceded the "third option," and that was the idea of diversification. We were also concerned that all our foreign relations, whether in the economic field or the political field, should involve the whole of the country. We were very conscious of the importance of Western views. The close relationship between Western Canada and Japan was a fact, so that the development of relations on the Pacific side was really an extension of the idea that foreign policy is an extension of domestic policy. It indicated the interest of the West in trade across the Pacific. . . .

We've never had any serious political problems with the Japanese. Probably the most serious have arisen out of the Japanese resentment at the requests that we were always making to restrain their exports. But that was not unique to Canada. . . .

It is very difficult to break into the Japanese market for any foreigner. I remember . . . a Japanese said to me: "When we were seeking to get into the North American market, we were advised that we should learn to speak English," and I think the point is very well taken. If you're going to break into the Japanese market, you must become like a Japanese. The Japanese employed Canadian consultants and marketing experts and followed their advice.

I wouldn't be too optimistic about our ability to sell manufactured goods, and thus we are right in emphasizing things like the Canadian Deuterium Uranium Nuclear Reactor (CANDU). There we have a special technology which has been extremely successful and people must turn to us for this. When we sell the CANDU to Japan, and I think we will, that will change the nature of the relationship somewhat.

As to Mr. Trudeau's impact on the relationship, I would have thought there was only the impact of his personality, not on any specific direction to policy. In the 1968 election campaign our three priorities were (1) a review of NATO; (2) the establishment of diplomatic relations with the People's Republic of China; (3) a closer relationship with Latin America. Japan was not a specific subject, because there was really no need for it. Our relations with Japan were developing very well.[8]

Apart from improved communication, the fifth ministerial conference broke little new ground, holding to its principal purpose of familiarizing ministers with existing problems in their respective portfolios. The final communiqué proclaimed mutual commitment to such commonplaces as continuing expansion of Canadian-Japanese trade, along with Canada's desire for diversification of Canadian exports and liberalization of some import restrictions by Japan. Japan in turn noted its hope for reduction of the voluntary export restraints (VERs) imposed by Canada. The desirability of closer scientific, technological, and cultural links was also stressed, with special reference to an ongoing tour of Japan by the Toronto Symphony Orchestra under its young and internationally prominent conductor, Seiji Ozawa, a native of Japan. The Toronto Symphony's tour, which was Canada's first major cultural endeavor in Japan, proved highly successful.[9]

Sharp gave an address at the Foreign Correspondents' Club in Tokyo, in which he commented on Canada's growing Pacific involvements, which he deemed "attributable in economic terms to the amazing progress of Japan, and to the continuing development of other countries on the 'Pacific Rim' and to the remarkable growth in the extractive and manufacturing industries of Western Canada." Perhaps the most interesting sentence in that address, however, came at the end, when he said, "Both of us have the U.S.A. as our chief trading partner and both of us are concerned lest the economic world of the developed countries become a U.S.-E.E.C. dialogue."[10] This remark clearly foreshadows the "third option" concept, which was as yet three years in the future.

When Jean-Luc Pepin, the minister of industry, trade and commerce, returned from Japan, he addressed the Vancouver Board of Trade on May 5, 1969, and noted that Canada during 1968 did 8.4 percent of its trade with the Pacific area and that as a consequence the Pacific had become an important consideration in the government's current review of foreign policies.

We were anxious at the Ministerial meeting to encourage the Japanese ministers to favour a high level of Canadian processing in many of our exports to their country. We are considerably restricted in our ability to supply manufactured products owing to import controls. To achieve our own national economic objectives, a greater degree of processing in Canada is evidently required, whether this be in upgrading resource materials or in manufacturing. We gave Japan a list of products we would like liberalized. . . . We had discussions with Japanese ministers seeking a reduction of the tariff on rapeseed in Japan, and they have undertaken to review the present structure.[11]

A new Japanese ambassador to Canada, Shinichi Kondo, 60, was appointed in May 1969. Like all his predecessors a career Gaimusho official, Kondo was a graduate in economics from Tokyo Imperial University. He had initially been posted to Canada as counselor in 1954 and had served as ambassador to Denmark and New Zealand before coming to Ottawa. According to Kondo,

Japanese industry had greatly developed, leading to the need for a stable supply of resources for our industries and the recognition of the importance of Canada in this connection.

Kondo noted the emergence of a number of major joint ventures, including coal mines in Eastern British Columbia (Kaiser Resources and Mitsubishi Canada Ltd.) and paper mills in Cranbrook, B.C. (Crestbrook Forest Industries Ltd. and Honshu Seishi-Mitsubishi Canada Ltd).

There was Mr. Trudeau's new policy option emphasizing the Pacific and then there was Expo '70 in Osaka, and Mr. Trudeau went to Japan on his first official visit. . . . At the same time, Japanese automobiles and industrial and electronic manufactured goods began to go in large quantities to Canada. Textiles had previously been the most important item, but that changed now. So one of the tasks facing us at that time was how we could develop our political relations across the Pacific. . . .

There was a negative problem in that the Canadian textile industry was in a state of decline and while textiles were no longer such a major part of our exports, we did have to negotiate VERs with the Canadian government. . . . In Canada at the local level, as textile mills were forced to close down, this was an economic problem involving unemployment, and for the Canadian government this became a political problem, not entirely caused by Japan, since there were textile imports from other places, such as Korea and Taiwan, as well. Jean-Luc Pepin was minister of trade and commerce at the time, and we often argued about trade. Why doesn't Japan buy Canadian manufactured goods? Canada is selling lots of manufactured goods to the United States and Europe. Why isn't Japan buying our goods? It's a disgrace! he told me.

I used to answer him: "We'll make an effort as buyers. But the seller also has to make some effort. Canada is not really trying to develop new markets. You need to do market research and study our distribution system. If the seller doesn't make more of an effort to do these things, no matter how many times we send you trade missions it will have no effect." And these problems still remain today.

I think it is fair to say that Trudeau is a man with a special interest in Japan, since he visited Japan twice when he was younger and traveled around by himself, staying in Japanese inns and meeting the people directly. . . . He was particularly interested in Japanese Zen, Japanese Buddhism, Judo, and the like.

In regard to the Japanese Canadians, from my travels around Canada I derived the impression that while the wartime experience was most unhappy for them, being rounded up in camps like that, nevertheless in the long run this had beneficial results. . . . After the war the Japanese Canadians were scattered over the country all the way to the East, and this enabled them to be absorbed into the local communities. At the same time their social position was very much elevated, and they extended themselves into the professions, such as medicine and architecture. . . . One Japanese Canadian [Thomas Shoyama] has become deputy minister of finance.

As to how we might improve Japanese-Canadian relations

in the future, I would like to say the following: On a government-to-government level there is extremely close consultation. There are regular ministerial meetings every two years, and there is consultation at the level of officials every year. . . . There is no regular consultation machinery for private business between the two countries. We do have very close consultation with British Columbia, but for all Canada and particularly the East, it is lacking. I believe that to promote future Japanese-Canadian relations, we need to create citizen-level consultation machinery, separate from the business level. . . . There is very little in terms of academic exchanges. There are few professors in Canadian universities taking a special interest in Japan and on the Japanese side as well, there are very few educators taking an interest in Canada. The interest in cultural exchanges at the government and diplomatic levels is not highly developed. Tourism has developed. Particularly the Canadian Rockies have become an attraction. When you go to Banff all you see is Japanese, and you go to the fur dealer there and everything is marked in Japanese; that is not necessarily a good trend. But this tourism is only up to the Rockies.

Finally, on the Canada-Japan Society, I have been its president since the retirement of Mr. Yoshizawa. Our society is not as active as I would wish it to be. When Prime Minister Trudeau comes to visit, or a provincial premier or a trade mission comes over here, we sponsor a reception or luncheon. We have both Japanese members and Canadian members and there is a social program for maintaining mutual contacts. Vancouver has a Canada-Japan Society, and so we try to arrange cooperative efforts between the two societies. . . . Our role is one of offering good offices and the society does not have funds of its own.

Clearly when I was ambassador, the outlook in Japan seemed far more rosy and there was greater enthusiasm for investment. . . . Even if economic expansion in Japan is slowed down at present, it will undoubtedly continue, and since Japan lacks resources, if we think ten or fifteen years into the future, Canada's resources will again be needed.

Japan so far has been getting most of her coking coal from

southern British Columbia, Sparwood. There are, however, very substantial reserves of coal in northern British Columbia at a place called Quintet, which the present premier, Mr. [William ("Bill")] Bennett, is very eager to develop with Japanese cooperation. This happens to be in an underdeveloped region of British Columbia, so it would serve regional development if this were done. This coal would be shipped through Prince Rupert rather than Roberts Bank.

There is also clearly a need for improvement in the investment climate, and when that occurs I am sure there will be further expansion, through not at the rates at which it was happening in the sixties.[12]

Japan's participation in Expo '67 in Montreal had been the occasion for close cooperation between the Canadian organizers of that world's fair and the prospective organizers of Expo '70 in Osaka, Japan. The Japanese closely monitored Expo '67 to learn any lessons that might be useful for their own extravaganza. Canada in turn threw itself into participation at Osaka with great enthusiasm, contributing four very attractive pavilions—a national pavilion and one each from British Columbia, Ontario, and Quebec. In number of pavilions and space occupied, Canada was the largest participant at Expo '70 except for Japan. May 28, 1970, was Canada Day at Expo '70, and Prime Minister Trudeau visited the exposition grounds on that day and spoke at the Canada Day ceremony.[13]

EXPO '70 is a direct descendant of EXPO '67, just as Canada's happening carried on the tradition of Brussels and Chicago, of Paris and St. Louis. But EXPO '70 is different and very special in an important respect: it is occurring in Asia. . . . As I look about me, . . . one is able to detect the same dynamism and the same sense of youthfulness that distinguished the Canadian EXPO from its predecessors. . . .

Japan is east of Canada only if it is approached by the long route—long in terms of distance, and long in terms of history. As a result of Canadian participation at EXPO '70, Japan and the Pacific countries in Asia shall be referred to by Canadians, I hope, not as the Far East, but as our New West.[14]

The principal sponsors of Canada's participation in Osaka were DEA and the Department of Trade and Commerce, and the funds allotted for federal involvement were in excess of $11 million. Since the Canadian federal and provincial exhibits were exceedingly popular, highly publicized, and visited by many thousands of Expo viewers, it was assumed by many Canadians that Canada's Expo showing would lead to great breakthroughs in Canada-Japan relations and to development of trade across the Pacific. In the decade since 1970, Canada-Japan trade has at least quintupled (see Appendix, Table 11), to $7.1 billion, and the number of Japanese tourists coming to Canada has increased eightfold, to 185,000 per year (see Appendix, Table 14). To what extent these increases can be credited to Expo '70 is impossible to determine, but surely the stunning pavilions showing Canada at her youthful, exuberant best did no harm. The Emperor of Japan started with the Japanese pavilion and visited the Canadian pavilion second.

There is little doubt that Expo '70 made its contribution to the very favorable image of Canada in Japan. Ambassador Moran recalls that Prime Minister Trudeau's performance in 1970 was "absolutely superb." Contributing to it was Trudeau's own great interest in Japan, which he openly displayed so that the Japanese could see that he was enjoying himself and was interested in them.

> Trudeau was one of a number of heads of government who came to Expo, all of whom were accorded the same treatment during their stay in Japan, including a dinner given by the prime minister. . . . Trudeau gave a very thoughtful speech that had to do with the role of youth in the world today and what was troubling youth. Not only was it a departure from a tedious routine which had obtained at previous dinners, but Trudeau had selected a topic of particular current interest, because the Japanese had been experiencing a lot of trouble with student demonstrations in the universities and the emergence of terrorist groups such as the United Red Army [Rengō Sekigun], so they listened intently to this. Having an interest in Zen Buddhism, he had asked that a minimum of an hour be set aside to give him time for a private meeting with a Zen priest. At the end of Trudeau's visit, when he made his call on the emperor, it was the first thing the emperor mentioned.

Prime Minister Trudeau had a brown belt in judo [the Japanese art of manual self-defense wrestling, also known as jujitsu]. The embassy therefore approached the Japan Judo Association and asked it to put on an exhibition at the Suidō-bashi Kōdōkan in Tokyo, its national headquarters, knowing that the prime minister would be interested. The judo association gladly complied. Trudeau was presented with a black belt at the beginning of the match.[15] In accepting, the prime minister said, "I'm not deserving of this, and the only promise I can give you is that I will return to Canada and I will practise and practise at my judo until one day I'll feel that I'm deserving of this great honor you've bestowed on me today." When the matches were over, Trudeau came out of his box and onto the floor, kicked off his slippers, and grabbed one of the fellows and threw him. And the fellow got up and grabbed Trudeau and threw him. The next day the pictures published all across Japan were of Prime Minister Trudeau, almost perpendicular, plummeting headfirst into the mat. So, many people said, wonderful, since among the Japanese it represented him as a person who was different, who had an interest in their religion, their sports, and their esthetics.

Trudeau wanted to sit down with some of the figures who had created the Japanese economic miracle and have a joint meeting with a small group of Canadians. On the Canadian side there were Trudeau, Andrew Kniewasser,[16] Gordon Robertson,[17] and Ambassador Moran. The eight Japanese included the presidents of the two largest trading companies, Akio Morita of Sony, the governor of the Bank of Japan, the economist Saburo Okita. Trudeau's astute questions made this meeting a success. Trudeau also met with Prime Minister Satō for an exchange of views and held a press conference. As it turned out the Japanese were charmed and favorably impressed with the Canadian prime minister, and Canada's image in Japan, already at a high level, got a further boost.[18]

Throughout 1970 there was an increasing number of visits to Japan by both federal and provincial Canadian officials, including provincial premiers and federal ministers, mostly on visits to Expo '70.

During 1970 the two-way trade expanded to a total of $1,395 million, of which $793 million was in Canadian exports, including copper, wood pulp, lumber, rapeseed, aluminum, coal, and nickel as major items. Canadian imports, by contrast, were increasingly in the area of consumer durables, such as automobiles ($85 million), iron and steel ($68 million), television sets ($22 million), tape recorders ($21 million), radios ($12 million), and motorcycles ($9 million), with a corresponding drop in nondurables such as textiles, clothing, and footwear, which were beginning to be supplied by Taiwan, Hong Kong, and Korea.

During the first two weeks of December 1970, J. J. Greene, the minister of energy, mines, and resources, led a mission of Canadian officials and businessmen with a primary interest in mining and energy problems on a tour to Japan. Greene told his Japanese hosts that they could best assure a continued supply of Canadian raw materials for their industries by not trying to control the mining companies producing them, using minority holdings and debt financing as their avenue of participation. On returning to Canada, Greene noted that Japan had imported 110,000 tons of Canadian copper concentrate during 1970 and that the figure might rise to 420,000 tons by 1975. He expressed the hope that environmental considerations in Japan might make it possible to do more of the smelting and refining in Canada in the years to come. Commenting on Japan's growing imports of natural uranium from Canada, Greene noted that much of this uranium was being enriched in plants in the United States. He suggested that it was desirable to build a uranium enrichment plant in Canada with the Japanese market in mind, which would involve an investment of $1 billion, hinting that Japanese capital would be more than welcome for that purpose.[19]

Reflecting the high expectations and keen interest in Canada-Japan trade at the time, Chujiro Fujino, president of Mitsubishi Corporation, led a high-level economic delegation to Canada during June 1971, with the Canadian government making the arrangements for meetings with Canadian business leaders and manufacturers. During a meeting in Vancouver, Fujino stated: "We are prepared to accept a much greater percentage of high labour-content products from Canada. The intention of Japanese business is principally to assure the supply of raw materials and progressively semi-finished products in keeping with Canadian policy."[20]

The sixth Japan-Canada ministerial conference was held in Toronto on September 13–14, 1971, with SSEA Sharp and Foreign Minister Takeo Fukuda heading the two delegations. Among the main topics discussed by the ministers were the impact of the "Nixon shocks" on both Canada and Japan and the desirability of an early removal of the 10 percent surcharge. Other subjects included trade liberalization, maintenance of flexible currency exchange rates, development assistance programs, and the potential for increased trade in agricultural products. Canada made its usual pitch for diversification and processing of her exports, and Japan announced another round of trade liberalization. The committee also agreed to establish a subcommittee on resources and energy matters.[21]

The two-way trade between Canada and Japan rose again during 1971, reaching the unprecedented total of $1.6 billion, with exports and imports almost perfectly balanced for the first time in more than twenty years. Japanese exports to Canada increased by more than $200 million over 1970, with automobiles, motorcycles, and steel products leading the way, while Canadian exports remained roughly at the level of the previous year. (See Appendix, Table 11.)

Pepin, the minister of industry, trade, and commerce, headed a sixty-member Canadian trade mission to Japan in January 1972, the largest economic mission Canada had ever sent anywhere in the world, which included both government officials and business leaders. The mission reiterated Canada's desire to sell more manufactured goods in Japan and its hope of encouraging more processing of Canadian resource materials before export to Japan.[22] This dual objective had by this time become the theme song for Canadian ambassadors, ministers, officials and some academics and was to dominate the Canada-Japan dialogue for the entire decade 1968–78 and beyond. Pepin sounded this message so forcefully that he was given the name Typhoon Pepin by his Japanese hosts during the 1972 visit. The Japanese listened and smiled, and the trade mix stayed the same.

Pepin admired the Japanese trading system, which involves trading houses in marketing Japanese goods all over the world. He hoped to see this system adopted in Canada but did not find his officials at the Department of Industry, Trade and Commerce responsive to the idea.

So . . . three friends and I created Interimco, to demonstrate that it could work. Interimco has generated $150 million worth of sales since its creation, which is not a bad start I think. But the Interimco type of operation has not found a sufficient degree of acceptance in the Canadian community. The idea of collective marketing of manufactured products has not become a national objective, as the Japanese trading houses are in Japan. In Canada there is a certain laziness. If we have a deficit in trade, we can always send the world more coal, or gas, or oil, or copper, or wheat. There is not here the kind of dedication which you have in Japan, because in Japan the issue is survival. One thing that the Japanese will probably learn sooner or later is what I learned personally through the "Connally shock" (the Nixon 10 percent surcharge of 1972), that in international trade you must not do too well or you will attract jealousy and retaliation.[23]

When the Pepin mission finally returned to Canada, its members had met 1,200 Japanese executives in 288 separate meetings.[24] There is no doubt that Pepin charmed many executives and made other people sit up and take notice, but the percentage of fully manufactured end products, which before the Pepin mission had stood at 3 percent, three years later was still gradually declining towards 2 percent;[25] even by the most optimistic accounts,[26] it has never yet exceeded 4 percent.

The reactions of Japanese business and government to the Typhoon Pepin approach were perhaps most accurately reflected in remarks made by Japanese Ambassador Shinichi Kondo, who said,

We Japanese cannot agree with the argument that we are treating Canada as a Japanese colony, exploiting Canadian natural resources and stealing Canadian jobs. We believe that Japan's purchase of resource materials and products helps create jobs in Canada.

According to the Mining Association of Canada, some 150,000 persons are directly employed in mining and for every person thus employed, six other jobs are created in the service and secondary industries. These additional jobs are spread across Canada.

He insisted that it was not true that Japan followed a deliberate policy of not buying Canadian manufactured goods.

> Japan's import of machinery . . . in 1970 . . . amounted to 2.3 billion dollars, a 40% increase over the previous year. United States sales increased by 45%; West Germany's by 40%; France's by 57%. To my regret, Canada's sales declined by 20%.
>
> Why has Canada failed to increase its share in Japan's expanding market? It may be that Canada has not tried hard enough to supply the higher technology-oriented products that Japan now requires, . . . has neglected to identify specific demands and has not launched a determined sales-campaign in support of specific export products, . . . has not succeeded in projecting in Japan, the image of an industrially and technologically advanced country.
>
> I would urge Canadian businessmen not to rely solely upon Japanese efforts. It is mainly Canada's responsibility to establish itself in the Japanese market.

Kondo finally quoted P. G. Campbell, assistant commercial secretary at the Canadian embassy in Tokyo,

> who wrote . . . in *Canada Commerce*, "Most important, however, in Canada's failure to share the Japanese market for manufactured goods is the disinterest or unwillingness of some Canadian businessmen to visit Japan to promote their products personally. Often when visiting potential customers for Canadian manufactured goods, Embassy officers have found that Americans, Germans, British and French businessmen in considerable numbers have preceded them, visits from Canadian businessmen have been rare."[27]

It is true that it takes a great deal of time, money, patience, and hard work to crack the Japanese market. The handful of Canadian companies in the Japanese market today are the ones that were equal to that challenge.

The Pepin mission was followed on March 6, 1972, by the first Canadian science and technology mission, led by Alastair Gillespie, the minister of state for science and technology. This delegation of forty-five Canadians, representing the federal and provincial governments, industry, and the universities, visited Japan for ten days at the invitation of the Japanese government. Both sides agreed to a continuing exchange of information, and personnel and bilateral exchanges have been carried on since this first mission in 1972.[28]

Following up on possible sales of manufactures, late in 1972 the International Defence Programmes Branch of the Department of Industry, Trade and Commerce sent a four-man mission headed by F. T. Jackman, its director, to Japan to explore the possibility that there might be a market for Canadian defense equipment in Japan. MITI and Defence Agency officials, in their final meetings with the Canadian delegates, conveyed the impression that sales of defense products might be difficult. It is likely that the predominant interest of the United States in such sales played a role in Japan's reluctance to develop military equipment sales from Canada.[29]

Canada sent a team of some fifty Canadian skiers and skaters to the Winter Olympic Games in Sapporo, Hokkaido, during the first two weeks of February 1972. Karen Magnussen, the figure skater, was the only member of the Canadian team to achieve high distinction, winning a silver medal in figure skating. The rest of the Canadian team achieved two fourth placings, giving the Canadian team sixteenth place in point standing and seventeenth place in medals standing. (Japan was respectively eleventh and twelfth.) Since Canada was scheduled to be the host of the Summer Olympics in 1976, it came as a surprise to some people in Japan that the Canadian team at Sapporo did not make a stronger showing.[30]

For some eighteen months starting in October 1971, the Standing Senate Committee on Foreign Affairs, under John B. Aird, chairman, held hearings on Canadian relations with countries of the Pacific region, inviting as witnesses a number of Canadian politicians, bureaucrats, businessmen, and academics with knowledge and experience in the area.

The final report of the committee, issued in March 1972, included a number of specific conclusions and recommendations in regard to the course of Canadian policy. On the economic side, the report recognized Japan's ever-increasing importance and predicted that Japan would become Canada's second most important market in short order. It noted the predominance of unprocessed raw materials in Canadian exports to Japan (65 percent) and of manufactured items (96 percent) among Canadian imports from Japan, and it pointed out, moreover, that 80 percent of the exports originated in Western Canada. It expressed concern for the upgrading and diversification of Canadian exports.

> There is no longer any justification for the great bulk (as much as 65%) of Canadian exports to be shipped to Japan, as the policy paper says, "in their rawest transportable and least profitable forms." The time has come for Canada to begin redressing this imbalance. A concerted national effort will be required, however, and the Committee considers this an urgent priority for action by industries concerned and by governments at all levels.
>
> With respect to the serious problem represented by the unsatisfactory level of Canada's manufactured exports to Japan (less than 3% of the total), the Committee believes that the Canadian Government is justified in pressing for further tariff liberalization by Japan and for the elimination of its many "nontariff barriers." Other clear needs, however, are to overcome the lack of familiarity, imagination and aggressiveness on the part of Canadian businessmen in the area, and to attack the general problem of lagging scientific and technical innovation in Canadian industry.[31]

The Senate report concluded that in awareness and understanding of Japan and other countries of the Pacific region, Canada had fallen behind most other developed countries of the Pacific in generating a regional consciousness and acquiring the necessary expertise in Pacific affairs. It pointed out that facilities and financing for training in the Chinese and Japanese languages were badly lacking and recommended that special grants be made to a small number of existing centers to upgrade and expand language programs and to make such courses available to business representatives and provincial officials. It was further suggested that library facilities and centers for Asian and Pacific studies be expanded and improved. As additional measures to shore up Canadian expertise in the area, the report recommended scholarships and fellowships at the graduate or postdoctoral levels providing opportunities for study in the

Pacific area, continuing education for people already involved in professions, and compilation of a national directory of Canadian institutions and individuals with competence in different aspects of Pacific affairs.[32]

The report also noted the relative lack of media coverage of Pacific area events, apart from the occasional crises, and the reliance, almost exclusively, on foreign news services. It recommended expansion of exchanges of public information and an increase in cultural exchanges, including sports competitions.

Turning finally to security matters, the report states:

> The Canadian Government does not envisage participation in military alliances with Pacific countries, or any other extensive military involvement, in the region. It has instead given priority to cooperative political and economic action to alleviate the deep-rooted causes of social and international tension.[33]

While the Senate report revealed no new discoveries, it did put together a coherent program of recommendations, many of which were implemented as government policy by the Trudeau administration in the period after 1973. Keith A. J. Hay of Carleton University provided a logical explanation of Japan's failure to buy more Canadian manufactured goods.

> At the end of the 1960's the market for manufactured exports to Japan . . . was equal to $15 billion. . . . If one looks at the structure of that market one finds that it is dominated by three suppliers who have been supplying the market for 15 years, the United States, West Germany, and the United Kingdom. . . . The reasons why the Japanese concentrated on these three suppliers is again very simple to understand: those three countries lead the world in investment in research and development and they are, in order, those countries which produce the largest number of patents, new ideas and new technology each year. . . . Unless we concentrate a little more on developing highly sophisticated specialized manufactured goods it will be difficult for us to get back a substantial portion of the Japanese market for manufactures.[34]

The year 1972 was in many ways pivotal to the Canada-Japan relationship, reflecting changes in Canadian and Japanese policy, as well as in the domestic politics of both countries. In Japan the return of Okinawa to Japanese sovereignty, free of nuclear weapons, as Prime Minister Satō had insisted, symbolized the end of the postwar era, as Japan reestablished its standing in the international community. Prime Minister Satō resigned in midsummer, after almost eight years at the helm, and was replaced by the ebullient self-made millionaire and grass-roots politician Kakuei Tanaka. Within four months of becoming premier, Tanaka broke the impasse in Sino-Japanese relations. He was invited to the People's Republic by Premier Chou En-lai, where he accepted China's conditions for the establishment of diplomatic relations with Japan and promised to work for the early conclusion of a peace treaty. Meanwhile, Japan's alliance with the United States, long the cornerstone of Japan's postwar foreign policy, was rocked by what came to be called the "Nixon shocks": the sudden announcement of President Richard M. Nixon's intention to visit Peking in 1972, the floating of the U.S. dollar, the imposition of a 10 percent surcharge on foreign imports to the United States, and the threat of compulsory quotas on Japanese textiles, all of which occurred during the summer and early fall of 1971. The announcement of the Nixon Doctrine on the Island of Guam in July 1969 had also indicated that the U.S. commitment to Asia was in the process of downward revision. The time for a rethinking of Japan's basic foreign policy posture was therefore clearly at hand.

In Canada, meanwhile, the first flush of Trudeaumania had subsided, and the Liberals were headed for a dead-heat election and a minority government on October 30. The postwar supremacy of the United States was clearly in decline as its inability to prevail in Vietnam became evident. Meanwhile, the imposition of the 10 percent surcharge made a reexamination of Canada-U.S. relations seem desirable. This led in the fall of 1972 to the publication of one of the most important foreign policy documents of the Trudeau era, Mitchell Sharp's article, "Canada-U.S. Relations: Options for the Future," which in a thorough soul-searching fashion looked at Canada's relationship to the United States and asked some agonizing questions.

The real question facing Canadians is one of the direction. In practice three broad options are open to us:
a. We can seek to maintain more or less our present relationship with the United States, with a minimum of policy adjustments.
b. We can move deliberately towards closer integration with the U.S.
c. We can pursue a comprehensive long-term strategy to develop and strengthen the Canadian economy and other aspects of our national life, and in the process to reduce the present Canadian vulnerability.[35]

Rejecting both the first and second options as less advantageous or viable from the Canadian viewpoint, Sharp indicated preference for the "third option" of strengthening Canada and reducing its vulnerability, adding that this option was in no sense anti-American. The basic aim of the third option would be "over time to lessen the vulnerability of the Canadian economy to external factors, including in particular, the impact of the U.S. . . . and develop a more confident sense of national identity."[36]

Bruce I. Rankin, Canada's ambassador to Japan from 1976 to 1981, has said, "Canadians dealing with Japanese affairs think of Japan as the other pillar, along with Europe, of the 'Third Option' policy."[37]

The word "vulnerability" in the "third option" paper is clearly in reference to Canada's excessive dependence upon the U.S. economy, making Canada vulnerable to such actions as the 10 percent surcharge, the oil shipment limitations, possible changes in the auto pact, and the Domestic International Sales Corporation (DISC) measures.[38] The "options" paper clearly implied that reducing vulnerability meant seeking alternative markets and political involvements. Derek Burney, who was the senior departmental assistant and media spokesman of the office of the SSEA when I interviewed him in 1977 and became Canadian ambassador to the ROK the next year, commented as follows:

With the third option, we had Japan in mind as well as Europe, as potential counterweights to the U.S.A. Until the

early sixties I used to talk of our relationship with Japan as
"smiling diplomacy"—we were getting along well; . . . by
and large we had no problems. We did not recognize any need
to share information with the Japanese. We regarded the Japanese politically, economically, and defensively very much in
a tight American orbit, and the Japanese seemed very com-
fortable in that role themselves. But as they began to become
more of a power in Korea and in Southeast Asia . . . and we
similarly tried to expand our own relations in Southeast Asia
and Korea, [we] saw a natural commonality there. . . . I
know that it's a relationship that we have decided consciously
to cultivate and nurture to a specific end. We want more out
of the relationship with Japan. I'm not convinced frankly
that the Japanese are reciprocating. They're reciprocating to
the extent that it serves their immediate interests, as they
always will. But I don't think their attitude is changed all that
much.

If you want to look twenty-five years down the road and
not two, however, you have to insist on the upgrading of the
economic relationship, if you believe that Canadian society
has to expand in some direction. Meanwhile, we're quite will-
ing to sell what we've got. It would be ridiculous to do otherwise. And if we have an industrial strategy at some point, in
this country, which gives the Japanese the impression that
we're serious about wanting to sell more than "rocks and
logs," then we're fighting them on their own grounds.
They've got an industrial strategy, and they know what
they're doing with it. But they don't see much evidence of the
same here. No matter what you hear, and no matter what
public statements of ministers and prime ministers say about
how we want to change the economic relationship [with
Japan], most of the people who are involved as businessmen
in that relationship are quite satisfied with it the way it is.
Well, this plays directly into the hands of the Japanese, who
are absolutely superbly content with the relationship the way
it is and say there is no need whatsoever to change it.[39]

In 1972 Canada suffered a rare balance-of-trade deficit with
Japan, amounting to $106.3 million (see Appendix, Table 11), but

in 1973 Canada recouped that loss eight times over, with an $800 million surplus. The Canadian surplus has persisted ever since. While trade has continued to prosper and has steadily increased in volume, 1972 also marks the development of certain negative trends in the economic relationship between the two countries. This applies particularly to the investment climate, with an increasing reluctance by Japanese investors to sink large amounts of funds into resource development in Canada because of a number of economic uncertainties, such as strikes, plant closings, and provincial or federal restrictions interfering with the profitable operation of resource businesses in Canada.

Ambassador Kondo was recalled to Tokyo in midsummer (where he died in 1981), and a new Japanese ambassador, Akira Nishiyama, arrived in Ottawa on August 26, 1972. Nishiyama, 59, a Gaimusho career officer, had served as ambassador in Indonesia and Switzerland before coming to Canada in 1972. When he came to Ottawa, Ambassador Nishiyama recalls that Canada, in the development of its resources, was gradually moving to a policy of preserving them for export as manufactured goods and that this created some problems. Nishiyama acknowledges that the cultural agreement (ratified in November 1977), the exchange of many missions, and the holding of ministerial conferences have indeed made Japanese-Canadian relations more close than they were, but he also points to a litany of Canadian shortcomings: the absence of Canadian partners Japanese business leaders can talk to; Canada's unwillingness to commit her oil resources for export; the poor quality and high price of Canadian manufactures; the unwillingness of Canadian coal miners to work and the many strikes in Canada's public sector (airlines, railroads, the postal service); and the bad climate, which is so cold as to make it difficult to develop Canadian resources.

> Clearly, both countries have their bad points. We possibly lack frontier spirit and the Canadians do not have the sense of urgency or the motivation. Instead of trying to build bigger markets or create competitive manufactures, Canadians may prefer to go to Florida or Palm Springs to relax and enjoy the sunshine and there is something to be said for that as well.[40]

Ambassador Moran was recalled to Ottawa at the end of 1972 and was replaced in January 1973 by Ross Campbell, who had served since 1967 as Canada's permanent representative and ambassador to NATO in Paris and later in Brussels. The appointment of this experienced, top-notch diplomat indicates the high priority the Trudeau administration attached to the implementation of its "third option" policy in Japan. Ambassador Campbell recalls that upon his arrival in Tokyo at the beginning of 1973 it was his hope that the "unbalanced relationship," in which Canada served merely as a "resource producer" for Japan, would be transformed to enable Canada to do some primary manufacturing for export to Japan. He further hoped that the "third option" concept of a truly broader and deeper relationship between Canada and Japan could be implemented.

> I think it is almost unique, what we did in offering a kind of partnership to Japan, that any other industrial country would have jumped at. Not so the Japanese. They're insular in this respect, . . . and they've had to stand on their own feet with nothing and they've made something truly wonderful by being wholly self-sufficient. But it isn't that kind of a world that we live in any more. They have too much to lose by being purely materialistic. I've been rather astonished at their inability to grasp that, or to grasp the hand that was offered, for they have not grasped it, far from it. . . . I think Japan is going to regret not having seized a moment in time, which is passing, to forge a much more equitable relationship with Canada.

Ambassador Campbell also hoped that Japan would buy Canada's CANDU nuclear reactors (he still thinks they may eventually) or the water bombers (planes used in spraying water or chemicals), which they ordered and tested and subsequently cancelled, deciding to build their own, and he was clearly disappointed that it proved impossible during his three years in Tokyo to sell Canadian high technology to Japan.[41]

The continuing Subcommittee on Mineral and Energy Policy (SMEP), which had been set up in 1971 when Energy Minister Greene visited Japan, met in Vancouver in September 1972 and noted that oil "surplus to Canadian needs" was unlikely to become available during the 1970s, that Canada had shipped only 64 percent of its contractual commitments in coal to Japan in 1972 (8.3 million tons), and that the natural gas outlook was not promising. Chances for increased processing of copper in Canada or Japanese investment in such processing or in the Athabasca tar sands also appeared dim.[42]

Clearly the most important development in Canada-Japan relations during 1973 was the fact that after twenty years as Canada's third-biggest customer, following the United States and the United Kingdom, Japan finally moved into the number two spot behind the United States, with a total of $2.8 billion in the two-way trade and an $800 million balance-of-payments surplus in Canada's favor. Both the Canadian surplus and Japan's position as Canada's number two trading partner have been maintained ever since.

A meeting of the Japan-Canada Ministerial Committee (last convened in September 1971) was scheduled for September 1973 but had to be postponed because of a national railroad strike in Canada. SSEA Sharp visited Japan on September 8, 1973, to meet with Prime Minister Tanaka and Foreign Minister Masayoshi Ohira for discussions on U.S. Secretary of State designate Henry Kissinger's plan for cooperative guidelines among industrial democracies. Sharp informed Ohira of Canada's desire to fly Boeing 747 jumbo jets between Canada and Japan. Ohira stressed Japan's concern about the supply of energy and mineral resources and the desirability of the establishment of intergovernmental organizations to study future cooperation in exploration for natural resources.[43]

With the outbreak of the Yom Kippur War scarcely a month later and the Arab oil embargo that followed, Japan's realization of its extreme vulnerability led to a global Japanese effort to assure itself of new and diverse sources of oil and other fossil fuels, not least by participation in the development of the Alberta oil sands and other energy-related projects in Canada. A contract between Denison Mines and the Tokyo Electric Power Company for the purchase of some $800 million worth of uranium over a twenty-year period was symptomatic of the general trend. When an international oil conference was called in Washington by the U.S. government in February 1974, SSEA Sharp met with Japan's foreign minister, Masayoshi Ohira, who brought up the subject of possible Japanese participation in the development of the Athabasca oil sands. Sharp replied that massive foreign capital investment in the oil sands was premature and might have negative economic effects.[44]

Ivan Head, special assistant to Prime Minister Trudeau, visited Japan in April 1974 to lay the groundwork for a meeting of the two prime ministers in Paris on April 7, 1974, when both were to be in that city for the state funeral of President Georges Pompidou of France. In Paris Trudeau informed Tanaka that Canada had decided to participate in the Ocean Expo 1975 in Okinawa. He also spoke of Canada's new Pan Pacific Policy, placing greater emphasis on the importance of Japan. Both prime ministers agreed on the desirability of upgrading Canada-Japan relations, and Trudeau reiterated an invitation to Tanaka to visit Canada at the earliest possible date in 1974. On May 8, 1974, a nonconfidence motion in the Trudeau government led to the dissolution of Canada's Parliament, with the calling of general elections for July 8, 1974, leading to yet another postponement of the seventh ministerial conference. In an article in the October 1974 issue of *Pacific Community*, Head stressed the common international commitments of the two countries, including their decision not to produce nuclear weapons.

> Of all of Canada's trans-Pacific relations, that with Japan promises to be among the most rewarding in terms of mutual potential advantage in the next ten years, yet without question it contains innumerable problems which must be overcome before those advantages will be enjoyed fully. . . . One of those is bound in the unhealthy (in the long run) preponderantly economic tone of the relationship.
>
> Japan needs much more than industrial minerals. It needs food. It needs energy. It needs, as we all do, understanding neighbours. Japan is approaching the social and environmental limits of its carrying capacity for pollution, is close to its maximum food production, and faces immense pressures for increased and upgraded housing. In each of these areas, Canada offers some solutions. The imaginative application of Canadian assets such as space, energy and unique technology could be instrumental in the solution of many of Japan's current problems.[45]

Japan's response to Canada's overtures was "tentative," to use Ambassador Nishiyama's euphemism, since Japan saw Canada as a U.S. satellite—and the importance of the United States in economic, strategic, and political terms so far exceeds the comparative importance of Canada to Japan that it was simply unthinkable that Japan would permit itself to be harnessed to Canada's "third option" wagon. Canada did have some significance as a trade partner to Japan, being the seventh largest importer of Japanese goods and the sixth largest exporter to Japan, but 97 percent of Japan's export trade and 95 percent of Japan's import trade in 1974 were done with countries other than Canada.

Meanwhile, the year 1974 developed into the busiest and most successful year to date in terms of the trade figures and commercial and consultative activity across the Pacific in both directions. Premier Dave Barrett of British Columbia dashed across to Japan for a two-week visit in April to promote Japanese investment in his province.[46]

During the first week of March, Guy Saint-Pierre, minister of industry and commerce of the province of Quebec, led a delegation of some 200 government officials, bankers, and industrialists from Quebec to Tokyo. The conference, called Tokyo '74, was the largest meeting of Japanese and Canadian businessmen ever held and also marked the official opening in Tokyo of Quebec House, a provincial trade center similar to the previously established Ontario and Alberta provincial offices.[47]

During 1973 Quebec had done $64 million worth of business with Japan, mostly in such resource commodities as asbestos, iron ore, copper, zinc, and pulp and paper. Hitachi Television, the YKK Zipper Company, Sanyo Electronics, Bruck Mills, and the Fuji Dye and Printing Company all operate factories in Quebec in which Japanese are major shareholders.[48] The operation of provincial offices in Japan is a somewhat controversial subject, since some Canadian diplomats feel that the Canadian embassy should be the only voice speaking for Canada in Japan. Provincial officials, on the other hand, feel that the embassy cannot adequately represent ten provinces, particularly when they compete for sales. Normand Bernier, the Quebec delegate in Tokyo, has pointed out that the Japanese market is extremely large and that even a hundred more salesmen for Canada and the ten provinces could not adequately cover it.[49]

Economic and political trends in Japan and the rest of the world were confusing and contradictory throughout Prime Minister Tanaka's two-and-a-half-year term of office (July 1972–December 1974). His popularity as a self-made man and "commoner premier" was high in October 1972, when he visited Peking to restore diplomatic relations with China, but by the time of the general elections of December 1972, his popularity was rapidly declining. His ambitious plans for a "remodeling of the Japanese Archipelago"[50] by decentralization of Japanese industry, a revamping of Japan's transportation network, urban remodeling, and regional development had led to an unprecedented speculative land-price spiral that boosted inflation to some 23 percent and forced the floating of the yen in February 1973. The outbreak of the Arab-Israeli War on October 6, 1973, with the resulting curtailment of oil shipments and oil price increases,[51] resulted in a net decline in gross national product and predictions that the Japanese economy faced disaster. At the same time there was grumbling in the LDP that Premier Tanaka had failed to consult with other politicians and the minority parties in the Diet. In short, the premier, his party, and Japan's economy were all in deep trouble. Moreover, as Tanaka traveled abroad, he encountered anti-Japanese demonstrations in Southeast Asia and a polite but cool reception in Europe, which had become wary of "Japan Incorporated." Even relations with Washington were precarious, as Japan's balance of trade surplus troubled the United States, and President Nixon was already under the Watergate cloud, which eroded his prestige and forced Tanaka to cancel a planned exchange of visits by President Nixon and the Emperor of Japan. Nevertheless, during the first half of 1974 Japan essentially recovered her balance from the oil shock and the Tanaka administration put in place a series of economic measures that put Japan on the road to recovery in an amazingly short time.

On July 8, 1974, Prime Minister Trudeau won a majority government for his party in Canada, and on July 9 Prime Minister Tanaka was able to maintain the LDP's majority in the Japanese House of Councilors election. This cleared the decks for the long-contemplated visit of Tanaka to Canada. Tanaka arrived in Ottawa on September 23, where he held summit talks with Trudeau. The lengthy joint communiqué issued by the two prime ministers indicated that they had discussed virtually all major matters of mutual interest and were committed to the usual salutary issues, such as peace and friendship. "They hoped that a new era in Japan-Canada relations would thus be ushered in."[52] It was agreed that the Seventh Canada-Japan Ministerial Conference would be held in Tokyo in 1975, and Prime Minister Trudeau accepted an invitation to visit Japan at an as yet unspecified date.

The communiqué included only one new announcement, regarding the initiation of matching and complementary programs of approximately $1 million each for promoting academic relations. These funds were to be used primarily for the development of Japanese studies in Canada and Canadian studies in Japan. It was added that new negotiations would eventually be started for the conclusion of a cultural agreement.[53] Ottawa's perennial complaint about the trade mix evoked only the usual lecture about trying harder.

After his visit to Ottawa, Prime Minister Tanaka visited the Prince Hotel in Toronto, newly built for $27 million by Japan's Prince Hotel Chain, collected an honorary doctorate of laws from the University of Toronto, and moved on to Vancouver's University of British Columbia to inaugurate the Asian Center.[54] On November 26, 1974, Tanaka announced his intention to resign as LDP party president and prime minister because of charges of bribery and conflict of interest made against him in the Japanese press. Since his resignation he has remained a member of the National Diet, where he continues (as of 1982) to head the largest faction in the LDP.

Tanaka's successor, Miki, was chosen on December 9, 1974. He had the reputation of being a political moderate with no hint of corruption in his background and was thus referred to as "Clean Miki."

The year 1974 had been a busy and confusing one on the political as well as the economic scene, in Japan as well as in the rest of the world. In terms of Canadian-Japanese relations, Prime Ministers Trudeau and Tanaka had spoken of "the beginning of a new era." While it is not clear what was meant by that, the phrase was not justified by any change in the political relationship, but in the economic relationship it can be argued that a new era was indeed under way. Total two-way trade between the two countries reached the unprecedented level of $3.6 billion, increasing Canadian imports

from Japan by 41 percent and exports by 23 percent in a single
year. Japanese investment in Canada increased by approximately
30 percent, to a level of some $300 million, and Canadian-Japanese
joint ventures could now be found in virtually every province of
Canada. An intimate political relationship had not really been
achieved, nor was Japan prepared to do much about the trade mix,
but trade and investment had really taken off, far beyond what
anyone could have expected a few years earlier.

When asked to comment on Canada, several years after his resignation as prime minister, Tanaka made the following statement:

> If I had to look for a place to live outside of Japan, I would
> choose Canada's Vancouver—that dream of my youth has
> not changed to this day.
>
> Canada is the world's greatest land of resources. Japan,
> which has no resources whatsoever and Canada should be-
> come brothers. In the new world of the future, Canada's re-
> sources will make a great contribution. In my view in such
> areas as oil sands, uranium, and nuclear cooperation the
> future outlook for Japanese-Canadian cooperation is very
> bright. . . . The oil sands alone constitute a great lure. Japan
> is importing copper ore from Canada. If about half of it
> could be smelted at the source by a Japanese-Canadian joint
> venture, I think this would improve understanding by the Ca-
> nadian people and Japanese friendship would be expanded.[55]

The abrupt departure of Tanaka from Japan's political scene at
the end of 1974 was genuinely regretted by a number of Canadian
high officials, who had seen the developing rapport between Trudeau and Tanaka as beneficial to Canada-Japan relations. However, there was no hiatus in the continuing close consultations between the two governments. Due to the global recession, trade
slightly declined during 1975, Canadian exports falling by 25 percent and Japanese exports by 6 percent, with a total two-way trade
of $3.3 billion (a drop of some $320 million).

Meanwhile, Ambassador Nishiyama was recalled to Japan and
replaced by Ambassador Yasuhiko Nara, 58, who arrived in Ottawa on February 25, 1975. A career Gaimusho officer, Nara had
been consul general in New York (1966), and ambassador to Singa-

pore (1969). Reflecting the Japanese approach to the "new era" in Canada-Japan relations, Nara said (in March 1977) that there were no diplomatic problems between the two countries and that the flow of raw materials was proceeding smoothly. Japan did not mind that Canada had a two-to-one export surplus. Cultural relations were also going well, though he thought "we do not do enough" in that area. There was the problem of uranium shipments suspended by Canada to negotiate a new safeguards agreement, but he anticipated the problem could be solved.

> We are well satisfied with the relationship as it stands. The Canadians on the other hand are evidently not satisfied. . . . [They say Japan] only wants "rocks and logs" from Canada and is not interested in more sophisticated goods. . . . From our viewpoint, where the Canadians are not doing enough is in the area of market research.

Basically Ambassador Nara did not think much of the idea that Canada could sell manufactured goods in Japan. Apart from this he commented favorably on the variety of close consultations between the two countries but added, "The trade pattern in my view, will not change."[56]

The major event in Canada-Japan relations during 1975 was the Seventh Canada-Japan Ministerial Conference, held in Tokyo on June 23–24. Kiichi Miyazawa, minister for foreign affairs, was chairman, and the Canadian delegation was led by SSEA Allan J. MacEachen. After exploring a number of international problems, the ministers decided to revise the agreement on commerce between Canada and Japan and to "discourage protectionist moves." Canada still wanted to sell more processed goods and continued to promote CANDU and De Havilland Aircraft of Canada's STOL Dash-7 aircraft. Canada also now invited Japanese investment in the Alberta tar sands. Japan, on the other hand, voiced its desire for stable supplies of copper, uranium, coal, wheat, and timber from Canada and expressed the hope that Canada's new Foreign Investment Review Act (FIRA) would not interfere with Japanese investments in Canada. On the tar sands, Japan was not prepared to invest heavily unless some assurance could be given by Canada that the oil could be exported to Japan.[57]

Meanwhile, MacEachen sought to project a modern image of Canada as a technologically advanced and industrially sophisticated country, producing CANDU reactors, communications satellites, modern mining and forestry machinery, high-voltage electrical transmission equipment, and other products of a mature industrialized economy. He also explained that the "third option" was not anti-American but rather similar to Japan's *takaku gaikō* (diplomacy of diversification). He finally offered Japan not only the usual resources but "space" for processing industries to handle metals, iron, zinc, aluminum, pulp, paper, and agricultural products, looking to joint ventures in those areas.[58]

A meeting of Japanese and Canadian officials from five ministries was held in Tokyo November 25–28 to follow up on previous proposals to identify sectors for future economic cooperation. The sectors selected for mutually beneficial cooperation included aluminum, oil sands, copper, zinc, uranium, coal, petrochemicals, aircraft, electronics, shipbuilding, marine components, paper, forest products, housing, grain, rapeseed, tobacco, and pork.[59]

Meanwhile Canada-Japan consultations continued in a number of forums, including the UN General Assembly. Foreign policy experts from both countries also met in Ottawa during April, and the finance ministers of both countries continued to consult. The Sub-Committee on Resources and Energy met twice. The Canadian chief of the defense staff visited Japan for consultations. Japanese Maritime self-defense forces exchanged courtesy visits with Canadian ships that had called in Japan earlier in the year. Canada participated in Japan's Ocean Expo '75 in Okinawa with a major exhibition of icebreakers, research submarines, and semisubmersible oil-drilling rigs.[60]

While the tone of the relationship continued to be upbeat and optimistic from the Canadian side, there were increasing indications that Japanese business leaders had lost interest in Canadian finished goods and were taking a sober second look at investment in Canada. The president of Mitsubishi Corporation put it very bluntly: "Frankly, Canadian-made highly developed manufactured products are either economically too costly or not necessarily more competitive than comparable products made in Europe or the United States."[61]

Many of the plans for joint-venture copper smelting plants, steel mills, and other processing facilities in Canada's "available space" never materialized. By 1975–76 Japanese investment in Canada had reached the $400 million level, but the pace had slowed down, and so many deals had gone sour that Japanese investors would become progressively cautious or even openly dubious of the wisdom of investing in Canada.

Early in 1976 Ambassador Campbell returned to Ottawa to accept appointment as chairman of the board of Atomic Energy of Canada Limited. Campbell is reported to have been disappointed with the "third option" and the "new era" and therefore requested reassignment to Ottawa. Canada's new ambassador to Japan was Bruce I. Rankin, 57, who arrived in Tokyo in February 1976. Ambassador Rankin had been Canada's consul general in New York since 1970.

When interviewed after fifteen months in the Tokyo embassy, he said that Canada-Japan relations were going extremely well and were amazingly quiet. Apart from some minor difficulties on textile restrictions and the ongoing concerns about nuclear safeguards, which were in the process of solution, there were really no items of contention between the two governments. Rankin foresaw no danger that Canadian protectionism would inhibit trade relations, although he conceded that Canadian restrictions on Japanese textile shipments were not appreciated in Japan. Rankin thought he had the best staff of any post in the Canadian foreign service. He predicted a bright future for nuclear cooperation between Japan and Canada and expected that CANDU reactors would eventually prove attractive to the Japanese.

Realizing that Canadian manufactured products would have to be competitive to sell in the Japanese market, he noted that Japan would no doubt continue to import Canadian raw materials and might gradually accept the processing of some of these materials in Canada before shipment to Japan. The Western provinces being the principal shippers of coal, wheat, barley, and rapeseed, which are Canada's main resource exports, he noted that pork and some high technology products were being shipped from Ontario and Quebec. Quebec also supplied some $50 million annually in iron ore as well as asbestos.

Ambassador Rankin particularly emphasized the expansion of his embassy's public affairs program and of cultural exchanges in both directions. He was enthusiastic about the success of Prime Minister Trudeau's visit to Japan in October 1976, feeling that it had set the tone the embassy had hoped to achieve. Finally, he questioned the cost benefit of provincial offices abroad.[62]

When I interviewed him in 1977, Harry R. Nellis, the Ontario representative in Tokyo, had toured all but two of Japan's prefectures in his search for Japanese technology to be licensed in Ontario and felt that his work in Japan was needed to create jobs in Ontario and that it could not be done by the embassy, which represents all of Canada. Ninety-five Japanese licenses had gone to Ontario in 1976, and scores of Ontario manufacturers had been put in touch with Japanese businesses or had been helped to establish agencies in Japan.[63]

There was a slight recovery of economic momentum in Canada-Japan trade during 1976, though the recession continued in Japan. Two-way trade rose to the unprecedented level of $3.9 billion, though much of the increase over the previous year was nominal and due to inflation. Japan, meanwhile, had become Canada's largest market for agricultural products. During 1976 more than $845 million worth of Canadian agricultural and fishery products were sold to Japan, comprising some 40 percent of the total Canadian exports.[64]

When interviewed in 1977, Counsellor (Commercial) William R. Parkinson, of the Canadian embassy in Tokyo, noted the rapid increase in the percentage of agricultural products, from 30 percent to 40 percent of Canadian exports since the early 1970s. He saw room for further expansion in such areas as processed foods, marine products, beer and liquors, cattle hides, and apples.[65]

There continued to be some limitations on Canada's agricultural exports to Japan, including Japan's import quotas on beef and health and sanitary requirements that effectively excluded Canadian apples and cherries. Japanese government regulations will continue to protect Japan's domestic producers for political reasons as well as the government's desire not to permit Japan to become excessively dependent on foreign food imports.[66]

The Japan-Canada Parliamentarians' League was established in Tokyo during March 1976, and 150 Diet members from all political parties joined this association for the cultivation of relations between the two parliaments. In April a delegation of seven Canadian parliamentarians, led by Speaker of the Senate Renaude Lapointe and Speaker of the House of Commons James A. Jerome and including Edward Broadbent, leader of the New Democratic Party, visited Japan at the invitation of the speakers of both houses of the Japanese National Diet.[67] Three months later Kenzo Kohno, president of the House of Councillors, paid a return visit to Ottawa and Montreal.

With the increase of business activity by Canadians in Japan during the early 1970s, an increasing number of Canadian corporations established branch offices in Japan and a number of Canadians took up residence in Japan to pursue private business interests. After consultation with interested officials in the Canadian embassy, this led in February 1976 to the establishment of the Canadian Businessmen's Association in Japan (CBAJ), with an initial corporate membership of twenty-seven and forty-one individual and special members, including the embassy's commercial officers. The CBAJ hoped to initiate a number of activities helpful to Canadian businessmen in their work in Japan.[68]

The annual policy planning talks between Gaimusho officials and their counterparts in the DEA were held in May in Tokyo. Consultations on UN questions were continued in New York and provided an opportunity for the SSEA to meet his Japanese counterpart, Zentaro Kasaka, for a review of problems of mutual interest. Prime Minister Trudeau, meanwhile, had a chance to meet Japan's new prime minister, Miki, on June 27 and 28 at the summit meeting of heads of state of the industrialized democracies (United States, United Kingdom, West Germany, France, Japan, Canada, and Italy) in Puerto Rico, where they discussed multilateral economic problems. A state visit to Japan by Trudeau was scheduled for October 1976. Consultation on a cultural agreement and a revision of the existing agreement on commerce was under way.

In Japan public disclosure of bribes given by executives of the Lockheed Aircraft Corporation to a number of "high government officials" deeply troubled the ruling LDP. Prime Minister Miki vowed to investigate all allegations and punish wrongdoing by any government official. In August 1976 former Prime Minister Tanaka was arrested and indicted as the recipient of a $1.67 million bribe from Lockheed. This brought about fighting among LDP leaders and a call for Miki's resignation.

A state visit by Prime Minister Trudeau right in the middle of a political crisis was risky, but Ottawa decided, with Tokyo's concurrence, to go ahead with the visit. Since the "broadening and deepening" of the Japanese-Canadian relationship was proceeding apace, to delay the visit might have seriously impeded the momentum of the process.

The Canadian studies program in Japan was under way, with courses taught at Tsukuba and Keiō Universities. Canadian books were being translated into Japanese for use in the program, and thousands of Canadian books were being donated to major libraries. The number of Canadian government scholarships for Japanese students to study in Canada were being virtually doubled every year after 1973. The National Research Council of Canada was granting additional fellowships every year to Japanese scientists. On May 22, 1975, the National Research Council and the Japan Society for the Promotion of Science signed an agreement on scientific cooperation providing for the exchange of scientists, for joint research projects, and for joint seminars on scientific topics; this agreement entered into force in April 1976.[69] At the same time, there had been an accelerating pace of cultural and athletic exchanges.

Starting in October 1975 a Japanese-language publication called *Bulletin Canada* was issued by the Canadian embassy, with an initial circulation of ten thousand copies every two months. There was a significant acceleration of media relations through the initiation of a regular flow of background papers, photographs, slides, and films to a growing number of media organizations. Japanese media representatives were invited to Canada by the DEA to cover such events as the Olympic Games and the Habitat Conference in Vancouver. The Canadian embassy's language officers were made available for lectures on Canada to Japanese audiences. A Canadian Press newsprinter was installed in the embassy to improve the embassy's ability to supply information on current events in Canada. The embassy's film library acquired some seven hundred films about Canada, forty of them dubbed in Japanese, some two hundred per month of which were being lent to various Japanese groups. An exhibit entitled "Stones of History," on the Canadian houses of Parliament, was shown all over Japan.

This media, cultural, educational, and public affairs "blitz" was coupled with increased political consultations at all levels in Tokyo by diplomats with Ministry of Foreign Affairs officials, as well as by Canadian diplomats with officials in other capitals, to develop the habit of exchanging views on matters of mutual interest, including exchanges of documents containing analyses by Canadian researchers on political affairs in various parts of the world. There was also a stepping up of Japanese language training of Canadian embassy personnel, with seven embassy officers taking intensive Japanese language courses. There were also plans to build an elaborate new embassy chancery and cultural and trade center, but these were frequently postponed for financial reasons and eventually shelved.[70]

Prime Minister Trudeau's state visit to Japan October 20–26, 1976, was to celebrate the flowering of the Canada-Japan relationship by the symbolic signing of the Framework for Economic Cooperation and the Canada-Japan Cultural Agreement. During his week-long visit to Japan, Trudeau had lengthy discussions with both Prime Minister Miki and Miki's successor-to-be, Deputy Premier Fukuda. Immediately after his arrival, Trudeau paid an official visit to their Imperial Majesties the Emperor and Empress of Japan. The prime minister also spoke to Keidanren, Japan's top business association, and addressed the students of Keiō University to symbolize the initiation of the Canadian Studies Program at that university, which awarded him an honorary degree.

The Framework for Economic Cooperation (the Japanese quite understandably insisted it should not be called an agreement) that Prime Minister Trudeau and Prime Minister Miki signed on October 21, 1976, is a document expressing the intention of both governments to promote friendly mutual cooperation in trade. It expresses their desire to reduce obstacles to trade, to diversity their commercial exchanges, to work under the GATT, to eliminate supply and access problems, to promote industrial cooperation and joint ventures, to explore fish product cooperation, and to exchange information. The only concrete new commitment in what is basically a public relations document established a joint committee to promote and keep under review economic cooperation activities between Canada and Japan, with the proviso that the committee would normally meet once a year.

The second document to come out of the Trudeau visit was the cultural agreement, which speaks of the common desire of the Canadian and Japanese governments to cooperate in the fields of culture and education. Canada and Japan commit themselves to encouraging the exchange of scholars, teachers, researchers, students, artists, and scientists, as well as fostering cooperation among the relevant institutions. Efforts are to be made to provide scholarships, professorial chairs, and language courses; to grant equivalence for academic purposes and access to cultural establishments; to provide books, radio programs, films, art exhibitions, lectures, concerts, festivals, translations of major books, youth and youth organization exchanges, and exchanges of press, radio, and television personnel; to promote tourism, and to consult on progress in achieving all of these aims. The agreement was subject to ratification and was to remain in force for five years. It was signed by Ambassador Rankin and Japan's foreign minister, Kosaka, on October 26, 1976, in the presence of Prime Minister Trudeau.

Both of the above documents are attempts to create a closer relationship and greater mutual accommodation and understanding by means of public exhortation. While their direct or binding effect on the economic and cultural relationship is unlikely to be earth shattering, they do provide statements that can guide future policy and serve as the basis for funding, particularly in the area of cultural and educational exchange. The resource stringencies in the educational sector and in government expenditures in Canada since the late 1970s are, however, likely to inhibit the implementation of some of the provisions. The instruments of ratification of the cultural agreement were exchanged in Ottawa on November 16, 1977, by Ambassador Nara and SSEA Donald Jamieson.[71] No ratification was required, since the economic document was not in fact a treaty, being rather in the nature of a voluntary declaration, not binding on either party, but the language used created certain expectations and implied a moral obligation of both governments to act in the spirit of its text.

There can be no doubt that Prime Minister Trudeau scored a personal success with Prime Minister Miki and with many of the other people attending his press conferences, banquets, and other personal appearances during his visit. His highly intelligent remarks and the grace, style, and wit he displayed made a most favorable impression. Speaking to the press he said:

Even more than the breadth of the North Pacific, . . . our most significant barrier today is indifference. So long as we fail, in each of our countries, to understand the benefits of an increased community, so do we diminish our own potential. . . . We in Canada, and you in Japan, have looked at one another for a long time, . . . but often with more polite curiosity than informed interest.

Noting that Japan had become Canada's second largest trading partner, he also stressed the complementarity of the two economies and the important things the two countries have in common, such as the necessity of protecting their distinctive identities from nearby giant powers, their decision not to produce nuclear weapons, and their efforts to aid the less developed countries. He finally made the point that Canada and Japan have a great deal to offer each other, in economics, in technology, in diplomacy, and in the unique political position each enjoys in its own sphere.[72]

At a banquet in honor of Prime Minister Miki on October 25, 1976, Prime Minister Trudeau spoke of the Japanese Canadians. His remarks unleashed a chorus of criticism in Canada to the effect that Trudeau should not have "apologized" to the Japanese for Canadian actions during World War II. What he did say in part reads as follows:

I wish I could say Prime Minister, that the many Japanese who followed the first settler to Canada were made welcome and were recognized for the hard-working law-abiding people they were. I cannot, for the record of intolerance in Pacific Canada in the decades around the turn of the century was not a proud one. No more exemplary was the decision taken by the Federal Government in the heat and fright of World War II to evacuate Japanese-Canadians inland from coastal communities and to deprive so many of their civil rights. In the past 30 years, however, the record has been a much happier one. In that period Nisei have been accepted with enthusiasm into Canadian communities and have demonstrated again and again their talents and their skills. In the highest ranks of business, academia and the public service are found persons with Japanese names. A number of them are so well known as to be virtual national celebrities. . . .

You give me the opportunity to thank Japan, on behalf of all Canadians, for the contribution made to Canada by men and women of Japanese origin who have shown through their courage, their tenacity, their industry, and their skills what gifted Canadians they are. Their contribution to Canada is out of all proportion to their numbers and we are grateful to them for their many qualities. . . .

Today Nisei are valued members of the Canadian community.[73]

It can be argued that "benign neglect" would have been a better way to deal with this subject. Perhaps so, but there is merit also in soberly stating the truth, as one sees it, in the hope that people may yet learn to benefit from historical experience.

The twenty-four-point joint communiqué issued by the two prime ministers on October 26, 1976, in Tokyo cited all the major points of mutual interest, such as bilateral cooperation and the extent of mutual consultations, and ended with an invitation to Prime Minister Miki to visit Canada in the future.

Prime Minister Trudeau's state visit to Japan marked a climactic high point in the Canada-Japan relationship during the postwar era. Trade had reached almost $4 billion, a level only nominally exceed in 1977 (with $4.3 billion). With the signing of the framework and the cultural agreement, all that government could really do to promote the relationship by exhortation had now been done. Mutual consultations between ministers and officials of both countries were now regularly occurring in dozens of forums in Japan, Canada, and other locations all over the world. The ambitious public affairs program of the DEA, carried out by the embassy in Tokyo, was reaching an increasing audience of influential Japanese, and Canada's image was indeed very high in Japan. The "broadening and deepening" exercise conceived by the Trudeau administration had gone about as far as it could go, and it was now a matter of carrying on with the established approaches.

An election was called in Japan by Prime Minister Miki for December 5, 1976, and the results barely enabled the LDP to retain control of the House of Representatives. Miki assumed responsibility for his party's setback and resigned a few days later. By Christmas Day 1976 Deputy Prime Minister Fukuda had succeeded Miki.

Of greater importance to Canada-Japan relations was the dispatch on October 24, 1976, of a high-powered Japanese economic mission to Canada, headed by Hisao Makita, president of Nippon Kokan Steel Company, Eiichi Hashimoto, chairman of the board of directors of Mitsui and Company, who toured various centers in Canada for twelve days and after their return to Japan wrote a profoundly critical report on Canada, which was widely distributed in Japan. The Makita Report, as it came to be known, included a number of negative findings on Canadian business, labor, management, efficiency, productivity, policy conflicts, and future potential, which saddled Canada with an image it will take years of determined efforts and high achievements to overcome. When during the last week of September 1977 the Ontario government sent an economic mission to Japan, headed by Premier William Davis, Hashimoto had not forgotten his negative conclusions from a year earlier and lectured Premier Davis on Canada's and Ontario's shortcomings. Canada, he said, was not a good place to invest because of labor disputes, timid businessmen, high taxes, stringent environmental policies, and its relatively small market for manufactured goods.

> Our biggest complaint is the labour problem. Strikes, high wages, and lack of productivity continue to make Ontario and Canada unattractive investment propositions for the Japanese. Fundamentally the first thing to do is to make a profit. We are not a charity.[74]

He said high taxes in Canada made the United States a much more attractive area for investment and for the establishment of branch plant companies. He claimed that because of taxes a company in Canada has to gross 150 percent more than one in the United States to make some profit. Hashimoto said the United States is also more attractive to Japanese investors than Canada because, particularly in the southern states, labor is cheaper and the environmental restrictions on companies are not as stringent. Hashimoto said the major area of interest for Japanese investors in Canada is British Columbia because it is relatively close to Japan. He did not expect investment to go into central Canada for some time.[75]

Another unfortunate consequence of Makita's negative view of the Canadian economy and of the world economic recession of the middle and later 1970s was his company's decision, announced toward the end of 1977, to shelve its plans for the building of a Nippon Kokan branch plant steel mill in British Columbia. Although overall Japanese investment in Canada rose to the $500 million level in 1977, the very hastiness with which some of these investments were made, shortly after the oil crisis, led to several spectacular economic failures, which tended to reinforce the image of Canada as a bad place to invest. The biggest of these was the investment of $250 million made by Ataka Trading Company in John Shaheen's now-bankrupt oil refinery in Come-By-Chance, Newfoundland. In order to survive that disaster, Ataka Trading had to be merged with C. Itoh and Company. Other similar failures involved the Canadian Motor Industries Automobile Assembly Plant (Toyota) in Point Edward, Nova Scotia, which after operating at a loss for several years closed at the end of 1975. There was also Cirtex Knitting in New Brunswick, which never opened because of labor union problems, and Japan Alberta Oil Mill Company, a rapeseed crushing plant built jointly by C. Itoh and Company and the Alberta Wheat Pool, which was rendered uneconomical before it even opened when freight rates were suddenly changed on the transport of oil as opposed to rapeseed. In spite of these horror stories, more than 200 other Canadian-Japanese joint ventures have survived and appear to be making money.

Another negative development, from the Japanese point of view, was the announcement in January 1977 that Canada was suspending the shipment of uranium (enriched in the United States) for use in Japan's nuclear electricity generating plants, pending the negotiation of a new nuclear safeguards agreement between Ottawa and Tokyo. The Japanese were baffled that the Canadian government, which had been begging Japan for years to buy Canada's CANDU reactors, would suddenly choose to be difficult about selling the uranium without which Japan's nuclear generating capacity might be seriously jeopardized and without which CANDU simply does not work. The reasons were largely political and involved India's action in misusing Canada's technology to produce a nuclear explosion in 1974 and Canada's strong international commitment to the cause of nuclear nonproliferation. The negotiations for the new nuclear safeguards agreement dragged on for just over a year, until January 26, 1978, when a protocol to the existing Nuclear Cooperation Agreement between Canada and Japan (1959) was signed by SSEA Jamieson and Japan's foreign minister, Sunao Sonoda, in Tokyo. In the protocol Japan agreed to all the additional safeguards requested by Ottawa and the Canadian government announced that uranium shipments from Canada to Japan would be resumed immediately, thus removing a major irritant in the bilateral relations.[76]

Ambassador Nara was recalled to Japan in July 1978 and was replaced on August 18, 1978, by Ambassador Michiaki Suma, 59, like most of his predecessors a graduate of the faculty of law at the University of Tokyo and a career Gaimusho official, who had served as ambassador in Tanzania and Malaysia. When interviewed in Ottawa on November 3, 1978, Ambassador Suma observed that there were no longer any great bilateral problems and that it was now a very quiet and happy time in Japanese-Canadian relations. Suma noted that Canadian press reporting on Japan was neither adequate nor accurate and attributed this to the fact that there was not a single Canadian correspondent in Japan. He expressed hope that Canada would be prepared to share its ample resources of uranium, coal, oil, and tar sands with Japan and mentioned Japanese cooperation in the development of the tar sands oil resources and the oil and natural gas explorations in the Arctic area. On the ministerial conferences, Suma said: "I believe that kind of formal conference format has really become unnecessary." When anything important comes up, ministers can commute in either direction.

It was only in the area of Japanese investment in Canada that Ambassador Suma perceived problems.

> Japan now has a very excellent and no longer cheap established labor force, but when we come here, that is not the case—the quality of the labor force is inferior, lacking in diligence and efficiency, and therefore the quality of products is affected. In Japan, when you subcontract, you get precisely what you order and on schedule. But that is not the way here, so that if you think of anything beyond mere assembly, you cannot expect the kind of quality that you get in goods manufactured in Japan. They simply don't make things well. Then there is the problem of labor, with the constant strikes. As a result the Japanese businessman will hesitate. He'll worry about the quality of goods produced, about the labor problems and

about meeting the agreed delivery dates—delivering goods when promised. . . . So that leaves us with tremendous problems. One might think that since we are both advanced countries, things will go smoothly between us, but that is simply not so.[77]

The Makitas, the Hashimotos, and the Sumas are all reading Canada the same lesson, and they appear to believe what they are saying, unless these statements are all part of a coordinated campaign to provide a rationale for Japan to avoid investing in Canada or buying Canadian manufactured goods. If Canada wants to play Japan's game, the game of trade in manufactured goods—and Canada does keep telling Japan that this is what it wants to do—Canadians will simply have to get up a little earlier in the morning and work a little harder. Otherwise they will remain purveyors of "rocks and logs" and Japan will regard Canada as a mere resource supplier.

What Ambassador Suma did not say, though he surely knew it, is that Canadians should learn a few things from the Japanese, such as how to maintain labor peace, industrial discipline, quality control, productivity, and unity of purpose and action on a national scale. Pride is part of the answer—personal pride, pride of workmanship, national pride, company pride. When Canada develops a greater degree of those qualities, it will make a better industrial partner for the Japanese and the relationship will thrive as never before.

It is noteworthy, however, that apart from the trade composition aspect, Canadian-Japanese relations have never been better or closer nor the trade figures higher than as the relationship entered its fiftieth year in 1978. The fact that this is recognized in both countries and that both governments fully appreciate the mutual benefits of their unprecedented economic and political cooperation augurs well for the second half-century of the diplomatic history of Canada and Japan.

NOTES

1. Canada, DEA, *Statements and Speeches*, no. 68/17, May 29, 1968, p. 3.
2. Mitchell Sharp, *Foreign Policy for Canadians.*

3. Sharp, *Foreign Policy for Canadians*, booklet 1, p. 39.

4. Ibid., booklet 5 (Pacific), p. 11.

5. Canada, Department of Defence, *White Paper on Defence*, p. 1.

6. *International Journal* 26, no. 1: 19.

7. Sharp, *Foreign Policy for Canadians*, booklet 5 (Pacific), pp. 16, 22, 23.

8. Tape-recorded interview with Mitchell Sharp, Ottawa, July 25, 1978.

9. *External Affairs* 21, no. 5 (1969): 200-203; 21, no. 7 (1969): 274-75.

10. *External Affairs* 21, no. 5 (1969): 194-99.

11. *External Affairs* 21, no. 6 (1969): 235-42.

12. Tape-recorded interview with Shinichi Kondo, Tokyo, April 22, 1977.

13. *External Affairs* 20, no. 3 (1968): 145-46.

14. Canada, Office of the Prime Minister, Transcript of the prime minister's remarks on Canada Day, Osaka, Japan, May 28, 1970.

15. The black belt is the symbol worn by those holding a degree of "dan" (ichi-dan, ni-dan, sandan, etc.), which signifies attainment of high skill.

16. Senior assistant deputy minister, Department of Trade and Commerce.

17. Clerk of the Privy Council and secretary to the cabinet.

18. Tape-recorded interview with Herbert O. Moran, Tequesta, Fla., December 13, 1977.

19. *Globe and Mail*, December 18, 1970, pp. B2-B3.

20. *Financial Post*, Toronto, June 12, 1971, p. 10.

21. *External Affairs* 23, no. 10 (1971): 384-88.

22. Japan Trade Center, *100 Years of Trade and Commerce Between Canada and Japan*, pp. 18-19.

23. Interview with Jean-Luc Pepin, Ottawa, July 24, 1978.

24. *Financial Post*, February 6, 1972, p. 5.

25. Keith A. J. Hay, "Canada's Economic Ties with Japan," in Norman Hillmer, ed., *A Foremost Nation*, p. 284.

26. Keith A. J. Hay, *Canada-Japan: The Export Import Picture*, p. 25. The reference to "optimistic" accounts recognizes that some economists classify a greater number of goods as "manufactured" or "end" products than do others. The same is true of the concept of "processed" goods. Is dressed pork "processed," or does it have to become canned ham before earning that classification?

27. "The Canada-Japan Trade Partnership," an address by Shinichi Kondo, Ambassador of Japan, to the Advertising and Sales Executive Club of Montreal, Queen Elizabeth Hotel, Montreal, Quebec, April 12, 1972. See also P. G. Campbell, "Japan Looks Beyond Its Borders," *Canada Commerce* (Canada, Department of Industry, Trade and Commerce) 136, no. 2 (1972): 8.

28. Canada, House of Commons, *Debates*, March 20, 1972, pp. 947–48.

29. Canada, Department of Industry, Trade and Commerce, Report of the International Defence Programmes Branch mission to Japan, November 25–December 8, 1972, pp. 2–6.

30. *Globe and Mail*, Toronto, February 14, 1972, p. S1.

31. Canada, Standing Senate Committee on Foreign Affairs, *Report on Canadian Relations with the Countries of the Pacific Region*, pp. 45–47.

32. Ibid., p. 6, testimony of John Howes, Associate Professor of History, University of British Columbia, March 11, 1971.

33. Ibid., p. 51.

34. Ibid., pp. 19–20.

35. Mitchell Sharp, "Canada-U.S. Relations: Options for the Future," *International Perspectives*, special issue, autumn 1972, p. 13.

36. *Globe and Mail*, October 18, 1972, p. 2.

37. Address by Bruce I. Rankin, Empire Club of Toronto, March 10, 1977, Canada, DEA, *Statements and Speeches*, no. 77/2, p. 7.

38. The DISC regulations allow a U.S. corporation to set up a special export subsidiary, the profits of which are partially exempt from tax. In Canada DISC was regarded as a "beggar thy neighbor" policy.

39. Tape-recorded interview with Derek Burney, Ottawa, November 18, 1977. In August 1978 Burney became Canadian ambassador to the ROK.

40. Tape-recorded interview with Akira Nishiyama, Tokyo, May 28, 1977. Nishiyama had meanwhile become ambassador to South Korea.

41. Tape-recorded interview with Ross Campbell, Ottawa, March 18, 1977.

42. Report by the Canadian Delegation on the First Meeting of the Canada-Japan Sub-committee on Mineral and Energy Policy in Vancouver, September 14–15, 1972, DEAF, 31-1-1-JPN, 48.

43. *Mainichi Daily News*, Tokyo, September 9, 1973, p. 1; September 11, 1973, p. 1.

44. *Globe and Mail*, Feb. 11, 1974.

45. Ivan Head, "Canada's Pacific Perspective," *Pacific Community* 6, no. 1 (1974): 16–19.

46. *Toronto Star*, April 13, 1974, p. C19.

47. *Mainichi Daily News*, Tokyo, March 6, 1974, p. 6.

48. *Financial Post*, March 30, 1974, report on Quebec, p. Q23.

49. Tape-recorded interview with Normand Bernier, Tokyo, June 3, 1977.

50. Kakuei Tanaka, *Building a New Japan*.

51. The oil price increased by 400 percent in one year.

52. Canada, Office of the Prime Minister, press release, Joint Communique Between Prime Minister Kakuei Tanaka and Prime Minister Pierre Elliott Trudeau, Ottawa, September 24, 1974, p. 1.

53. Ibid., pp. 2–6.

54. *Toronto Star*, September 26, 1974, pp. 1, 6.

55. Tape-recorded interview with Kakuei Tanaka, May 30, 1977.

56. Tape-recorded interview with Yasuhiko Nara, Ottawa, March 3, 1977.

57. Canada, DEA, Joint Communique of the Seventh Meeting of the Canada-Japan Ministerial Committee, June 24, 1975, pp. 1–5.

58. "Towards a New Japan-Canada Partnership," speech by SSEA Allan J. MacEachen to the Japanese Press Club, Tokyo, June 25, 1975.

59. Speech by SSEA MacEachen to the Alberta Liberal Association, Calgary, November 30, 1975.

60. Canada, DEA, *Annual Review*, 1975, p. 11.

61. "Curtain has risen on a new era in Japan-Canada relations," panel discussion in *Kokusai Keizai* (International Economy) 12, no. 8 (1975), special issue on Canada, Canadian embassy translation.

62. Tape-recorded interview with Bruce I. Rankin, Tokyo, May 3, 1977.

63. Tape-recorded interview with Harry R. Nellis, Tokyo, May 19, 1977.

64. Canada, Ministry of Supply and Services, *Exports by Country*, January to December 1976, Statistics Canada, Ottawa, 65–003.

65. Tape-recorded interview with William R. Parkinson, Counsellor (Commercial), Canadian Embassy, Tokyo, May 13, 1977.

66. Keith A. J. Hay, *Canadian Agriculture and Japan*, pp. 3–26.

67. English press release, Secretariat, House of Representatives, Japanese National Diet, April 15, 1976, pp. 1–3.

68. Canadian Businessmen's Association in Japan, Canada, DEA, Files, 37-16-1-JPN, David J. S. Winfield, Counsellor (Commercial), to Chief, DEA, Pacific Division, May 24, 1976, pp. 1–3.

69. Canada, DEA, Files, 67-11-1-JPN, press release, Signing of Japan/Canada Scientific Cooperation Agreement, May 22, 1975.

70. Data on the Canadian public affairs program in Japan (media, culture, education, and so on) were supplied by Jack Derksen, first secretary, Canadian embassy, in a tape-recorded interview, Tokyo, June 9, 1977.

71. Canada, DEA, Exchange of instruments of ratification of the Canada/Japan cultural agreement, Communique no. 103, November 16, 1977.

72. Canada, Office of the Prime Minister, press release, October 26, 1976, notes for remarks by the prime minister to the Japan National Press Club.

73. Canada, Office of the Prime Minister, press release, notes for the prime minister's remarks at dinner in honor of Prime Minister Miki, Tokyo, October 25, 1976.

74. *Toronto Star*, September 27, 1977, pp. A1, A3.

75. Ibid., p. A3.

76. Canada, DEA, Conclusion of a Nuclear Agreement Between Canada and Japan, Communique No. 10, January 26, 1978.

77. Tape-recorded interview with Michiaki Suma, Ottawa, November 3, 1978.

6

Conclusions and Projections

Canada-Japan relations in the postwar period can be regarded to have been successful and beneficial for both countries. The quick reestablishment of normal relations and the political rapport developed after 1952 attest to the diligence and skill of both Canadian and Japanese diplomats, as the wounds of war were healed and a web of trade and friendship took their place.

During the 1950s Canada was most helpful to Japan in smoothing its reentry into the community of democratic nations associated with the United Nations, NATO, and the British Commonwealth. The mutual confidence and good will established in those years has proved to be a durable feature of the relationship.

The "broadening and deepening" exercise initiated by Canada in pursuit of the "third option" since the early 1970s has led to an unprecedented pattern of close consultation at virtually every level of both societies. Consequently, mutual understanding and cooperation have flourished as never before, particularly between the respective governmental, bureaucratic, and commercial elites. Along with this greater intimacy, however, some frictions have developed as the two countries became aware of one another's virtues and weaknesses. Thus Japan remains unwilling to regard Canada as anything more than a resource hinterland of the United States and is as yet not disposed to consider Canada as a major potential supplier of manufactured and processed goods for the Japanese market, nor as a sophisticated industrial nation, distinct and separate from the United States. The fact that so many major industries in Canada are owned or controlled by U.S. parent companies largely accounts for Japan's attitude in this area.

At the same time, Canada has been unable to attract Japanese capital investment in Canadian manufacturing and processing industries at levels anticipated in the early 1970s. As of 1982, more than $1 billion has been invested in Canada by Japanese companies, largely in the resource development sector, while approximately $100 million has been invested in Japan by Canadian companies.[1] The relatively modest level of Japanese investment in Canada is partly attributable to the recession of the middle 1970s, which reduced Japanese investment abroad. While Canada's FIRA has not created legal impediments to Japanese investment, it is nevertheless perceived as a barrier by many Japanese businessmen, but in my judgment Canada's labor unrest and low rates of productivity, widely advertised by the Makita Report, have been more significant factors in discouraging investment. Finally, Japanese policy is to invest in resource development only where firm commitments are given that the resources will be made available for export to Japan.

In a larger sense, Japanese investment in Canada appears to have been strongly affected by what could be called the "rhythm" and the "mood" of the relationship, which were positive and exuberant in the late 1960s and early 1970s but which have become somewhat more negative, cautious and more keenly calculating since then. Expo '67 and Canada's centennial celebrations projected Canada forcefully and favorably onto the international scene. Japan, in the process of diversifying its international involvements, discovered Canada and its tremendous potential at that time.

During the decade after 1968 the Trudeau administration played a vital if ambivalent role in the development of the Canada-Japan relationship. The personal efforts of Prime Minister Trudeau; his adviser Ivan Head; and Minister of Industry, Trade, and Commerce Pepin brought about unprecedentedly close cooperation and awakened both Canadians and Japanese to the fact that an exclusively commercial relationship was undesirable.

In regard to the investment picture, I believe that Hay's statement is the most accurate analysis:

> There has been a distinct lull in Japanese investment interest in Canada since 1974. At first, this seemed to be directly related to Japan's adverse balance-of-payments situation. But Japan did invest considerable sums overseas in 1975 and 1976. It was not a lack of capital, but lack of confidence that caused the Japanese to shrink from investment in Canada.
>
> There are several factors that Japan weighs negatively in evaluating the Canadian investment climate: disproportionate public sector spending, the uncertainties caused by wage and price controls; economic nationalism symbolized by the Foreign Investment Review Agency (FIRA); apparent government uncertainty about an energy development policy; tax jurisdiction conflicts, and in some provinces, public ownership policies which afflict resource developments; high labour costs; poor industrial relations; and most recently, uncertainty about Canadian political unity.[2]

In speaking of Canada's failure to export a significant volume of manufactured or finished goods to Japan, it should be kept in mind that many Canadian manufacturing companies, such as Ford Motor Company of Canada, General Motors of Canada, Canadian General Electric Company, and Westinghouse Canada, are branch plants of U.S. parent companies, which will naturally give first priority on export orders to goods originating in their U.S. factories. Conversely, if Japan wishes to buy a U.S. product, it will order in the United States, not in Canada.

The major problem in the development of the Canada-Japan relationship during the early Trudeau years was that Japan's political and economic status was rapidly rising at the same time that Canada's political and economic influence in the world was entering a prolonged decline. The Japanese have a high regard for success and victory, and they tend to be disdainful of failures and losers; this makes it important that Canada be perceived as successful. The Trudeau administration retrenched Canada's military commitments in NATO and elsewhere, thereby limiting Canada's strategic and political influence on the international scene.

Neither the Canadian public nor the Canadian press or business circles appeared overly interested in Japan, in spite of the fact that the growth of the Canada-Japan trade was truly phenomenal during the early 1970s. In the decade from 1972 to 1981 the two-way trade quadrupled, from $2 billion to almost $8 billion, which is impressive even when inflation is taken into account. These trade figures reflect Japan's ever-growing appetite for Canada's "rocks and logs" and other resources and foods. Even as the resource trade flourished, Canada's balance-of-payments surplus averaged $1 billion each year from 1973 through 1981. Fortunate though these statistics are, Canadian officials remain dissatisfied, because the percentage of finished manufactured goods exported to Japan since 1973 has averaged only 2.3 percent annually, with no sign that this trade pattern is likely to change. Those most knowledgeable in the field of Canada-Japan trade[3] share my view that while modest increases in the resource trade will continue, no substantial change in the trading pattern can be expected in the near future. This is entirely acceptable to Japan, but some Canadians will surely continue to complain about it. The very substantial growth of Japanese automobile exports to Canada during 1980 and 1981 (close to 200,000 passenger vehicles annually, constituting a market share of 22 percent or more), coinciding as they do with serious unemployment in the Canadian and U.S. automobile industries, will also create serious problems for Canada-Japan trade relations. A trade war could be provoked if Japan's automobile exporters do not agree to the usual voluntary export restraints. It appears likely that bilateral consultations can cope with this kind of perennially recurring trade friction by the usual "orderly marketing" formula.

While I do not wish to dwell on the most unfortunate episode in Canada-Japan relations, my own conclusions on the evacuation of Japanese Canadians in 1942 are that what made the evacuation inevitable was not the security threat posed by Japanese Canadians but the strong anti-Japanese feelings harbored by a small group of white people in British Columbia, who saw this as a chance to displace the Orientals from British Columbia once and for all. Most immediately to blame were a small number of liberal politicians, who threatened that if the federal government did not act there might be rioting or lynchings of Japanese Canadians as well as a collapse of support for the Liberal party.

Every Japanese Canadian who went through this experience was either scarred or traumatized by it for life. While people were not deliberately mistreated, they suffered the frustration of losing their liberty and being treated as "enemy aliens" although most of them were Canadian citizens.

The Japanese Canadians are very well off today and continue to improve their image, their performance, and their importance to Canada. Intermarriage with Caucasians, the declining birthrate, the tendency toward Canadian homogenization, and the decline of immigration from Japan will probably mean that the Japanese-Canadian population will hover around fifty thousand and may decline before the end of the century. There will probably always be some Canadians who will have racist attitudes, but the phenomenon is declining.

If there is serious economic or political trouble with Japan again, racism might reemerge, but a repetition of 1942 is inconceivable to me. The history of the evacuation should be taught to every Canadian as an example of the kind of injustice and inequity that should not be permitted to recur in an open society committed to constitutional government. Japanese Canadians should feel free to take pride not only in who they are but in Japanese culture, the Japanese language, and the history of their forefathers. The growth of trade between Canada and Japan in the years to come will provide employment and business opportunities for Japanese Canadians who prepare themselves properly. They can play a vital role in helping this important relationship to prosper and in educating the rest of Canada toward greater understanding of Japan and a keener appreciation of what the two countries mean to each other.

The final balance sheet of the Trudeau years is not yet in, but a number of conclusions can be ventured in the spring of 1982. Many of the major aims of the Trudeau government with regard to Canada-Japan relations appear to have been achieved, but others have not and may well have to be abandoned as hopeless causes, because in all essential aspects of the relationship Japan is very much in control and appears unlikely to change its policies. The "third option" has clearly failed, and Canada is back to closer relations with the United States. The attempt to restructure the trade pattern has totally failed, and while Canadian officials still yearn to sell CANDU reactors and Dash 7 STOL aircraft, this is wishful thinking.

By the conclusion of the revised Bilateral Atomic Energy Agreement with Japan on January 26, 1978, Canada has succeeded in establishing the controls she had been seeking over enrichment, reprocessing, and stockpiling of Canadian-supplied natural uranium and the transfer of nuclear information on the CANDU reactor to third countries. Unfortunately, this agreement was achieved only after Canada had placed an embargo on uranium shipments to Japan during 1977, costing Canada both credibility and good will in Japan.

On April 28, 1978, Japan and Canada signed a bilateral agreement restricting Japan's fishing within the Canadian 200-mile zone. Japan, moreover, has had to agree to similar restrictions in other areas of the Pacific. Canada takes the view that such restrictions are necessary for conservation, but the Japanese suspect that they are being deliberately excluded from large areas of the Pacific fishery.

On the positive side, Canadian news items are now found frequently in the Japanese press and media. One Japanese major daily in Tokyo, *Nihon Keizai Shimbun*, maintains a regular staff correspondent in Toronto, who keeps the Japanese business world informed on what is going on in Canada. Meanwhile, the Canadian general public is not yet receptive to, nor indeed supplied with, much information on Japan. I consider it regrettable that Andrew Horvath can only place an occasional item with his employers, Southam Press, and remains the only Canadian "correspondent" in the capital city of Canada's second most important trading partner. The high cost of maintaining a full-time correspondent in Tokyo makes this understandable, but Canada as a whole loses out by being inadequately informed about what goes on in Japan.

The business communities in Canada and Japan have recently been linked by an organization called the Japan-Canada Businessmen's Conference, which has held meetings every spring since 1978, alternately in Japan and Canada. Headed by David M. Culver, president of Alcan Aluminum, and Makita, of Nippon Kokan Steel Company, the conference includes about 100 prominent business executives from both countries and institutionalizes an opportunity for the Canadian business elite to socialize with the Japanese business elite without diplomats and politicians from either country interfering in the process.

Much has been achieved during the last decade of Canada-Japan relations, but much more remains to be done. The future outlook for the relationship is excellent, and the connection has never been better or closer. Naturally there are problems, and there always will be, but these problems are manageable. When $8 billion worth of business is done without serious trouble between the partners, there is much to be thankful for. There is every reason to believe that the good relations will continue for the rest of the century and beyond.

The communication gap between the two countries and their peoples still finds them using each other for their respective commercial purposes without pursuing genuine intimacy and friendship, however. If people in Canada and Japan make the effort to learn more about each other and come to appreciate the importance of their interrelationship, this might lead to the formation of genuine friendship and neighborliness across the Pacific. I believe it is worthwhile to work toward that objective and hope that Canadians and Japanese will join in that common enterprise.

NOTES

1. The more than thirty Canadian companies with investments in Japan include Moore Corporation; Seagram Distilleries; Alcan; Inco; MacMillan Paper; Polysar International; Cominco; Brascan International; S. C. Johnson Co.; Isopol Chemicals; Council of Forest Industries, B.C.; Pizza Patio; EMCO Wheaton; Tottrup and Associates; Seabord Timber and Plywood; and Northwood Mills, plus more than a dozen other firms, including several of Canada's chartered banks, which have representative offices in Japan.

2. Keith A. J. Hay, "Friends or Acquaintances? Canada and Japan's Other Trading Partners in the Early 1980's," p. 26.

3. Tape-recorded interviews were conducted with Reid Morden, Counsellor Economic and Financial to the Canadian Embassy in Tokyo (May 1977); Brian A. Smith, Japan Desk Officer, Department of External Affairs, Ottawa (November 1977); N. Gregor Guthrie, Vice President, Canada-Japan Trade Council, Ottawa (October 1977); Col. Robert L. Houston, President, Canada-Japan Trade Council, Ottawa (December 1977); Frank Langdon, Professor of Political Science, University of British Columbia, Vancouver (May 1979); and W. W. Johnston, Japan Desk, Department of Industry, Trade and Commerce, Ottawa (November 1977 and July 1978).

APPENDIX

Statistical Tables

Table 5
Trade Between Canada and Japan, 1921–1940 (in millions of dollars)

Fiscal Year	Exports to Japan	Imports from Japan
1921	6.4	11.3
1922	14.8	8.2
1923	14.5	7.2
1924	26.9	6.3
1925	22.0	6.9
1926	34.6	9.5
1927	29.9	11.1
1928	32.9	12.5
1929	42.2	12.9
1930	30.4	12.5
1931	18.9	9.3
1932	16.5	5.9
1933	10.3	3.8
1934	13.8	3.3
1935	16.9	4.4
1936	14.8	3.4
1937	21.6	4.8
1938	26.6	5.7
1939	21.0	4.4
1940	26.0	5.0
Total	441.0	149.0

Source: Canada, Bureau of Statistics, *Canada Yearbook*, for the years given.

Table 6
Canadian Exports of Selected Metals to Japan, 1929-1939 (in dollars)

Metal	1929	1936	1937	1938	1939
Scrap Iron	96,345	324,876	673,530	643,317	565,201
Copper	44,323	23,258	167,262	1,300,473	2,383,122
Lead	3,278,464	2,149,993	3,976,269	2,864,947	2,672,322
Nickel	324,814	631,999	2,049,993	5,439,127	8,792,740
Zinc	1,429,459	789,885	1,091,693	1,294,188	1,273,662
Aluminum	—	1,967,078	1,947,847	4,777,464	7,801,052

Source: Canada, Bureau of Statistics, *Canada Yearbook*, for the years given.

Note: During this period Canada increased its scrap iron exports to Japan by 600 percent, its copper by 5,300 percent, and its nickel by 2,700 percent, while its zinc and lead exports remained steady. Aluminum exports increased by 400 percent in three years (1937-39). The annual average of exports exceeded $22 million, while the annual average of imports was $7.4 million. The highest year for exports ($42 million) and also for imports ($12.9 million) was 1929, while the lowest year for exports ($10.3 million) was 1933 and the lowest for imports ($3.3 million) was 1934.

Table 7
Canadian Trade Composition with Japan in Peace (1926) and War (1939)
(in millions of dollars)

1926 Exports		1926 Imports	
Wheat	16.3	Silk and silk products	5.7
Lead	4.2	Tea	.6
Wood pulp	2.2	Rice	.4
Zinc	1.6	China and pottery	.3
Fish	1.4	Oranges	.2
Logs	1.1	Brushes	.1
Planks and boards	.9	Buttons	.1
Aluminum	.8	Fish	.1
Shook	.8	Beans	.1
Timber	.8	Cotton fabrics	.09
Others	4.0	Others	1.5
Total	34.6	Total	9.5

1939 Exports		1939 Imports	
Nickel	8.7	Tea	.3
Aluminum	7.8	Flax, hemp, jute, and	
Lead	2.6	related products	.3
Copper	2.3	Oranges	.2
Asbestos	2.0	Canned tuna	.2
Zinc	1.2	Cotton fabrics	.2
Scrap iron	.5	China and pottery	.2
Wood pulp	.4	Silk	.1
Logs	.4	Rayon	.1
Hides and skins	.2	Toys	.1
Sea herring	.1	Cotton handkerchiefs	.1
Others	1.2	Electric lamps	.1
Total	28.1	Others	2.5
		Total	4.8

Source: Japan Trade Center, *100 Years of Trade and Commerce Between Canada and Japan*, pp. 9 and 10.

Table 8
Japanese Immigration to Canada, 1926–1942

Year	Number
1926	443
1927	511
1928	535
1929	180
1930	218
1931	174
1932	119
1933	106
1934	126
1935	70
1936	103
1937	146
1938	57
1939	44
1940	44
1941	4
1942	0

Source: Canada, Bureau of Statistics, *Canada Year-book*, for the years given.

Table 9
Japanese in Canada, 1901–1941

Year	Males in British Columbia	Females in British Columbia	Total in British Columbia	Total in the Rest of Canada	Total for All of Canada
1901	virtually all males		4,597	141	4,738
1911	virtually all males		8,587	434	9,021
1921	10,500	5,300[a]	15,006	862	15,868
1931	13,000 (58.7%)	9,200 (41.3%)	22,205	1,137	23,342
1941	12,426	9,670	22,096	1,053	23,149

Source: Canada, Bureau of Statistics, *Canada Yearbook*, for the years given.

[a]The dramatic increase in females reflects the arrival of picture brides during the twenties.

Table 10
Composition of Japanese Population in Canada, 1941

Category	Number	Percentage
Canadian born (all Canada)	13,687	59.1
Naturalized Canadian (all Canada)	3,694	16.0
Japanese nationals (all Canada)	5,768	24.9
Canadian born (British Columbia only)	13,309	60.2
Naturalized Canadian (British Columbia only)	3,223	14.6
Japanese nationals (British Columbia only)	5,564	25.2

Source: Canada, Bureau of Statistics, *Canada Yearbook*, for the years given.

Table 11
Canada-Japan Trade in the Postwar Era, 1946–1981 (in millions of dollars)

Year	Canadian Exports	Canadian Imports	Total Two-Way Trade
1946	1.0	.003	1.0
1947	.559	.350	.909
1948	8.0	3.1	11.1
1949	5.8	5.5	11.3
1950	20.5	12.0	32.5
1951	72.9	12.5	85.4
1952	102.6	13.1	115.7
1953	118.5	13.6	132.1
1954	96.4	19.1	115.5
1955	91.0	37.0	128.0
1956	127.8	60.8	188.6
1957	139.1	61.6	200.7
1958	105.0	70.2	175.2
1959	139.7	103.0	243.0
1960	178.8	110.0	290.0
1961	231.5	116.6	306.0
1962	214.5	125.3	339.8
1963	296.0	130.4	426.4
1964	330.2	174.3	506.0
1965	316.1	230.2	547.0
1966	393.8	253.0	648.0
1967	572.1	305.0	879.0
1968	606.1	360.0	968.0
1969	624.7	495.8	1,122.0
1970	810.1	581.7	1,395.0
1971	828.6	803.0	1,633.0
1972	964.7	1,071.0	2,035.7
1973	1,804.0	1,018.0	2,822.0
1974	2,219.7	1,423.0	3,646.6
1975	2,117.3	1,204.7	3,322.0
1976	2,388.0	1,525.6	3,913.0
1977	2,513.0	1,800.0	4,300.0
1978	3,051.2	2,268.4	5,319.6
1979	4,080.5	2,156.9	6,237.4
1980	4,370.5	2,792.1	7,162.6
1981	4,464.0	3,399.0	7,863.0

Source: Canada, Ministry of Supply and Services, Statistics Canada, *Trade of Canada: Exports and Imports.*

Table 12
Japanese Immigration to Canada, 1946–1979

Year	Number	Year	Number
1946	3	1963	171
1947	2	1964	140
1948	6	1965	188
1949	13	1966	500
1950	13	1967	858
1951	3	1968	628
1952	7	1969	698
1953	49	1970	785
1954	73	1971	815
1955	102	1972	718
1956	124	1973	1,105
1957	185	1974	810
1958	193	1975	635
1959	197	1976	498
1960	169	1977	412 (387)[a]
1961	114	1978	359
1962	141	1979	666 (576)

Source: Canada, Bureau of Statistics, *Canada Yearbook*, for the years given; and Ministry of Supply and Services, Statistics Canada.

Note: Total immigration from 1946 to 1977 was 10,327; the annual average for those years was 322.7. The peak immigration year, 1973, was also the postwar peak trade year; there have been only nominal increases in trade since then. The post-1973 decline coincides with the decline in the Canadian economy.

[a]Figures in parentheses are immigrants with Japanese citizenship; others are immigrants from Japan.

Table 13
Sister City Affiliations Between Canada and Japan, 1962–1982
(including towns, provinces, and wards)

City, Town, or Ward in Canada	City, Town, or Ward in Japan	Year of Affiliation
New Westminster, B.C.	Moriguchi, Osaka Prefecture	1962
Vancouver, B.C.	Yokohama, Kanagawa Prefecture	1965
Burnaby, B.C.	Kushiro, Hokkaido	1965
Dundas, Ont.	Kaga, Ishikawa Prefecture	1968
Prince Rupert, B.C.	Owase, Mie Prefecture	1968
Lindsay, Ont.	Nayoro, Hokkaido	1969
North Vancouver, B.C.	Chiba, Chiba Prefecture	1970
Winnipeg, Man.	Setagaya-Ku, Ward in Tokyo	1970
Jasper, Alta.	Hakone Town, Kanagawa Prefecture	1972
Richmond, B.C.	Wakayama, Wakayama Prefecture	1973
Penticton, B.C.	Ikeda-cho, Hokkaido	1975
Hamilton, Ont.	Fukuyama, Hiroshima Prefecture	1976
Banff, Alta.	Obama-cho, Nagasaki Prefecture	1976
Saskatoon, Sask.	Otaru, Hokkaido	1980
Sparwood, B.C.	Kamisunakawa Town, Hokkaido	1980
Alberta Province	Hokkaido	1980
Taber, Alta.	Notogawa, Shiga Prefecture	1981
Kelowna, B.C.	Kasugai City, Aichi Prefecture	1981
Collingwood, Ont.	Katano City, Osaka Prefecture	1981
Timmins, Ont.	Naoshima Town, Kagawa Prefecture	1981
Quesnel, B.C.	Shiraoi Town, Hokkaido	1981
Mississauga, Ont.	Kariya, Aichi Prefecture	1982

Sources: Japan Report (Japan Information Center, Toronto) 25, no. 6 (1978):
3, 4; Japan Municipal League for International Friendship, *Jamlif 1975*
(Tokyo), p. 16; *Jamlif 1978*; *New Canadian*, April 10, 1981, p. 6; April 6,
1982, p. 1.

Table 14
Tourism Between Canada and Japan, 1940–1981

Year	Japanese Visitors to Canada	Canadian Visitors to Japan
1940	—	385
1952	—	498
1960	400	5,064
1961	—	6,606
1962	—	7,048
1963	1,403	6,789
1964	1,981	8,752
1965	3,206	9,767
1966	2,799	11,831
1967	18,979	11,054
1968	12,515	13,272
1969	18,525	16,938
1970	22,011	44,016
1971	25,855	16,940
1972	52,438	19,942
1973	71,095	21,317
1974	77,543	20,490
1975	90,411	24,301
1976	106,783	29,791
1977	97,532	35,143
1978	127,827	34,464
1979	158,582	34,476
1980	162,253	41,045
1981	146,461	44,869

Sources: Statistics Canada, *Travel Between Canada and Other Countries*; Japan, Ministry of Transport, Department of Research and Data Processing, *Statistics on Foreign Visitors to Japan.*

Table 15
Canadian Coal Exports to Japan, 1958–1980

Year	Average Price per Ton (in dollars)[a]	Tonnage Shipped[b]	Value Shipped (in dollars)
1958	3.28	18,939	62,207
1959	5.11	190,722	971,460
1960	7.39	604,397	4,464,157
1961	9.07	685,263	6,211,435
1962	9.30	639,040	5,946,157
1963	9.62	772,470	7,424,480
1964	9.48	984,846	9,326,401
1965	10.37	1,023,134	10,613,890
1966	10.77	1,059,502	11,413,089
1967	11.42	1,167,000	13,333,096
1968	11.60	1,273,000	14,767,804
1969	12.06	1,160,000	14,000,000
1970	13.70	4,123,000	56,700,000
1971	11.09	7,400,000	82,063,000
1972	12.51	8,300,000	103,835,000
1973	13.68	11,700,000	160,046,000
1974	21.08	10,900,000	229,880,000
1975	38.56	11,800,000	455,001,000
1976	44.40	11,700,000	519,566,000
1977	55.70	9,500,000	529,200,000
1978	46.93	12,000,000	562,100,000
1979	59.60	9,500,000	569,900,000
1980	51.21	11,500,000	589,000,000

Source: Canada, Bureau of Statistics, later Canada, Ministry of Supply and Services, Statistics Canada, *Trade of Canada: Exports*, for the years given.

[a]Price per ton has been computed from tonnage and value figures. It should be kept in mind that the price per ton differs from mine to mine, from contract to contract, and according to the particular qualities of the coal shipped.

[b]Post 1967 figures on tonnage have been rounded off to nearest thousand, post-1971 figures to nearest one hundred thousand.

Table 16
Japanese Motor Vehicles Imported by Canada, 1970–1981

Year	Passenger Vehicles	Value of Passenger Vehicles (in millions of dollars)a	Passenger Vehicles Market Share (in percentages)	Trucks	Motorcycles
1970	65,569	78	10.3	—	—
1971	115,000	152	14.3	8,500	63,000
1972	146,000	235	14.4	16,600	91,000
1973	83,000	160	11.8	12,500	91,000
1974	105,000	212	9.4	19,500	99,000
1975	72,226	162	8.6	11,300	69,000
1976	120,005	270	16.1	13,761	70,220
1977	119,333	305	15.8	11,197	104,058
1978	129,308	453	17.4	14,188	96,269
1979	61,400	255	8.0	11,050	82,000
1980	150,600	589	14.8	26,557	91,972
1981	174,000	1,500b	23.0	46,578	117,366

Sources: Statistics Canada, *Trade of Canada: Imports*; Automobile Importers of Canada, Press Release.

aEstimated.

bValue of all automobiles and parts sold in Canada.

Glossary of Japanese Words

banzai "Ten thousand years," a cheer for the emperor's long life, given during an assault on the enemy

gaimushō Japan's Ministry of Foreign Affairs

gyokusai The death of honor of the soldier who spurns surrender

issei First-generation Japanese (immigrant to Canada)

nisei Second-generation Japanese (born in Canada to an *issei*)

takaku gaikō Diplomacy of diversification

zaibatsu Financial clique in Japan

Bibliography

BOOKS

Adachi, Ken. *The Enemy That Never Was: A History of the Japanese Canadians.* Toronto: McClelland and Stewart, 1976.

_____. *A History of the Japanese-Canadians in British Columbia: 1877–1958.* Toronto: National Japanese-Canadian Citizens Association, 1958.

Angus, H. F. *Canada and the Far East, 1940–1953.* Toronto: University of Toronto Press, 1953.

Blanchette, Arthur E. *Canadian Foreign Policy, 1955–65.* Carleton Library, no. 103. Toronto: McClelland and Stewart, 1977.

Broadfoot, Barry. *Years of Sorrow, Years of Shame. The Story of the Japanese Canadians in World War II.* Toronto: Doubleday Canada, 1977.

Cameron, M. E. *China, Japan, and the Powers.* 2nd ed. New York: Ronald Press, 1960.

Canadian Annual Review, The. Toronto: Canadian Review Co., 1930.

Dawson, R. M. *Canada in World Affairs.* Vol. 2. Toronto: Oxford University Press, 1943.

Eayrs, James. *Canada in World Affairs, October 1955–June 1957.* Toronto: Oxford University Press, 1959.

_____. *In Defence of Canada.* Vol. 2, *Appeasement and Rearmament.* Vol. 3, *Peacemaking and Deterrence.* Toronto: University of Toronto Press, 1965.

Glazebrook, George Parkin de Twenabrouker. *A History of Canadian Ex-*

ternal Relations. Toronto: Oxford University Press, 1950.

Hadley, Eleanor M. *Anti-Trust in Japan*. Princeton: Princeton University Press, 1970.

Hay, Keith A. J. *Canada-Japan: The Export Import Picture, 1977*. Ottawa: Canada-Japan Trade Council, 1977.

_____. *Canadian Agriculture and Japan*. Ottawa: Canada-Japan Trade Council, 1978.

Hill, O. Mary. *Canada's Salesman to the World*. Montreal: McGill–Queens University Press, 1977.

Hillmer, Norman, ed. *A Foremost Nation: Canadian Foreign Policy and a Changing World*. Toronto: McClelland and Stewart, 1977.

Hōkakeizai Shisetsudan Hōkokusho (Report of the Economic Mission to Canada, 1964). Tokyo: 1965.

Holmes, John W. *The Shaping of Peace: Canada and the Search for World Order, 1943-1957*. Toronto: University of Toronto Press, 1979.

Japan. Ministry of Foreign Affairs. *Gaimushō Nenkan* (Ministry of Foreign Affairs Yearbook). Tokyo: published annually.

Japan Biographical Encyclopaedia and Who's Who. 3rd ed., 1964–65. Tokyo: Rengo Press, 1965.

Japan Trade Center. *100 Years of Trade and Commerce Between Canada and Japan*. Toronto: Japan Trade Center, 1977.

Kaneko, Hisakazu. *Manjiro—The Man Who Discovered America*. Boston: Houghton Mifflin, 1956.

Keirstead, B. S. *Canada in World Affairs*. Vol. 7, 1951–52. Toronto: Oxford University Press, 1956.

Kim, Young Hum. *East Asia's Turbulent Century*. New York: Appleton-Century-Crofts, 1966.

La Violette, Forrest E. *The Canadian Japanese and World War II*. Toronto: University of Toronto Press, 1948.

Lingard, C. Cecil, and Trotter, Reginald. *Canada in World Affairs 1941-1944*. Vol. 3. Toronto: Oxford University Press, 1950.

Lloyd, Trevor. *Canada in World Affairs, 1957-1959*. Toronto: Oxford University Press, 1968.

Lower, A.R.M. *Canada and the Far East—1940*. New York: Institute of Pacific Relations, 1940.

MacArthur, Douglas. *Reminiscences*. Greenwich, Conn.: Fawcett Publications, Crest Books, 1964.

Macdonald, Donald S. *White Paper on Defence*. Ottawa: Information Canada, 1971.

Mackay, R. A. *Canadian Foreign Policy, 1945-54*. Toronto: McClelland and Stewart, 1960.

Nakayama, Jinshiro. *Kanada no Hōko* (The Treasure House of Canada). Tokyo: Japan Times-sha, 1922.

Norman, E. Herbert. *Japan's Emergence as a Modern State*. New York: Institute of Pacific Relations, 1940.

_____. *Soldier and Peasant in Japan*. New York: Institute of Pacific Relations, 1943.

_____. *Andoshoeki and the Anatomy of Japanese Feudalism*. Tokyo: The Asiatic Society of Japan, 1949.

Ōkubō, Genji, trans. *Haabaato Nooman Zenshu* (The Complete Writings of E. Herbert Norman). Vols. 1–4. Tokyo: Iwanami Shoten, 1977–78.

Pearson, Lester B. *Mike*, Vol. 3. Toronto: University of Toronto Press, 1972.

Pickersgill, J. W. *The Mackenzie King Record*. 4 vols. Toronto: University of Toronto Press, 1960–1970.

Preston, Richard A. *Canada in World Affairs, 1959–61*. Toronto: Oxford University Press, 1965.

Reader's Digest. *The Canadians at War 1939–45*, Vol. 1. Montreal: Reader's Digest Association, Canada, 1969.

Roy, R. H. *For Most Conspicuous Bravery*. Vancouver: University of British Columbia Press, 1977.

Sharp, Mitchell. *Foreign Policy for Canadians*. 6 bookets. Ottawa: Queen's Printer, 1970.

Skilling, H. Gordon. *Canadian Representation Abroad: From Agency to Embassy*. Toronto: Ryerson Press, 1945.

Stacey, C. P. *Arms, Men and Governments: The War Policies of Canada 1939–45*. Ottawa: Queen's Printer, 1970.

_____. *Six Years of War: The Army in Canada, Britain and the Pacific*. Vol. 1. Ottawa: Queen's Printer, 1967.

Tanaka, Kakuei. *Building a New Japan*. Tokyo: Simul Press, 1973.

Taylor, Charles. *Six Journeys: A Canadian Pattern*. Toronto: Anansi, 1977.

Thomson, Dale C. *Louis St. Laurent: Canadian*. Toronto: Macmillan, 1967.

Toland, John. *The Rising Sun: The Decline and Fall of the Japanese Empire, 1936–45*. New York: Random House, 1970.

Tucker, G. N. *The Naval Service of Canada: Its Official History*. Ottawa: King's Printer, 1952.

Warriner, E. V. *Voyage to Destiny*. New York: Bobbs-Merrill, 1956.

Watanabe, Rui, and Mizuno, Tae. *Witnesses of the Way in Japan*. Toronto: United Church of Canada, Committee on Missionary Education, c. 1940.

Woodsworth, Charles J. *Canada and the Orient*. Toronto: Macmillan, 1941.

Yamashita, Keitaro. *Kanada Fugen* (The Natural Resources of Canada). Tokyo: Maruzen Shosha Shoten, 1893.

Young, Charles H.; Reid, Helen R. Y.; and Carrothers, W. A. *The Japanese Canadians*. Toronto: University of Toronto Press, 1938.

DOCUMENTS

Canada. British Columbia Security Commission. *Report of the Removal of Japanese from Protected Areas*. Vancouver: BCSC, 1942.
Canada. Bureau of Statistics. *Canada Yearbook*. Ottawa: annual.
Canada. Department of Defence. *White Paper on Defence*. By the authority of Minister of National Defence Donald S. McDonald. Ottawa: Information Canada, 1971.
Canada. Department of External Affairs. *Annual Review*, 1975. Ottawa: 1976.
_____. *Canada Treaty Series*. Ottawa: annual.
_____. *Conclusion of a Nuclear Agreement Between Canada and Japan*. Communique no. 10, January 26, 1978.
_____. *Documents on Canadian External Relations (DCER)*. Vols. 4–8. Ottawa: 1971–76.
_____. *Exchange of Instruments of Ratification of the Canada-Japan Cultural Agreement*. Communique no. 103, November 16, 1977.
_____. *Files (1929–1941)*. Ottawa.
_____. *Joint Communique of the Seventh Meeting of the Canada-Japan Ministerial Committee, June 24, 1975*. Ottawa: 1975.
_____. *Records (1941–1948)*. Ottawa.
_____. *Statements and Speeches*. Ottawa: Information Services Division, Department of External Affairs, annual..
Canada. Department of Justice. Bird, Henry I. *Report upon the Investigation into Claims of Persons of the Japanese Race. Pursuant to Terms of the Order in Council, P.C. 1810, July 18, 1947, As Amended*. Ottawa: April 6, 1950.
Canada. Department of Labour. *The Re-establishment of Japanese in Canada, 1944–1946*. Ottawa: 1947.
_____. *Report of the Department of Labour for the Calendar Year Ending March 31st, 1944*. Ottawa: King's Printer, 1945.
_____. *Report of the Royal Commission Appointed Pursuant to Order in Council P.C. No. 9498 to Enquire into the Provisions Made for the Welfare and Maintenance of Persons of the Japanese Race Resident in Settlements in the Province of British Columbia*. Ottawa: 1944.
Canada. House of Commons. *Debates* (Hansard).
Canada. Ministry of Industry, Trade, and Commerce. *Report of the International Defense Programmes Branch, Ministry of Industry, Trade, and Commerce, Mission to Japan, November 25–December 8, 1972*. Ottawa: 1973.

Canada. Ministry of Supply and Services. Statistics Canada. *Travel Between Canada and Other Countries*. Ottawa: Queen's Printer.
_____. *Trade of Canada: Exports*. Ottawa: Queen's Printer.
Canada. Office of the Prime Minister. Press release. Joint communiqué between Prime Minister Kakuei Tanaka and Prime Minister Pierre Elliott Trudeau, Ottawa, September 24, 1974.
_____. Press release. Notes for the prime minister's remarks at dinner in honor of Prime Minister Miki, Tokyo, October 25, 1976. Ottawa: 1976.
_____. Press release. Notes for remarks by the prime minister to the Japan National Press Club, October 26, 1976. Ottawa: 1976.
_____. Transcript of the Prime Minister's remarks on Canada Day, Osaka, Japan, May 28, 1970. Ottawa: 1970.
Canada. *Report of the Royal Commission on Chinese and Japanese Immigration*. Ottawa: 1902.
Canada. Special Committee on Orientals in British Columbia. *Report and Recommendations, December 1940*. Ottawa: 1941.
Canada. Standing Senate Committee on Foreign Affairs. *Report on Canadian Relations with the Countries of the Pacific Region*. Ottawa: Queen's Printer, 1972.
Japan. Gaimushō (Ministry of Foreign Affairs). Files of the Diplomatic Records Office, Tokyo.
Japan. Ministry of Transport. Department of Research and Data Processing. *Statistics on Foreign Visitors to Japan*.
League of Nations. *Verbatim Record of the Special Session of the Assembly*, December 8, 1932, Geneva.
Public Archives of Canada. Diary of W. L. Mackenzie King, Ottawa.
_____. Ian Mackenzie papers, Ottawa.
_____. Laurier Papers, Ottawa.
U.S. Department of State. *Occupation of Japan: Policy and Progress*, Publication 267. Washington: Government Printing Office, n.d.

ARTICLES

Bamba, Nobuya. "Nippon, Kanada Kankei no Tenkai" (The Development of Japanese-Canadian Relations). *Kokusai Mondai* (Tokyo), no. 203 (February 1977).
_____. "Senryoo to Nooman" (The Occupation and Norman). *Shisoo* (Tokyo), no. 634 (April 1977). Special issue on the twentieth anniversary of the death of E. Herbert Norman.
Brebner, J. B. "Canada, The Anglo-Japanese Alliance and the Washington Conference." *Political Science Quarterly* 50 (March 1935).
Granatstein, J. L. "Defence Against the Imagined Internal Enemy: How

the Japanese Candians Were Treated.'' *Canadian Defence Quarterly* 4, no. 3 (1974).

Hay, Keith A. J. ''Friends or Acquaintances? Canada and Japan's Other Trading Partners in the Early 1980's.'' Occasional Paper No. 6, Institute for Research on Public Policy, Montreal, December 1978, p. 26.

Head, Ivan. ''Canada's Pacific Perspective.'' *Pacific Community* (Tokyo) 6, no. 1 (1974).

Prince Mikasa. ''Nooman Sensei no Omoide'' (Recollections of Professor Norman). *Iwanami Shoten Monthly Bulletin* (Tokyo) 1, no. 1 (1977).

Sharp, Mitchell. ''Canada-U.S. Relations: Options for the Future.'' *International Perspectives* (Ottawa, Information Canada), special issue, autumn 1972.

Soward, F. H. ''Forty Years On: The Cahan Blunder Re-examined.'' *B.C. Studies*, no. 32 (Winter 1976–77).

Ward, W. Peter. ''British Columbia and the Japanese Evacuation.'' *Canadian Historical Review* 57, no. 3 (1976).

PERIODICALS

Asahi Shimbun (daily, Tokyo)
Canada Commerce (bimonthly, Ottawa)
The Daily Yomiuri (English edition, Tokyo)
External Affairs (monthly, Ottawa)
The Financial Post (weekly, Toronto)
Foreign Trade (bimonthly, Ottawa)
Globe and Mail (daily, Toronto)
The Japan Times (daily, Tokyo)
The Mainichi Daily News (English edition, Tokyo)
Mainichi Shimbun (daily, Tokyo)
The Toronto Star (daily, Toronto)
The Vancouver Sun (daily, Vancouver, B.C.)
Yomiuri Japan News (daily, Tokyo)

UNPUBLISHED PAPERS

Canadian Embassy, Tokyo. ''Diplomatic Procedure in Japan.'' Tokyo: Files of the Canadian Legation, 1929. Courtesy of Richard Gorham, Minister of the Canadian Embassy.

Norman, Gwen R. P. ''A Brief History of the Canadian Academy.'' Toronto: 1977. Courtesy of Mrs. G. P. Norman.

INTERVIEWS

Tape-recorded interviews were conducted with the following government officials, diplomats, and academics of Canada and Japan. Dates of the interviews are cited in the notes.

Bernier, Normand, Quebec representative, Tokyo
Bull, William F., former ambassador to Japan
Burney, Derek, senior departmental assistant and media spokesman, Canada Department of External Affairs
Campbell, Ross, former ambassador to Japan
Derksen, Jack, former first secretary, Canadian Embassy, Tokyo
Diefenbaker, John G., former prime minister of Canada
Guthrie, N. Gregor, vice president, Canada-Japan Trade Council
Hagiwara, Tokru, former ambassador to Canada
Houston, Robert L., president, Canada-Japan Trade Council
Itagaki, Osamu, former ambassador to Canada
Johnston, W. W., Japan desk officer, Department of Industry, Trade, and Commerce, Ottawa
Keenleyside, Hugh L., former chargé d'affaires in Tokyo legation
Kondo, Shinichi, former ambassador to Canada
Langdon, Frank, Professor of Political Science, University of British Columbia
Matsudaira, Kōto, former ambassador to Canada
Moran, Herbert O., former ambassador to Japan
Morden, Reid, counsellor, economic, Canadian Embassy in Japan
Nara, Yasuhiko, former ambassador to Japan
Nellis, Harry R., former manager, Ontario Provincial Office, Tokyo
Newton, T.F.M., former chargé d'affaires, Canadian Embassy, Tokyo
Nishiyama, Akira, former ambassador to Canada
Norman, W. Howard, former principal, Canadian Academy, Kobe
Ōkubō, Genji, translator/analyst, Canadian Embassy, Tokyo
Pepin, Jean-Luc, former minister of industry, trade and commerce, currently minister of transport
Parkinson, William R., counsellor, commercial, Canadian Embassy, Tokyo
Rankin, Bruce I., former ambassador to Japan
Sharp, Mitchell, former secretary of state for external affairs
Shimazu, Hisanaga, former ambassador to Canada
Smith, Brian, Japan desk officer, DEA
Suma, Michiaki, former ambassador to Canada
Tachibana, Masatada, former first secretary, Japanese Embassy, Ottawa
Tanaka, Kakuei, former prime minister of Japan
Ushiba, Nobuhiko, former ambassador to Canada

Yoshizawa, Seijiro, former minister to Canada

The following persons were contacted by mail and answered sets of questions in writing or on tape.

Bower, Richard P., former ambassador to Japan
Iguchi, Sadao, former ambassador to Canada
Menzies, Arthur R., former ambassador to Japan

Index

230   Index

International Air Transport
Association (IATA), 130
International Defence Programmes
Branch, Department of Industry,
Trade and Commerce, 163
International Military Tribunal Far
East (IMTFE), 98, 105; Canadian
judge at, 98, 99
International Nickel Company of
Canada, Ltd. (INCO), 201 n.1
International North Pacific Fisheries
Convention, 134, 137
International Red Cross Committee,
80, 82
International Wheat Agreement, 114
Internment camps. *See* Interior
housing centers
Internment of Japanese males in
British Columbia, 71
Ishibashi, Tanzan, 122, 123
Isopol Chemicals, 201 n.1
Issei, 75
Itagaki, Osamu, 142, 144
Italy, declares war on U.S., 67
Ito, Hirobumi, 27
I-26 (Japanese submarine), 87
Iwakura, Prince Tomosada, 27
Izumo (Japanese battleship), 21

Jackman, F. T., 163
Jackson, J. W., 82
Jamieson, Donald, 184, 189
Japan: annexes Korea, 22; attacks
China (1937), 42; as Canada's
number two trading partner, 171,
185; citizens of, in Canada, 70, 79,
93; contract laborers from, 5, 7, 8;
and East Asian expansion, 68;
emigrants from (*see* Immigrants,
Japanese); exports automobiles to
Canada, 198, 215; and fear of subversion in Canada, 55, 68; and free
access to Canadian market, 135; as
imperialist nation, 12, 22; and import taxes, 44, 45; invades French
Indo-China, 55; invests in Canada,
177, 178, 179, 187, 188, 189;

mandated territories of, 41; market
of, 162; occupation of (*see* Occupa-
tion of Japan); protests treatment
of Japanese in Canada, 79; and
research reactor, 129; sends consuls
to Canada, 18; surrenders, 91, 98;
treatment of Canadian internees by,
80; trials of war criminals of, 98
Japan Airlines service, Tokyo-
Vancouver, 145
Japan Alberta Oil Mill Co., 188
Japan-Canada Agreement on
Commerce (Trade Treaty), 1954,
117, 118, 119, 121, 133, 135
Japan-Canada Businessmen's
Conference, 200
Japan-Canada Parliamentarians
League, 180
Japan-Canada Society (Canada-Japan
Society), 58, 130, 134, 155; Cana-
dian ambassador as honorary
president of, 131; reactivation of,
131
Japan-Canada Trade Council, 134
Japanese books on Canada, 5
Japanese Canadian Citizens Council,
(JCCC), 75
Japanese Canadian Committee for
Democracy, (JCCD), 93
Japanese Canadians, 4, 78, 106; in
armed forces, 21, 22, 107 n.6;
awarded military medal, 22; in
British Columbia, 52, 69, 70;
centennial of, 4; civil rights of, 52,
76, 87; classified as enemy aliens,
198, 199; community of, 4; confisca-
tion of property of, 54; deportation
(repatriation) of, 81, 86, 87, 92, 93,
134; deprivation of legal rights of,
94; discrimination against, 110 n.40;
enfranchisement of, 94; and evacuation exemptions, 107 n.11; government policy of dispersal of, 86, 87,
92, 94; hostility towards, 51, 71;
living conditions of, 82; loss of
citizenship rights of, 73, 76, 92;
loyalty of, 52, 68, 84; perceived as